My Pursuit
of the
Axis of Evil

And Other True Stories From Asia and Alaska

Bill Cox

My Pursuit
of the
Axis of Evil

And Other True Stories From Asia and Alaska

Bill Cox

PUBLICATION
CONSULTANTS
We Believe In The Power Of Authors
PO Box 221974 Anchorage, Alaska 99522-1974
books@publicationconsultants.com—www.publicationconsultants.com

ISBN: 978-1-63747-095-4
eISBN: 978-1-63747-096-1

Library of Congress Catalog Card Number: 2022917045

Copyright 2022 Bill Cox
—First Edition—

Manufactured in the United States of America.

DEDICATION

I dedicate this book to all the good people I've encountered on my travels. You took me into your homes, shared meals, stories, and taught me. You are the vast majority.

Acknowledgements

I acknowledge, in no particular order or ranking, the many people who helped me in the preparation of this book. Starting, perhaps, with those who provided the raw material for the book itself—whether you invited me into your home in Burma, Barrow or the Soviet Far East or talked to me from inside a dumpster in midtown Anchorage—you all had a story to share. Or perhaps our meeting was a story in the making.

I thank my wife, Amy, who accompanied me on many of these trips and could put up with the unexpected inconvenience and keep her cool—like the time we camped out in a tent in the Mongolian wilderness and a very tenacious mouse spent the entire night trying to chew its way into the tent.

I thank my Fordham University-educated daughter, Colleen, who first edited my stories maybe some ten years ago and picked up many typos and had good suggestions for improving syntax and rephrasing.

I thank my publisher, Evan Swensen, of Publication Consultants for his extensive expertise, advice, guidance and suggestions. And his patience.

And finally, I thank my non-human digital assistant, Grammarly, who was literally at my fingertips for the last editing. I had already purged scores of commas and she tried to get me to restore them, but I held my ground. She kept pushing dashes, too. But she did pick up several typos and misspellings, for which I was grateful. And she sends me regular updates praising my writing skills and word choices, which goes right to my head and feeds my ego. Thanks, Grammarly!

And if I've missed anybody—and I'm sure I have—send a nice email to my future website and I'll mention you in the next printing. I expect the first run to sell like hotcakes.

CONTENTS

MORE FAMOUS ALASKANS, INCLUDING 4 GOVERNORS

INTRODUCTION

I promise I'll keep it short so you can get on with the book.

My Pursuit of the Axis of Evil is primarily people-centered. The travels and adventures described center around the people involved. My original title was going to be something like *Pacific Rim Encounters – meetings and adventures with interesting people in Asia and Alaska*. But we decided to just use the first story's title as the title for the book: *My Pursuit of the Axis of Evil*. It's more catchy, more likely to cause you to grab it off the shelf, and if you're reading this introduction, that's proof that it worked. But it's only the first story. This is not a book about evil.

These stories are all true - as I experienced them first-hand.

Yes, you'll notice a little humor woven in. That's my style. Many were written some twenty years ago, and I've added epilogues. Where the mafia was involved, even peripherally, I have changed names and maybe a location. Nobody told me to, but it just seemed to make sense. And I took all the photos, except where I handed my camera (a Pentax ME Super or a Zoom 90 WR) to someone to take a photo that included me.

These stories can be read in no particular order, so feel free to pick and choose. In one or two cases, a story may make reference to something in the immediately preceding story. Enjoy.

Chapter 1
My Pursuit of The Axis of Evil

THE NORTH KOREANS (Axis of Evil #1)
Lao PDR (Laos) October 1998

I was riding on the back of Phetsavanh's motorcycle, streaming along in the sparse traffic that flowed out of Vientiane, the capital and largest city in Laos. Glimpses of the Mekong River were visible through the trees on our right. It was my second visit to this sleepy, backwater Southeast Asian paradise, so when a familiar neighborhood appeared on the left, I asked Phet to turn. I guided him through a maze of dusty gravel roads that I'd been through on a rented bicycle a year earlier. We soon pulled alongside the iron fence surrounding the building I was looking for: the Embassy of the Democratic Peoples' Republic of Korea (North Korea, as we know it in the west).

The main gate was open and the dilapidated little guard shack un-manned, so we drove on through and barreled across the wide-open courtyard, stopping at the base of a broad sweeping oval stairway that led up to the main entrance. As we stepped off the motorcycle, several people came up to the window of a ground-level office next to where we were standing. They picked me out right away and tried to tell me, in reason-ably good English, that I was mistaken. "The South Korean Embassy is that way," they pointed and gestured, trying to give me directions. "No, no," I replied, "this is where I want to be. The Embassy of North Korea."

The main door opened and an official-looking man with a Kim Jong Il haircut appeared and started down the stairs to see what the commotion was all about. It was First Secretary Kim. When he recognized me a broad smile appeared across his face and he motioned for us to follow, leading us inside.

Sitting on a spotless black upholstered couch, I pulled out my photos and set them out on the varnished coffee table in front of us. First Secretary Kim could scarcely contain his surprise at seeing photos of his friend and former classmate, Counselor Kim Myong Gil of the North Korean Mission in New York City, whose visit to Anchorage I had arranged just months before. He apologized that his French was better than his English and summoned his wife, who spoke better English, to join us. For the next twenty minutes we looked at photos, laughed, talked about families and jobs... only when I glanced at the wall over my right shoulder at the stern official portraits of Kim Il Sung and Kim Jong Il was I reminded that I was inside the North Korean Embassy.

I should admit that it all started with the Russians. I was, after all, a child of the H-bomb, Khruschev, and Sputnik. I grew up through thirty years of vicious, anti-Soviet propaganda. The Russians were the bad guys - from Hollywood to Washington, D.C.

Fast forward to 1985: Gorbachev, perestroika and glasnost. The courageous and forward-thinking Dr. Ted Mala of Anchorage virtually single-handedly melted the Ice Curtain. I gawked at the first delegation of Russians to arrive in Anchorage – as if they were from Mars. After seven visits to Siberia and the Russian Far East, scores of homestays and shared meals, I have found the Russians to be among the kindest and most hospitable people I have ever met.

So, in the late 1990s I became curious about North Korea, the residual Dark Kingdom. This was years before it became labeled as a member of the Axis of Evil by President George W. Bush.

VIENTIANE, LAO PDR (LAOS) JANUARY 1997

In communist Laos, eight years after the fall of the Soviet Union, I had a chance to check out this "Stalinist Dark Kingdom." It was some four years before it would be christened as part of the Axis of Evil. With rough directions to the North Korean Embassy, I took off on a rented bicycle.

The main gate was plastered with Soviet-style propaganda photos of lock-step soldiers in a military parade in Pyongyang, factories churning out rough consumer goods, and crowds of loyal, smiling citizens. A sleepy Lao guard cradling an ancient pre-World War II carbine made me leave my bicycle at the gate but otherwise waved me through. I had with me a letter written in Korean by a friend in Seoul detailing my involvement with medical exchanges in Russia and my desire to begin a medical and humanitarian exchange with North Korea.

Standing now in the middle of the courtyard of the North Korean Embassy with a manila envelope in my outstretched hands, I could not help feeling like Aldrich Ames. I pushed aside thoughts of the Pueblo. I felt somewhat awkward and vulnerable, but not fearful. Maybe a bit disconnected. Would I be greeted by a bullet or a commando team of highly trained North Korean security? The roof of the embassy was studded with a wide array of antennas: coiled ones and pointed ones and some that looked like those cooling trays for cookies and muffins that just came out of the oven. It reminded me of KGB Headquarters in Magadan in 1990, when Russia was still the Soviet Union.

I had bet myself that a 6'7" American standing in the middle of the courtyard of a North Korean Embassy with an envelope in his outstretched arms would generate some kind of response within five minutes. It was just the nature of the response that concerned me. But my time estimate was right. A late-middle-aged woman, about as threatening as a spinster librarian, walked out to confront me. I greeted her in Korean and we spoke briefly in Russian. She invited me inside.

My discussion with Mr. Jon, who spoke excellent English, was very friendly. The topic soon turned to the floods and famine that were plaguing North Korea at the time, and he urged me to contact North Korea's mission to the United Nations in New York City when I got back to the States.

BACK IN THE USA MAY 1998

When I next found myself back in New York City, I took the elevator to the 13th floor of a nondescript building on 2nd Avenue and rang the buzzer to the UN Mission of DPR Korea. I introduced myself and was ushered in. A very productive discussion ensued with Counselor Kim Myong Gil. I invited him to come to Alaska and when I returned to Alaska I worked with the Alaska World Affairs Council to make it happen. Mr. Kim not only gave a public speech in Anchorage, but also answered questions from the public. I suspect this was a first for a North Korean diplomat.

Driving east on 6th Avenue in downtown Anchorage after his talk, I was taking Counselor Kim and his colleague to a meeting at the University with former Alaska governors Steve Cowper and Wally Hickel. I braked suddenly as a man in a business suit and tie dashed across the road and ran down the sidewalk toward the 5th Avenue Mall. I thought I was witnessing a white-collar purse snatching, but as we inched forward I saw it was only Mayor Rick Mystrom.

"See that man running down the sidewalk, that's our mayor, the mayor of Anchorage," I said to Mr. Kim. "Really?" said a surprised Mr. Kim.

That evening, at a pot-luck reception for the North Korean delegation, the mayor arrived. True to his gracious, low-key and friendly style, Rick Mystrom grabbed a paper plate and got on the food line with everyone else. Finding himself next to me and Mr. Kim, he introduced himself. "Hi, I'm Rick Mystrom, the mayor of Anchorage," he said, extending his hand to Mr. Kim. "I know," said Mr. Kim, "we saw you running down the sidewalk this afternoon." Momentarily at a loss for words, the mayor recovered quickly and laughed, explaining he had had a quick errand to run at the Mall between meetings at City Hall.

THE IRANIANS (Axis of Evil #2)
BANGKOK, THAILAND NOVEMBER 2000

Turning left off Soi 33, I was headed on foot toward the small supermarket on Sukhumvit Blvd. It was the same one Father Joe Maier, the Bangkok slum priest, sent me into several years earlier to buy beer. His friend, Carthusian priest Father Denis Rackley, a colleague of Thomas Merton's, was with him. Father Denis was visiting from Burma, where he was studying vipassana meditation. I had been most fortunate then to share lunch and free-wheeling conversation with these two spiritual giants.

This time a sign caught my attention: Iranian Embassy. An arrow pointed across the traffic-congested boulevard.

I'd already engaged the North Koreans and now I wanted to hear what the Iranians had to say. Per Pythagoras' instructions, I checked all my prejudices at the tall iron gate. A uniformed Thai guard waved me into the Embassy of the Islamic Republic of Iran. I crossed a courtyard, aware that I was no longer under the authority, or protection, of the Kingdom of Thailand. I hesitated before an enormously high, floor-to-ceiling door that brought back memories of the Soviet Embassy in Stockholm in 1972. I went in and took a seat next to some young Iranians on a long couch. These fellas are just here to straighten out some passport or visa irregularities, I thought, naively.

A thick plexiglass window framed the main reception desk. Like the 7-11s in inner-city Detroit. Above this, striking anyone who entered this small sitting room, were three portraits: Center and highest was a black-and-white photo of Ayatollah Khomeini, the deceased but supreme prophet of the Islamic Republic of Iran. To the lower right was a photo of Iranian President Khatami and to the lower left was supreme cleric Ayatollah Khamenei.

I began to hear what sounded like an argument, in Farsi, coming from a room behind the reception desk. It escalated, followed by crashing sounds, like a body being thrown against a wall. One particularly loud crash almost dislodged Khomeini's portrait, which now listed ominously about 15 degrees. Meanwhile, the second voice in the argument dropped precipitously, changing to a desperate pleading, like someone begging for his life. Then silence.

I turned and looked through the steel bars on the window behind me and watched a uniformed Thai chauffeur pull a shiny black car up to a doorway that seemed to lead to the room where the argument had taken place. Stepping out of the car, he opened the trunk and sauntered off. At that point I averted my gaze, not wanting to witness a body being stuffed into the trunk to be driven out and dumped into one of Bangkok's putrid canals. I was starting to get a little nervous. I had told no one I was going into the Iranian Embassy. I thought about the American hostages taken in Tehran. I needed an exit strategy, and quickly.

I glanced over at the floor-to-ceiling doors when, out of the corner of my eye, I noticed a mustachioed man behind the plexiglass motioning for me to come forward. He handed me a phone. Just then, two men entered and stood behind him, staring at me. Shit, I muttered to myself. The short one made me nervous. He was obviously out of breath but struggling to maintain his composure, leaving little doubt in my mind that he was the one who had just killed someone in the next room. His eyes bore through me like two cold lasers, causing me to shudder. Then I remembered I had a phone in my hand. "Hello?" The voice on the other end asked me what I wanted. I stuttered, "I, uh, just wanted to talk and meet with you, but it seems you are busy." They apparently didn't notice my nervous sarcasm. "Maybe I can come back tomorrow," I suggested, knowing full well that the next day I was flying to Burma. "Come back tomorrow," said the unfriendly voice.

Still fearing for my safety, I pondered my next move. Should I make a mad dash for the exit or just wander out pretending to be nonchalant? I chose the latter course of action. My sweaty palms managed a grip on the doorknob and I stepped outside. I still had a short walk over to the main gate before I was clear. I did not look over my shoulder. When I finally reached the loud, smoggy, traffic-choked streets of Bangkok my knees buckled a bit and I breathed in a deep polluted gasp of relief.

Al, a well-connected ex-US military man, was a 30-year-plus expat in Bangkok. He was sipping his afternoon beer at a sidewalk café near my hotel when I walked by, still a little shaky. He dressed me down royally and read me the riot act for risking my life with "that bunch of thugs". I had to admit Al had a point and I nodded meekly.

Finding myself in Bangkok a year later, I wandered back over to the main gate, hoping to coax the Iranians outside their embassy to the relative safety of a local Thai restaurant. The guard, however, excitedly started waving me through the gate, but I hesitated. It was then I noticed his other hand slowly sliding across the wooden tabletop toward an Uzi submachine gun. It was a bad omen. I spooked and bolted back to the smog-choked safety of Sukhumvit Blvd. The Iranians would just have to wait.

THE IRAQIS (Axis of Evil #3)
NEW DELHI, INDIA MARCH 2003

Back in New Delhi with Roma human rights activist Dr. Ian Hancock after our meeting with His Holiness the Dalai Lama, we had a day to kill. I remembered the Dalai Lama's polar opposite, Saddam Hussein, had an embassy in this city. It was March 2003 and maybe my last chance to complete my circuit of the Axis of Evil.

I had glimpsed the Iraqi Embassy on a previous visit. I remembered a sandbagged outer perimeter and a guard stationed behind a tripod-mounted machine gun. But I was informed they had moved across town. We pulled up to the new Iraqi Embassy.

The neighborhood was quiet. A single tattered anti-war poster was plastered on a lamp post. A stray dog trotted by. No one would get out of the taxi.

I walked alone up to the main gate, which was slightly ajar. There was no one in sight, so I called for attention. An attendant came out and informed me it was a religious holiday and the embassy was closed. Damn, I thought, Bush was widely expected to launch his invasion of Baghdad the following day and this would be my last chance. When the attendant turned his back, I stuck my foot inside the gate for good measure, hoping that would count if I ever decided to go for a spot in the record books.

North Korean diplomat Kim Myong Gil and my daughter Colleen melt the ice at Portage Glacier, Alaska May 1998

CHAPTER 2

MY FLIGHT TO INDIA: ONANISM AT 30,000 FEET, AN ARMED CONFRONTATION ON THE STREETS OF NEW DELHI AND, FINALLY, TWO KINGFISHERS. FEBRUARY 1992

BANGKOK, THAILAND

I boarded the Air France Boeing 747 in Bangkok, Thailand, bound for New Delhi, India. It was the final leg of a long journey from Anchorage, Alaska. Delighted that they somehow assigned me to Business Class, I finally got to walk up the spiral staircase to the exclusive "upper deck" of the 747. Settling into the middle seat with no one on either side of me, I felt even luckier. Across the aisle, a lone gentleman also had the entire row to himself. I looked across, made eye contact, and smiled. First mistake.

It has been said that of all the countries and cultures on the planet, only the Taiwanese and the French have fully perfected the art of cooking. Confident that Air France was not going to disappoint its Business Class passengers, I was looking forward to a great meal. Once we reached cruising altitude, our Business Class steward unbuckled his seatbelt and set about to work.

I talked with the steward briefly as he was setting up shop. He insisted this was a "French" plane, even though it was built in Seattle. Fine, I thought, I knew the French were proud. Then he started raving about his time in San Francisco, about what a great place it was. He seemed somewhat effeminate. I glanced down at his briefcase leaning against the wall. A big flashy silver-framed bumper sticker pasted to the brown leather read "I got crabs at Fisherman's Wharf". I understood.

I never had any problem with gay people and respected and fully accepted them then as I do now. I knew that back then the florist industry and the airline attendant industry were two safe refuges of employment. But there was the entirely different problem of my seatmate–across–the aisle.

His face had Asian features, but I couldn't pinpoint them any further. He was drinking heavily. Liquor was free in Business Class and whiskeys kept coming his way. When he wasn't drinking, he was staring at me while gently massaging his crotch. I feared for the worst.

And the worst came to pass. The next time I glanced across the aisle I saw a naked penis as erect as a flagpole being vigorously rubbed as he glared at me. When the steward passed by with meal trays he quickly threw a pillow on his lap. My dinner finally arrived.

The French did not disappoint. A multi-course feast with Brie and Camembert cheeses as appetizers and a refillable glass of a fine French Chardonnay. But based on the dinnertime entertainment I was about to endure, I would have preferred a salad dressing other than "creamy Italian."

It's difficult to enjoy fine French cuisine, or even a bologna sandwich for that matter, when someone is sitting five feet away, staring at you and openly masturbating. I pondered my options: I could ignore him. Difficult. I could revert to my medical training and observe him with a cold, clinical eye. Better done with a Styrofoam cup of stale black coffee than an exquisite French meal tantalizing my taste buds. Or I could step across the aisle and punch his lights out. I opted against violence, as I did not know whose authority I was now under. Was it the French, as the steward–with–crabs led me to believe? French prisons are notorious. Or the Thais, from whose country we took off? Thai prisons are worse. Or the Indians, whose country we were now flying into?

There was no point in bothering the steward. I think he knew. There had already been a brief encounter between the two back in the galley that caused the poor steward to burst through the curtains and storm down the aisle, red-faced and angry. I gulped the rest of my Chardonnay. Outside the window I could see lightning in the distance. I wanted this flight to be over.

I passed the onanist in the jetway when I disembarked. I nodded and continued on. This was the land of Gandhi, I thought. Ahimsa, nonviolence. Besides, it should be no problem losing one asshole in a country of over one billion.

INDIRA GANDHI INTERNATIONAL AIRPORT

I knew from past experience it was best to get a pre-paid taxi voucher to whatever one's destination from the airport. The cabbies are desperate for a fare and often have no idea where they are going. "The Lodhi Hotel at the corner of Lala Lajpat Rai Marg and Lodhi Boulevard," I told the dispatcher. The fare was reasonable for a cab ride of almost an hour, and I paid him in rupees. Clutching the printed voucher, I walked up to the head of the queue. It was about midnight.

The cabbie looked all of 14-years old, barely understood English, and clearly had no idea where to go despite the hotel name and address I gave him. But he desperately wanted the fare. Convinced that he understood this was a pre-paid voucher, I settled into the back seat for what might be a long ride.

It was past 2 am and he'd already driven by my hotel twice. I could see it. I tried to point it out to him and explain that it was on a one-way street. All I got was a blank stare. I made myself comfortable in the back seat. At 3 am he pulled the cab over to the curb on a dark, deserted side street next to an abandoned kiosk. Saying something in broken English about asking directions, he hopped out, dashed across the street and disappeared into the bushes, leaving me alone in the back seat with the engine idling. Obviously, he had to take a leak. Or whatever. Probably whatever.

No sooner had he disappeared than two men swaddled in brown blankets pulled up alongside on a motorcycle. They stopped, dismounted, tossed their blankets aside and walked toward the cab. This was the early 1990s and I had not yet heard of the Taliban. But if I had, I would have sworn they were Taliban! To say they appeared menacing, intimidating and unfriendly would be an understatement.

One of them suddenly brandished two long sticks with steel tips. The second guy unshouldered a rifle. They saw me and approached. Realizing the vulnerable position I was in, defenseless in the back seat of an idling cab, all I could do was meekly smile. I still remember clearly the first thought that went through my mind. I remember thinking that, regardless of how this situation panned out, I was still glad to finally be here on the streets of New Delhi and not back in that damn plane.

Suddenly, the kid reappeared from the bushes, talked to the two men, and they drove off. As he got back behind the wheel, he told me they were cops. Whatever, I thought, but I owe you, kid. You just earned yourself a big tip. The steel-tipped sticks did resemble the lathis that Indian police were known to carry. Ten minutes later he got me to the hotel.

LODHI HOTEL, NEW DELHI

It was 3:30 am by the time I checked in, got my key, and was about to head to my room. The uniformed night attendant was sleepy. I told him that despite the late hour, I would like two beers - 650ml Kingfishers – brought to my room. They arrived within minutes. It had been a long day and I needed to unwind.

CHAPTER 3

AND BACK AGAIN: ORDAINED AT 30,000 FEET - AND DEFROCKED AT SEA-LEVEL

We took off from New Delhi in a white-out. Not the snowy Alaska kind - this wasn't Fairbanks in an ice fog. It was May, the hottest and driest month in India and the temperature was 114 degrees F. A thick, white haze smothered the airport – one could barely see across the runway.

I knew basic aerodynamics: Cold air is denser and provides better and quicker lift. Hot air is the opposite. Our fully-loaded Air India 747 screamed down the runway through the 114-degree haze, struggling to purchase lift. It seemed like we were going to run out of runway when we finally broke free of the ground – ever so slightly. When I finally heard the landing gear retract I could stop worrying about lift-off. And start worrying whether a radical Sikh had placed a bomb on board our plane. But worry is very irrational, non-productive and does not provide answers. So I asked the attractive sari-clad flight attendant for some scotch.

After a few scotches my seatmates asked me if I was nervous. I hadn't really paid them much attention: Two slightly chubby young American women with heavy Brooklyn accents, wearing nearly identical purple polka-dot cotton dresses. When I admitted I was a bit nervous, the one next to me asked if I'd like her to pray for me. I checked my watch. We were about 30 minutes out of Bangkok. Might help pass the time, I thought. "Yes," I said.

She placed her left hand on my right mid-thigh, bowed her head, raised her right hand, and prayed. In tongues. I'd heard about this phenomenon among the Pentecostalists. It was fluid, unforced, and very natural. It was also, well, bizarre. At intervals she would interrupt herself to translate. It was always: "He said this" or "He said that". She was obviously translating for a male. Must have been one of the Trinity. They were all male. Mary must have been minding her tongue.

After the translation she resumed praying in a strange, unrecognizable tongue. Nothing seemed fake or phony in this – there was no hesitancy. Each time she resumed praying her hand slid further up my thigh. Not that I had a problem with that - I just found it rather curious. When the prayer session was over, she ordained me. Just like that. On the spot. Who was I to argue?

As the big jet began to make its descent, she finished her final prayers and summarized: #1) Don't pray for anyone who is not Christian. That really struck me. Sorry, I thought, gonna have trouble with that one. Goes against the grain of everything I've ever been taught or felt. #2) Stop drinking scotch. OK with that one – at least until after I cleared customs in Bangkok. When I finally got to my hotel in Bangkok I had every intention of hitting the Singha beer.

I survived the harrowing, high-speed taxi ride from Bangkok's airport to my hotel downtown. Bangkok cabbies routinely drive like maniacs. A Roman Catholic priest, resident in Thailand, had previously advised me to just hold a newspaper or magazine in front of my face and not lower it until I arrived at my destination. I followed his advice. I sucked down many Singhas that night.

A month or so later, back in Anchorage, Alaska, a handwritten letter arrived from a church in Texas confirming my Ordination as a Minister. It was filled with misspellings and grammatical errors, but so what. Wow! Visions of Benny Hinn being lowered by a steel cable from a hovering chopper into a stadium full of adoring believers came to view – their raised fists clutching credit cards, cash and checks! But it was not to be. A few weeks later, before I even had a chance to apply for tax-exempt status, I received an equally poorly written letter revoking my ordination. I was summarily defrocked! Drats! A few tears and a few beers and I got over it. I wish I'd had the presence of mind to save those two handwritten letters. If so, they'd have been printed in the appendix of this book.

CHAPTER 4

INDIA: SCAMS AND BEGGARS, MORE SCAMS AND, FINALLY, THE ULTIMATE SCAM

India is a country of over a billion people. More people live in India than in all of Africa. And they have to eat – ideally at least once a day. Food is only free to beggars; others have to pay for it – in rupees. So all kinds of ways have been developed to earn rupees. A large subclass of the thousands of cottage industries humming along 24/7 in India might be labeled "Fleecing the Anglo–Western tourist". I'm not talking muggings, violence or guns. I'm talking street side and marketplace verbal fleecing. Been there, been fleeced, no regrets. God Bless India, the land of Gandhi.

THE GARMENT SHOPS

India is a land of garments and textiles of almost unimaginable variety. Ingenious and persuasive ways to get the tourist to buy a rug or a sari or whatever are among the most popular scams. The streets of India's cities are so hopelessly congested and chaotic that the best way to get around is to book a bicycle rickshaw for a couple hours or half a day. Tell the driver where you want to go or just sit back and plunge into the "happy Asiatic disorder" that Kipling's Kim extolled.

The bicycle rickshaw driver/tour guide will not be a fount of accurate historical or cultural information. Most questions will be met with a blank stare or an empty "yes". Asians do not like to say "no". It's a cultural thing. But they know where they are going. They do not get lost. And, should the rumbling gut from the previous day's indulgence in street food suddenly threaten to explode within minutes – a situation with potentially embarrassing consequences – the driver can find you a toilet in a hurry (for which he deserves a sizeable tip, by the way). He works for you.

But one thing all the bicycle rickshaw driver/tour guides have in common, without exception, is that they all have a friend in the garment business whose shop is conveniently nearby and a mandatory scheduled stop. When you arrive you are greeted effusively by the shop owner and ushered inside. Ideally for them, you're brought into one of the inner rooms or, if it's only a small shop, offered a seat as far away from the door as possible. (There are obvious psychological reasons for this – just check out the CIA Interrogation Manual.) Once you are comfortably seated, the sari–clad missus comes in with a soft drink or a cup of sweet milk tea on a silver tray and sets it before you. It would be very rude to refuse, but once you accept you owe them.

You've been politely saying all along that you are not interested in buying anything now but are happy to look. Bolt after bolt of fine silk cloth comes down off the shelves and is unrolled before you. You compliment its quality. Rugs and wall hangings are unfolded and laid out before you. A sari for your wife or daughter?

Soon you see sadness welling up in the merchant's eyes as he says in a resigned, almost pleading, tone that none of his merchandise is pleasing to you. The sadness soon transforms into impatience, sprinkled with a little anger. The place looks like a tornado just passed through – unrolled bolts of cloth, unfolded rugs and wall–hangings cover the floor in disarray. Your empty coke bottle sits on the small table next to you. This was all for you. You feel a small pang of guilt. Time to buy something, anything. You can always give it to one of the in-laws. You settle on the cheapest purchase you can get away with (less commission for the bicycle rickshaw driver who set you up for this). In my case, I bought a light cotton Nehru shirt I thought might be comfortable in the 110-degree heat. Paid about three times what it would have cost on the street. The stitching at the shoulder seam started to unravel after a few days. It was probably made in China.

THE EAR CLEANERS AT CONNAUGHT PLACE

Connaught Place is a vast traffic circle in the northern part of New Delhi. The center of the big circle is a large, grass-covered knoll that serves as an open space – a de facto public park. All kinds of interesting people pass through here, or hang out. Including the Connaught Place Ear Cleaners.

You can pick them out from afar by their flowing, white robes – chosen, perhaps, to mimic the authority of the physician's white coat. There was nothing professional, much less sterile, about these guys. I approached a tall, bearded and white-robed man named Abdul. It was the two instruments in his hand that caught my attention (being a physician, I had more than a passing knowledge of surgical instruments – and sterile procedure.)

About the length of a typical chopstick, these babies went after cerumen (ear wax), not rice or garlic chicken. The active end, beyond the handle, was about 4 inches long, maybe 1/8 inch wide, and very thin. Designed to be stuck into human ears and probably wiped clean on his white robe between patients.

Abdul exuded confidence and handed me a notebook of handwritten testimonials from his numerous patients. I perused it avidly. Some of his patients saw their businesses prosper after Abdul cleaned their ears. But most of them (in their own handwriting) described a rejuvenating metamorphosis in their sex lives! One guy (I can't remember if he was from Australia or Denmark) was now up to three orgasms a night delighting (or, possibly, exhausting his wife… or girlfriend). I remember thinking if these ear cleaners just banded together they could put the tiger penis, snake blood, and Viagra peddlers out of business overnight. Just a little promotional savvy and up pops another flashy building in New Delhi. An IPO on the stock exchange to follow. Sex sells.

Abdul had no intention of allowing me to sit on the grass and read his notebook of handwritten testimonials in its entirety. He wanted at my ears. But there was no way I was going to let those unhygienic metal chopsticks rupture my tympanic membranes and introduce infection. I could live with one orgasm a night. I responded with my feet. Briskly. In no time I reached the curb at the edge of Connaught Place. And into the middle of my next scam.

THE SHOE REPAIRERS

Along the innermost traffic circle, cars flying by, the shoe repair scammers set up shop. They will engage you in casual, friendly conversation and then suddenly point to a defect in one of your shoes or sandals. A small tear or scratch. Sometimes, you are not sure what they are pointing to. They offer to fix it for a pittance and you relent. At least they are working and not begging, you rationalize, so wanting to be helpful to the local people in a foreign land, you hand over your shoe and take a seat on the curb and read your Lonely Planet guidebook. Big mistake.

Twenty minutes later your shoe will come back riddled with rubber patches and the price tag is now ten times the original pittance you were quoted. If you want your shoe back, you pay. You've been had.

Forewarned, I was ready for them. I'd made sure I had a noticeable gash in one of my shoes. A young Hindu kid chatted me up a bit before pointing to the defect in my right shoe. I told him I liked the gash in my right shoe and asked him how much it would cost to damage my left shoe so it looked as bad as my right. He knew I was playing with him and just smiled, allowing me to walk away unmolested. Touché. I was beginning to catch on.

THE KIDS

There are kids all over India, many of them poor. Some are professional beggars, but many just seem to have figured out that with persistence and the right pose, hand-outs from exotic foreign tourists are easily gotten. It runs the whole gamut and kids, being innately smart and adaptable, have perfected the art. A common sight is a five-year-old girl holding a baby in one arm and begging with the other, a pose designed to tug at the guilty heartstrings of an American or European.

You don't have to be a rocket scientist to figure out that any money you give these kids is unlikely to be deposited in a bank account for their future education. More likely it would be taken from them by a bigger or stronger kid, or used to buy rum or tobacco by a dysfunctional parent. So I always carried a bunch of bananas in my pack. Small Indian bananas. Give a kid a banana and it goes from his hand into his mouth while you're standing there – no one can take it away from him then.

I obviously couldn't feed all the little kids in India and it was easy to run out of bananas. And some of them could be annoying and persistent – following you for blocks, tugging at your pants or grabbing at your ankles and not letting go. I discovered, quite by accident, a foolproof way of shaking these kids loose that comes with an ahimsa (non-violence) stamp–of–approval: Look for someone on the street wearing a uniform – any kind of uniform – and start walking briskly toward that person. It could be a hotel bellboy or doorman who just got off duty. These kids all seem to have a deeply instilled fear of cops. And anyone with a uniform was a cop until proven otherwise and they were not about to take any chances. The closer you get to the uniformed individual the farther back the kid would trail off. It worked every time.

Once, bereft of bananas, I had a little girl following me for blocks. I couldn't shake her and there was no one in sight wearing anything that resembled a uniform. Something about being followed made me uncomfortable, even though she was no obvious threat. So, I resorted to a less pleasant technique to shake her loose. Up ahead was a construction zone where a building was being torn down and the road was all dug up. The scene was littered with shards of concrete and twisted pieces of rusted Rebar up to a foot deep in places. Perfect. I had on a good pair of shoes and made a beeline for it, the little street urchin in hot pursuit. It quickly proved to be too much even for the calloused soles of her bare feet and I finally left her behind.

THE PROFESSIONALS

It's no secret that infants in India have been deliberately blinded or crippled so they will make good beggars. This horrible practice may be much less common today, but its victims, now in their teens or even middle ages, can still be seen on the streets. And that's probably what I witnessed on the sidewalk one steamy hot morning in Calcutta.

The Chowringhee is the main street in Calcutta. The Oberoi Grand, on the Chowringhee, is its main hotel. Sidewalk space in front of and extending for several blocks on either side of this five-star hotel was prime begging territory. It was well known that any beggars here were under the control of the local mafia. And I never confirmed it, but I suspected these beggars were dropped off like orange traffic cones in the morning and picked up near sunset.

Near noon, on my way back from Mother Teresa's Home for the Dying Destitutes, I saw a horribly deformed beggar lying face down on the hot pavement just blocks from the Oberoi Grand. His legs were so twisted and deformed they reminded me of one of those Philadelphia pretzels (always served with mustard) being hawked roadside on the margins of Pennsylvania's biggest city. His face lay not six inches from the pavement and his body oscillated rhythmically as he moaned, a puddle of drool collecting on the pavement below his lips. Some coins lay scattered nearby.

I wasn't about to give any money to the inhuman pimp who dropped off and controlled this guy. A block back there was a man on the sidewalk grinding fresh sugar cane juice. I couldn't fix the beggar's life, but I could do some small good and give the guy a refreshing drink. I knew I had Martin Buber and the Jewish mystics on my side: redeem the world, even just a few square meters, as you walk through time. My problem was, I didn't know if his arms were dysfunctional as well. I wandered in circles for a few minutes, pondering my options.

Suddenly, the pretzeled beggar sat up and, confidently using his arms as crutches, hobbled off into the shade of a nearby tree and lit up a cigarette. I was stunned! Even Calcutta street beggars get scheduled coffee or cigarette breaks? I was so taken aback that I found myself staring. And the human pretzel, smoking his cigarette and looking every bit comfortable and sure of himself, glared back at me.

Overwhelmed and blindsided again by Calcutta, I high-tailed it back to my hotel, my Raj-era oasis, the Fairlawn Hotel on Sudder Street. Patrick Swayze stayed here during the filming of "The City of Joy." (They pulled down the hotel's signs for the movie, but I immediately recognized the place on screen.) And rumor has it that Jerry Brown (former California governor, U.S. presidential candidate, mayor of Oakland, California attorney general under Arnold Schwarzenegger and later governor once again) stayed here. He was apparently on a post-Tomas a Kempis religious quest at the time. I was told there were no rooms for him and he was given a place on the roof or a balcony. Jerry would not have had a problem with that.

It was too early in the day to drink beer, so I opted for a long afternoon nap with the air-conditioner and ceiling fan on. It would help me re-set.

TURNING THE TABLES

Scams can be fun, especially if you see them coming with enough lead time to turn the tables on the perpetrators. For example, when you see a group of beggar kids heading your way, turn suddenly, stick out your hand, and say "rupee." It throws them off.

Once, our train stopped at a small station unexpectedly; within minutes, several little brown hands (actually, arms up to the elbows) thrust themselves between the welded steel bars that precluded our window from being used as an exit even in the direst of emergencies. Like a troop of agile monkeys, they swooped upon that train, swinging from window to window, zooming in on high-yield, pale-faced foreigners like myself and the British woman in our compartment. To pass the time I verbally worked over one little kid until he handed me a coin he held tightly in his sweaty palm. I turned it over in my own palm. It was the real thing and my first success as a beggar. The train suddenly lurched. I pressed the coin back into the little brown palm before we pulled out of the station.

In Old Delhi I once negotiated with a bicycle rickshaw driver for a 2-3 hour ride. We came to a verbal agreement. After a few blocks I ordered him to hop into the back seat while I pedaled, implying it was part of our agreement. It wasn't long before we were caught in a massive traffic jam on the Chandni Chowk, Old Delhi's main street.

The driver was very dark, possibly a Tamil, but darker than the typical northern Indian. This placed him lower in the illegal, but still accepted, caste system. People around us started staring and pointing and smiling and waving and cheering at the white, gray-haired "Sahib" pedaling furiously (it was harder than it looked) while the real driver sat in the back seat. Most of them were probably his friends. He was grinning from ear to ear.

I cooked up a plan for my next trip to India. My "partner-in-crime" and I are going to stop at one of the ubiquitous roadside stalls and admire some cheap trinkets. "How much?" I'll ask, pointing to a cheap trinket. Five rupees, or thereabouts, will be the answer. I'll scratch my head and, with a pained facial expression, explain that five rupees is too cheap. "Eight rupees," I'll throw out, upping the ante. Bewildered, he'll respond, "OK, eight rupees." My partner will then call me aside and, head-to-head, we'll confer. I'll go back to the merchant and explain that eight rupees is still too cheap. "Twelve rupees," I'll insist. Before he has a chance to respond, my partner will start gesticulating wildly and I'll go back to him. Then I'll return to the merchant with disappointing news. "Twelve rupees is still too cheap. It's not fair to you. We're going to go look around in the market." And we'll split before he has a chance to reply. Throw them off a little, I say. It can only make them stronger. They're good people.

THE ULTIMATE SCAM

My third trip to India took me to the desert state of Rajasthan in western India where I hoped to go camel trekking. With experience under my belt from two previous trips, I felt no one was going to pull the wool (or any other fabric) over my eyes. I could sense a scam like General Patton could smell a battlefield. And then I met Mohanlal Verhomal - Spice Merchant.

India has long been the land of spices. Columbus sailed west from Italy in 1492 hoping to secure a more convenient trade route. Unfortunately, for Columbus and the local indigenous people, North America got in his way. Profoundly ignorant of the immense variety and subtleties of Indian spices, I always perused the spice shops. As most of the writing was in Hindi, I let visual and olfactory clues educate me.

Mr. Mohanlal Verhomal sold spices near Jodhpur Fort. Jodhpur is the ancient sandstone kingdom-city of Rajasthan. Its magnificence is rivaled only by the phenomenal sandstone fortress-city of Jaisalmer further west. Mr. Verhomal's spice-cart, the largest I've ever seen on wheels, was parked at the base of the huge Jodhpur Fort.

Mohanlal Verhomal sold 34 different spices. The staple, curry, could be had in strong, medium or normal (not Hot at all). There were spices for Tandoori curry (strong and medium). Henna and Mace and Potato's Masala. And Asafoetida, about which I hadn't a clue. And #33, Winter Tonic - maybe something for Alaska?

All of the spices on the cart were marked down one-third to one-half - an old trick now so commonplace as to be the norm. Mr. Verhomal, a small, gentle and soft-spoken man, asked if he could help me find anything. "Just looking," I replied. "Take whatever you like, sir," the gentle spice merchant offered, "you don't have to pay me now. Just send me a money order when you get back to Delhi, or your home country."

Whoa, I thought, never had an offer like that. "You mean I can take some spices and send you a money order when I get back to America?" I questioned, trying to hide my incredulity and suspicion. "It's no problem, sir. I trust you. Here is my card with my address," he answered sincerely.

Now I was both baffled and intrigued. OK, I thought to myself, the only way to get to the bottom of this scam is to play along until he reveals himself. I chose a packet of spices for ginger tea. Added to Indian-style milk tea it makes a tasty hot drink. The Tibetans in Dharamsala introduced me to it. I also took a packet of curry he recommended to me.

Now for the moment of truth, I thought, as I said to him, "I'll take these two and I have your card. I'll send you a money order when I get back to America. Thank you." I turned and walked away …slowly… and listened carefully. After a half-dozen or so paces, I stopped and turned around. I waved to him. The gentle spice merchant simply smiled and waved back. I walked a little farther … slowly … still listening carefully. The next time I turned around he had his back to me, but by then I was lost in the crowds on the street.

He got me! I'd been had! General Patton would have probably slapped me, though gently, because this was a clever one. There I was with spices I really didn't need and a guilty conscience that drove me to Western Union the day after I got back to Anchorage. I had to hand it to Mr. Mohanlal Verhomal. It was the perfect scam, the ultimate scam. Because it was a scamless scam.

Beggar family in Nariman Square, Bombay, India. April 1994

CHAPTER 5
A SHAVE IN VARANASI

Varanasi, Benares, Kashi - call it what you will, it was for centuries (millennia?), and still is, the holiest Hindu city in India. It has my highest respect.

After I had already booked a 23-hour train trip from Pathankot, in the Punjab, to Varanasi, I met the vice director of the Federal Civil Service for the Indian State of Himachal Pradesh. We were talking in a restaurant in lower Dharamsala, which is Indian (upper Dharamsala, where I just had an audience with the Dalai Lama, is Tibetan). He offered me an armed escort to Golden Temple in Amristar – the holiest of holies to the Sikh religion. At the time there was still apparent tension stemming from Indira Gandhi's assassination.

Wow, I thought, a chance to visit the Golden Temple of the Sikhs. And under armed escort (my style, though, favored a more low-keyed and less ostentatious approach). I politely declined, as I already had my train ticket. And after 23 exhausting hours on Indian Railways, I arrived, bleary-eyed, in Varanasi.

Still, I was up very early the next morning. Sunrise over the Ganges River in Varanasi (about 6 am) was the holiest time of day on the holiest river in the holiest Hindu city.

On my way to the river in the pre-dawn darkness, I could hear music coming from every direction; I concluded it could only be coming from heaven above. I was out on the river in a small wooden boat when the sun came up and sent my lit *puja* (offering) downstream. Funeral pyres onshore were lit and one could see human feet sticking out between the flames.

Before returning to shore I emptied my plastic Nalgene 1-liter water bottle and filled it with Ganges River water. Physically and chemically polluted, but spiritually pure. I still have much of it. And it is available to any sincere and devout Hindu simply for the asking. Money pollutes spirituality. Call me.

But I digress. This is a story about a shave. Which I needed. Trudging back up toward my hotel after my time on the Ganges, I ducked into a non-descript barbershop. I was quickly ushered into a barber's chair and a thin sheet was fastened around my neck.

The barber grabbed a small hand-held wooden tub of shaving cream and added some hot water. Using a shaving brush (it may not have been genuine badger-hair, but was probably the Indian equivalent), he worked up a lather which he then began to apply to my face. He lathered and lathered the left side of my face before moving under my nose to the right side, which he lathered and lathered. Then back across my chin to the left and down the left and right sides of my neck. Just as I thought I was beginning to feel some slight sensitivity from the prolonged lathering, he stopped. This was a man, I remember thinking, who was not in a hurry.

Then out came a double-edged razor, the likes of which I'd only seen in old cowboy movies. He expertly sharpened it on a thick leather razor strop hanging from the chair (another scene from the same old black-and-white John Wayne western). And he proceeded to give me the closest shave I ever had. The combination of an extremely sharp razor and the skill in knowing exactly how to pull the skin taut and angle the razor made it feel like he was only sliding a smooth wooden pencil across my face.

Then, to my astonishment, out came the shaving brush and the tub of shaving cream, and the entire process was repeated.

After the second shaving, he reached up to some bottles on a shelf in front of his chair, poured some clear liquid into his hands, and splashed it across my face. It tingled delightfully. But we were not yet done.

He finished off with a skillful facial and scalp massage. Afterward, he pounded my head with his fists (which felt great – maybe because I thought it was supposed to feel good). And ended with a spinal massage down my neck to my lower back.

The shave, which lasted some 30 minutes, set me back a whopping 64 cents (converted from rupees). I rubbed my cheeks in amazement on the walk back to my hotel – they felt like a newborn baby's you-know-what.

On a later train ride in India, I shared this experience with my seatmate. He very matter-of-factly told me I'd gotten ripped off because I was a foreigner. Had I been Indian, I would have only been charged the equivalent of 16 cents. Damn, I thought with a smile and without regret, scammed again.

CHAPTER 6
IMAN AND SOBA

TRAIN TO JAISALMER, INDIA

The meter-gauge passenger train rolled slowly through the dry scrubland of southern Rajasthan. The temperature outside had to be at least 100 degrees, and our first-class compartment was not air-conditioned. Soot, dust and sand blew in through the windows, clinging to exposed, sweaty skin.

But in India, getting there is at least half the fun.

Where else in the world can a party of tired, late-arriving Brits crash out among the scattered homeless on the floor of a railway station, only to be awakened in the early morning by the station master who insisted on serving them breakfast in bed – a breakfast they ate sitting up in their sleeping bags as the rush-hour crowds passed tolerantly around? Where else does one find oneself in the position of the young British woman I met whose bicycle rickshaw driver grabbed a passing lorry and held on tight, giving them both a terrifying ride through the crowded streets of a large Indian city? This desert milk run was to prove interesting in its own right.

I hung out of the open doorway as the train chugged through the dry, forested mountains of western India where lions and tigers prowled at night. And I sat in the same doorway, legs dangling and hot wind blowing in my face, looking straight down as we crossed over deep chasms. Nobody telling me to take my seat. Ah, tolerant India, where the child in one can come alive and be expressed without fear of embarrassment or admonishment.

The train once stopped in the middle of nowhere, for no apparent reason, and a troop of monkeys, some with their young clinging to their chests, scampered up to the carriage for handouts. From chai wallahs at hodunk railway stations we would buy sweet milk tea in little clay cups – cups that, when emptied, were meant to be smashed on the tracks or on the concrete platforms - the ultimate disposable. (Again, the child in one comes alive.) And at one such stop I saw Shiva himself – a man sitting on a bench, naked and covered with ash from head to toe, giving the smooth skin of what looked like the hermaphroditic body of the great god himself a purplish-gray sheen. Only in India.

TO THE DUNES

I survived the gauntlet at Jaisalmer station. It was not the peak tourist season and the hotel touts were out in force, desperate to grab every tourist they could for a free jeep ride into town to their hotel, which had the best rate in town. During peak season it often got so bad that lathi-wielding cops had to beat them back. Some touts were known to hop aboard at the previous stop and begin the hustle on the train. I stuck to my guns and insisted on the Swastika Hotel and I was soon settled into a second-floor private room with a ceiling fan (shower and toilet in the lobby downstairs, and free morning tea). It was a steal at just under $2 a night.

At 4 pm the following day we piled into a jeep and drove out to the Sam dunes (yes, the sand dunes named Sam). It was here we would begin our camel trek. Ambling over to one of the higher dunes, we sat down to watch a beautiful sunset – the rapidly falling sun setting the horizon on fire as it dropped into the sand across the Pakistani border.

Dinner was at the Hotel Al-Fateh. The dome-shaped "hotel" was about 20 feet in diameter and constructed of branches and thatch with a dirt floor. There was no furniture, electricity, water or toilet. We ate under the light of a single lantern and listened to the stories of a Muslim camel driver named Namal. Namal was also a masseur, or so he said, and he willingly demonstrated his massaging skills on Lorna, a young British woman who was to be the other member of our expedition. It soon became obvious that he was enjoying it more than she was.

I grabbed a pile of dusty blankets and headed out into the darkness to sleep on the dunes. Lorna and Namal followed and, despite her polite protests and gentle suggestions, he continued his massage. Kneeling in the sand, his dark form was silhouetted against the starry sky. Lying back, I counted meteors to stay awake in case things got out of hand, but all was quiet after about half an hour. I pulled the blankets over my head to ward off the chill and, hoping I was the only living organism between these not-so-clean covers, drifted off to sleep.

THE TREK BEGINS

I awoke to sand, sun, camels and dark-skinned men in turbans speaking Hindi and Rajasthani. After a breakfast of toast, tea and hard-boiled eggs, we packed our camels and prepared to depart.

Now, camels get up on their hind legs first, so it's important to hold on tight to avoid being catapulted into a faceplant on the hard sand. Then they bring their front legs into a kneeling position, leveling off somewhat. Finally, they straighten out their front legs, instantly almost doubling their height. And there you sit, high upon a majestic furry throne, four sandy horizons beckoning.

With Iman and Soba, our camel drivers, leading the way, we quickly left the dunes and traveled through scrubland dotted with thornbush and small shrubs. To our right the sands stretched off to the lonely Pakistani border and beyond into the Sind.

Having gotten a late start, we were soon pushing the brutal midday sun. It was time to look for shelter. We stopped at a mud-and-thatch hut where we planned to have lunch and rest until it was cool enough to travel again. It was not unpleasant sitting under the thatched lean-to that adjoined the mud cooking hut, but I had already decided that I wanted to build a camel dung fire.

After a few slugs of warm water from my canteen, I grabbed a cardboard box and plunged into the glaring furnace around us. Waves of heat shimmered off the horizon, and even the vultures were sitting it out in a row on a grassy hillock. It didn't take long to half-fill the box with dry, flat dung cakes.

I tossed a few into the fire and watched them burn while Soba made tea. And minutes later I was sitting in the shade of the lean-to enjoying a cup of sweet milk tea brewed over a camel dung fire, trying not to dwell on the possible origins of the odd bit of ash floating on the surface. After a lunch of chapattis and curried vegetables, we settled down to siesta.

The sun reigned supreme. The heat would peak about 2 pm, then dissipate grudgingly as the slow roll toward evening played out across the timeless desert stage. These were lazy hours, drifting in and out of sleep, so I only reluctantly opened my eyes when I heard a commotion. Blinking in the glare, I saw a camel silhouetted against the sun and a man in a white turban walking toward us. There was no mistaking Namal - the storytelling camel driver and mad Muslim masseur. He greeted me and quickly turned his attention to Lorna, continuing the previous night's massage while going over details of the 30-day camel trek he was dreaming up for the two of them.

CAMPFIRE TALES

By 4 o'clock it was cool enough to set out again. At dusk, as we descended into a dry riverbed, we were engulfed by cool, damp air from a pool to our left. It was soothing and invigorating.

It felt so good to get off the camel that I immediately set off up and down the riverbank to collect driftwood, returning with quite a handful. It started getting dark quickly and it was nearly complete when two small boys on bicycles appeared – out of the darkness, out of nowhere – as we finished setting up camp.

"You like cold drink… Cola, Limca, Beer?" they asked.

"Beer? … Beer!" I said, not sure I wasn't talking to a mirage. "How much?"

"Fifty rupees," answered one boy.

"What kind?"

"Kingfisher," they assured me.

We ordered four beers and the two boys turned their bikes around and disappeared. Ten or 15 minutes later a motorscooter arrived with the beers. They weren't cold and they weren't Kingfishers, but they tasted great as we sat around our small fire, eating chapattis and vegetable curry while listening to the stories of the camel drivers and trying to learn Rajasthani folk songs.

RETURN

The next morning we trekked past abandoned, crumbling sandstone villages and through small living ones. Women in saris could be seen in the distance, balancing large clay jugs of water or bundles of grass on their heads. Children played. India moved through another morning.

The midday sun found us cooking lunch under a large tree in the courtyard of a beautiful sandstone Jain temple. As we ate (chapattis and curried vegetables), a beggar family hovered nearby, waiting for the first shot at our leftovers. An old woman and two small girls quietly accepted the curried vegetables Soba poured into their pots before they wandered off to beg the rest of their meal.

And while we dozed on our blankets, three or four little black billy goats wandered among us, licking our plates and pots clean. A few loose dogs circled farther out, waiting their turn. And I realized that after we left, the birds and squirrels and insects would finish the job. Nothing is wasted in India, neither food nor anything that can be recycled into cash.

Around mid-afternoon we climbed a rise in the desert, and I sensed there would be something spectacular at the crest. I was not disappointed. For on the near horizon stood the entire fortress-city of Jaisalmer, set on a pink sandstone pedestal that thrust up out of the flat desert as if to both dazzle and intimidate anyone who dared to approach. That moment was both the climax and the end of our trek, and we slowly trotted into town.

A typical train station in Jaisalmer, India April 1994

Bill Cox with tribal Bopas, Jaisalmer, India April 1994

Iman, Bill Cox, and Soba - Thar Desert camel trek,
Rajasthan, India April 1994

The Hotel Al-Fateh isn't exactly 5-star, but they did have an indoor band. Namal standing at doorway. Rajasthan, India April 1994

CHAPTER 7

FOUR DAYS IN CALCUTTA AND A MEETING WITH DR. JACK PREGER

The Coromandel Express was speeding through the West Bengal countryside, about an hour from Calcutta. It was late morning, and I was beginning to get apprehensive about my imminent arrival at Howrah Station, the massive railway station that serves Calcutta. I'd read and heard a lot about the place – its cavernous immensity teeming with masses of people. Squatters sleeping, cooking and making their homes on the pavement. Beggars, hustlers and pickpockets. I was alone with no hotel reservations and didn't know a soul in this city of some 10 million.

They were all over me as soon as I stepped off the train: "Taxi? Taxi, Sir? Hotel? Where are you going? Change money?" I brushed them off and walked quickly toward the main hall of the station. Here I paused, took a deep breath, and tried to comprehend the scene that surrounded me. I found out quickly, though, that when you're 6' 7", white and carrying a backpack, you don't stand still for very long at Howrah Station.

The touts were soon upon me again and I decided I'd better keep moving. I made a beeline for the front entrance and headed toward a long row of taxis, ignoring several offers before arbitrarily settling on a young Bengali with betel-stained teeth.

"How much to the Fairlawn Hotel?" I asked.

"50 rupees," he replied.

A quick mental conversion into dollars told me it was a reasonable fare (they refuse to use their meters), so I hopped in. We sat around for several minutes going nowhere until he asked for 10 rupees baksheesh (tip, or more accurately, bribe). I gave him a nasty look and began to haul my pack out of the cab. He waved his hands and said, "OK, OK." We took off for Calcutta.

Halfway into the city, the cabbie turned to me and said, through those widely spaced and deeply stained teeth, "50 rupees, uh, problem. 100 rupees."

"50 rupees," I insisted.

"100," he said again.

Not about to give up, but also unsure about my ultimate physical safety, especially after another Bengali hopped into the front seat, I said with some resignation, "Just take me to my hotel and I'll give you 100 rupees."

He seemed satisfied and in no time we arrived at the hotel. I told him to wait in the cab while I went in and checked on a room. I took my luggage with me. When he didn't protest this, I knew I had him. The English lady behind the desk confirmed my suspicion that I was being grossly overcharged. I asked for, and got, uniformed hotel "reinforcements" and proceeded out to the street to confront the cabbie. A heated argument commenced in Bengali and continued back into the hotel. Flanked by uniformed hotel guards, I was now in a much more favorable bargaining position than earlier in the back seat of the cab. I gave him 50 rupees, and he left, not very pleased. I didn't like making enemies in a foreign country, but neither did I like getting ripped off. But in a city of this size, I figured I needn't worry about one angry cab driver.

MOTHER TERESA

The next morning a group from the hotel was going to Mother Teresa's Home for the Dying Destitutes, so I decided to tag along. We took the subway. It was clean, spacious and uncrowded – distinctly out of place in Calcutta.

I was not emotionally prepared for Mother Teresa's. The first thing one sees after walking through the door are rows of dying bodies lying on cots. It almost reminded me of a Nazi concentration camp, but here these people were loved and cared for in a Christian environment. Or so it seemed. It wasn't until years later, after having my eyes opened by Christopher Hitchens and Aroup Chatterjee, that I learned what was really going on at Mother Teresa's. Her "Christian environment" prioritized conversions, last rites and prayer over saving lives and providing real medical care. She knew how to manipulate the media by glorifying the poor - boosting contributions into the millions. Most was squirreled away into bank accounts overseas. Very little was invested in medical supplies and medical services.

I asked some German volunteers what I could do to help. I was told there's no one here to tell you what to do, just do what you can. I started getting water for those who were thirsty, fetched urinals, helped change a dressing, pass medication. All the patients seemed content, even polite.

One I'll always remember is Sedrick. He was young, maybe in his late 20s. At first, he seemed hydrocephalic, but later I decided that his was just a normal-sized head on a very emaciated body. His bright eyes shone, he was cheerful and polite, and he spoke fluent English. All I remember him saying was that he was glad he was in Calcutta, that it was a good place to die.

I really regret not sitting down and spending more time with him, but my attention was distracted by an old Indian lying on a cot off to the side. He looked deathly ill. I knelt down beside him and held his hand. His pulse was weak and rapid, his skin cold and clammy – an ominous sign in Calcutta's heat. Soon he started making a clacking sound in the back of his throat - his lips opening and partially closing. I remembered seeing this in dying patients when I was a medical intern in Buffalo.

"Is he dying?" asked a young girl kneeling next to me, mopping the sweat off his brow.

"Yes," I said. "He's dying."

The clacking sound stopped, his eyes rolled slightly, he stopped breathing, and his head turned slightly to the left. Over a period of about thirty seconds he had made the transition from life to death. We stepped back while Brother Dominique and some aides wrapped him in a clean white sheet, leaving only his face exposed.

I stood there and stared for a few minutes at the body of an anonymous destitute swathed in a white sheet. At his gaunt face and sunken cheeks, his lifeless eyes staring up at the ceiling. Feeling helpless, confused and somewhat overwhelmed, I decided it was time to volunteer my services in the kitchen for a while. I grabbed a piece of coconut husk (poor man's Brillo), dipped it into a bucket of ashes and clay (poor man's dish soap) and began to vigorously scrub pots until noon, when it was time for the volunteers to leave.

I followed the Germans down a side street, as they seemed to know where they were going. They planned to take a bus back, which made me nervous. But first we were going to stop at a small shop where they said you could get the best milk in Calcutta. And it was the best! Ice cold milk in a little plastic pouch. Anything cold in Calcutta during the hot season was a treat. I sucked it down through a small straw as we walked to the bus stop.

We boarded, and someone motioned me toward a seat. I sat down and looked around. Closely spaced steel bars welded across the windows precluded their use as an emergency exit. That bothered me. The back-door exit didn't look too functional either. More people got on at each stop, and I began to feel increasingly uncomfortable and claustrophobic. Buses in Calcutta have been known to topple over because they were overloaded with people. I worked my way toward the door and got off one stop early. I walked back to my hotel, my British Raj-era hotel – a true oasis in chaotic, steamy Calcutta. I ate lunch, then laid down under the ceiling fan and slept. Slept until awakened by a knock on the door. It was the turbaned Indian waiter with my afternoon tea.

DR. JACK

Mohammed, a passionate Algerian journalist from London, had flown to Calcutta to interview Dr. Jack. He invited me to come along. I'd been hearing bits and pieces about Dr. Jack since I arrived in Calcutta. He was a British physician who had been conducting a streetside clinic for the poor in Calcutta for about eight years. He also provided medical care to foreigners passing through. He'd been variously described as a saint and as a man whose presence and personality was almost palpable as one approached him. He was the subject of a movie at the Cannes Film Festival and said to be a candidate for the next Nobel Peace Prize, even nominated by Queen Elizabeth. But he was also in serious trouble with the Indian government.

We arrived at Middleton Row about mid-morning. His patients were already lined up and down the street, squatting Indian-style on the curb. Cripples, asthmatics, people with tuberculosis, gastrointestinal bleeding, skin wounds. Women clutching sick infants. He had more than 6,000 patients, which might help explain the Indian government's paranoia about his continued presence in Calcutta. But there seemed to be other concerns, probably political in very political India, that I was not privy to.

A skinny Australian resident presided over a group of volunteers, treating patients as best as they could, fumbling through boxes of dog-eared medical records and jars of medications that had survived previous police raids.

Dr. Jack arrived. Dressed in soiled white pants and a plaid shirt clinging with sweat, he seemed a very unassuming individual. A Canadian journalist introduced me to him, and we chatted briefly. Then he spoke for a few minutes with the Australian resident before disappearing into the backseat of a taxi, off to an Indian courtroom to fight deportation.

Dr. Jack and I still keep in touch more than thirty years after we first met. I made it a point to send him a "cool" card or photo from Alaska once a year and in return, I would get a delightfully irreverent letter, a poem or a self-deprecating card signed by "Rambling Jack" or one of his many other epithets.

LOST IN THE CITY

I went for a long walk late one afternoon through the maze of winding, narrow streets that fill central Calcutta. I tried to make a mental note of landmarks and signs at each turn or intersection so I could find my way back.

Darkness falls quickly in the tropics. I turned around and started back. Soon all the streets began to look alike. Or, rather, they looked different; I'm not sure which. None looked very familiar. Yes, I was totally, unequivocally lost, on foot, in Calcutta after dark.

Panic begins in the loins, or lower abdomen, as a kind of a deep pulling or sucking feeling, qualitatively similar to a strong yearning. But then it starts to spread – down to the knees, which become wobbly, and up to the chest and neck, which tighten. It needs to be arrested while still in the loins.

I arrested its spread by assessing my situation. I was in no apparent physical danger. I had plenty of money and credit cards (so far, anyway).

I would just take a cab to my hotel if I had to. Besides, I'd been lost before in a big city after dark. That was in Nagasaki. Only then I didn't remember the name of the hotel (an obscure little Japanese inn), I didn't have it written down on me anywhere, and I didn't know the name of the street it was on. I made it back OK then and celebrated with a Kirin beer. I told myself I'd make it back to my hotel this night, too. And I would celebrate with an Indian beer.

Calcutta comes alive after dark. People start closing their little cubicle shops - the ones they sit cross-legged in all day sorting chick-peas or repairing sandals or any one of more than a thousand cottage industries. They stand around drinking tea and speak in animated Bengali. Big pots of stew are set to boil over charcoal fires on the sidewalk. Bells call the faithful to prayer in the Moslem neighborhoods. Children scamper about like they do all over the world. It's fascinating. Unfortunately, being lost kept me from fully enjoying it.

I finally found a rickshaw driver who could understand English (the streets were too narrow and congested to hope to get anywhere in a taxi). Central Calcutta is one of the last holdouts in the world for the man-powered rickshaw. I now had a good excuse to try one. I resolved to give him lots of baksheesh if he got me back to my hotel, then hopped into the back seat. And he started pulling me.

He took off in the opposite direction I had been walking – further proof of how disoriented I was. When we got back to my hotel, I thanked him profusely and gave him lots of extra 2, 5 and 10 rupee notes because I was so thankful. He kept wanting more, which I suppose was natural. I thanked him one last time and slipped through the hotel gates. Finding a chair in the outdoor courtyard, I sat down and called for a beer.

NIGHTFALL

On my last night in Calcutta we were all sitting outside in the courtyard drinking beer and talking about the problems of the world and just about any other subject that came up. There was Basil, the Scottish hotelier from Bangkok, whose stories about North Africa I listened to with envy. Mohammed, the passionate Algerian, was there. His intensity made me a little uncomfortable. There was the Briton whose exploits in the Nepalese Himalaya seemed a bit out of proportion to his portly frame, with the beer in one hand and the cigarette in the other. And then there was the Australian university lecturer who gave me insight into the unbelievable complexity of Indian politics, when he pointed out that the West Bengal communist party alone had seventeen factions.

Around midnight I stood up and excused myself. The beer had long since gone to my head, which it does very quickly in the hot and humid Calcutta summer. I was about to go to my room when something caught my ear outside the gates of the hotel: the quiet of the street.

I wandered over. The gates were chained and locked, so I pressed my face against the bars and craned my neck to see as much of the street and sidewalk as I could. And I saw feet. Feet attached to legs giving way to feet attached to ankles and finally just feet, where my peripheral vision was blocked by the cool steel bar.

The "sheeted dead" that Kipling described. Only they didn't have sheets. The lucky few slept on an old blanket or a piece of cardboard. Most just slept on the bare pavement. It was so quiet, warm and still. The city was asleep. It was the end of another day in Calcutta.

Dr. Jack Preger (in plaid shirt) at his streetside clinic, Middleton Row, Calcutta, India. May 1988

Dr. Jack Preger's patients line up on the sidewalk in Calcutta, India.
May 1988

Chapter 8
Dr. Yeshi Dhonden and Dr. Tenzin Choedrak

(Dharamsala, India February 1992)

The "Great Yeshi Dhonden" is how I've heard him described. A simple and humble maroon-robed monk, he is the former personal physician to the Dalai Lama and the senior and most famous practitioner of traditional Tibetan medicine. He now ran a busy private clinic in Dharamsala, India - home to the Tibetan government-in-exile and a large Tibetan refugee population. I would be spending the morning at his side, observing.

Tibetan medicine is based on the Buddhist Medicine Tree and its associated Tantras. It is vastly complex, yet its basis is simple. There are three humours that permeate all sentient beings: bile, wind and phlegm. When they are in balance, we are healthy. Yet, the slightest imbalance may account for the tens of thousands of diseases documented in the Tantras. The practitioner diagnoses the disease and prescribes the appropriate treatment to restore the balance, thereby restoring health. Tibet's first medical school was built in the 8th century, but Tibetan medicine was almost certainly long-established by then.

The premier diagnostic tool is pulse diagnosis. Studied for a solid year, it is said to take ten years to master. The middle three fingers are placed on the patient's radial artery at the wrist. Each presses down with a slightly different pressure. The inside and outside of each finger senses, or "reads", a different organ system (a division into hollow and solid organs does not necessarily correspond to Western medicine's understanding of anatomy). The combination of the humours is also read. There are hot and cold illnesses, seasonal pulses...

Next, the urine is examined and smelled. It is whisked and the way it bubbles or froths is noted. Finally, a prescription is written in Tibetan and the patient is sent to the pharmacy.

Dr. Dhonden saw dozens of patients that morning. There was very little doctor-patient discussion. It was as if Dr. Dhonden already knew why they came to see him and what to look for. Pulse diagnosis and urine examination seemed to be the mainstay, followed by more particular techniques that might be necessary. I watched him do facial acupuncture on a young monk.

Yeshi Dhonden has been to the big medical centers on the American East Coast and examined patients. His diagnostic abilities stunned University hospital doctors! His descriptions, translated from Tibetan, left his American medical colleagues no doubt they were talking about the same disease or underlying congenital anatomic defect.

Tibetan medicine is mostly herbal, and I followed the last patient of the morning over to the pharmacy where it was prepared and distributed. The raw materials were mostly gathered from the surrounding valleys and hillsides and assembled into the final product in this building. A strong but wonderfully pleasant herbal scent filled the air, like potpourri, and I wondered if it might be acting as a health-enhancing tonic on the workers who inhaled it all day. In one of Dr. Dhonden's final exams as a medical student, he was taken into a large tent near the medical institute in Tibet where he trained. Long tables were filled with roots, leaves and herbs of every kind. Blindfolded, he identified each and every one correctly by taste, smell and touch!

Early the following afternoon I showed up at the office/apartment of Dr. Tenzin Choedrak - the personal physician to His Holiness the Dalai Lama. This small, gentle man was imprisoned and brutally tortured by the Chinese Communists in Tibet before he was able to make his way to India. His smile filled the room with compassion as he took my hand in his, holding it and rubbing it gently until it reached the same temperature as his. His skin was the softest I ever felt.

A Nepali woman knelt beside us to translate, but I had no medical issues and said nothing. I just wanted to experience having my pulse taken... and who better than the Dalai Lama's personal physician to do it! Dr. Choedrak pressed his three fingers against my radial artery.

After what seemed like several long minutes of concentration, he removed his hand, looked at me and, through the translator, announced that I was suffering from constipation and maybe a mild gastritis. I was stunned! While virtually every westerner traveling in India gets diarrhea on one or more occasions, I'd been having the opposite problem. My bowels had been stopped up for several days, despite indulging in street food, and I was beginning to get concerned. As for the gastritis, it was almost 2 pm and my stomach was quietly rumbling with hunger. I went to the pharmacy of the Tibetan Medical and Astrological Institute and filled the prescription Dr. Choedrak gave me.

A final word to the wise: Don't mix Tibetan medicine, Larium (a vicious anti-malarial known to cause hair loss and exacerbate psychotic episodes) and strong, dark Indian rum! It caused me to miss rounds at Delek Hospital the following morning!

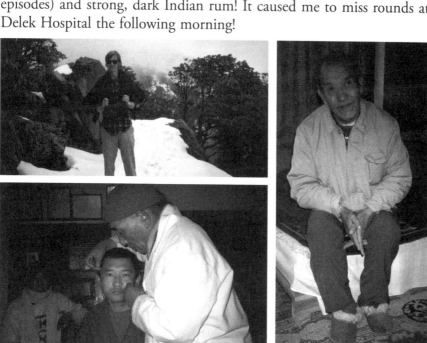

Top left: Bill Cox underdressed for a winter hike into the Himalayas. February 1992

Bottom left: Dr. Yeshi Dhonden doing acupuncture, Dharamsala, India February 1992

Right: Dr. Tenzin Choedrak, Dharamsala, India February 1992

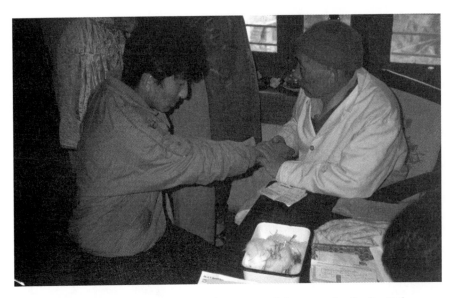

Dr. Yeshi Dhonden doing pulse diagnosis, Dharamsala, India February 1992

CHAPTER 9
THE DALAI LAMA, FIRST MEETING

In February 1992 I found myself in Dharamsala, India – home of His Holiness the Dalai Lama and the Tibetan exile community. I'd been active with the Alaska-Tibet Committee for some years, but wanted a first-hand, real-time look without going clear to Chinese-occupied Tibet and risking any missteps that might cause problems for the locals. India was (and is) a free country and a good place to start.

I wanted to visit the exiled political institutions and, especially, the monasteries that were preserving Tibet's religious and cultural traditions. And the Tibetan exiles themselves. I also harbored, I'll admit, a nearly impossible wish-dream to actually meet with the Dalai Lama himself.

Tempa Tsering, Secretary of the Department of Information and International Relations, was patient, kind and helpful to me. His job was similar to Secretary of State. I had read about Tempa in John Avedon's book, *In Exile from the Land of Snows*. About his family's harrowing escape from Chinese–brutalized and occupied Tibet. As a small boy he may, or may not, have remembered his sister slowly succumbing to hypothermia, and dying, on a brutally cold and windswept Himalayan mountain slope. How could he have possibly imagined, as a scared and freezing small boy, not only surviving, not only ending up safely in India, but being the first Tibetan to graduate from the Madras Christian College, in Tamil Nadu State? And not only that, but marrying Jetsun Pema, the Dalai Lama's younger sister!

In quiet Dharamsala, having everything to gain and nothing to lose, I ventured as close as I could get to the Dalai Lama. He was in town. Several layers of security away, I was stopped, politely, and I pleaded my case. I was given an appointment to return and talk with the Dalai

Lama's Private Secretary – a pre-requisite before any private audience would be considered. It was auspicious.

THE HIKE

It was spring in the lower foothills of the Himalayas, the rhododendron were starting to bloom, and I had a day to kill – I wanted to hike, preferably uphill. I made the rounds of some foreigners I'd befriended, but found no one who wanted to join me on short notice. With vague directions and minimal provisions, I took off alone.

Past the historic St. John of the Wilderness Church - cast into perpetual shadow by the huge and protected trees that surrounded it. Farther along, the dark green leaves and red blossoms of the rhododendron forest greeted me, along with scampering monkeys. I continued uphill.

As I gained altitude, the temperature cooled, and I nearly jumped with excitement when I saw, on the trail ahead, what I had come for. No, it wasn't Yeti scat, but a small patch of Himalayan snow – the real stuff. I caressed it, much as I did some years later with Hawaiian snow on a hike to the summit of Mauna Kea.

As I continued onward my "novelty" Himalayan snow soon covered the trail, which became narrower and steeper. Green-leaved rhododendrons, poking up from the snow, provided solace and encouragement. That is, until a big Mexican barreled down the trail towards me, warning me that conditions farther uptrail were hazardous. Mexico, as I recalled, was a hemisphere away, and he seemed a bit out of his element. We talked a bit, and he continued barreling downhill.

I paused, ruminating on the Mexican's warning, when an energetic German named Mischa shot by me in jeans and sneakers, heading uphill. We talked briefly. I decided to follow Mischa.

I remember one very challenging, short, snow-covered section where the trail narrowed down to about two feet – with a steep drop-off on the right. A fall, cushioned by snow and rhododendrons, would probably not have been lethal, but it might have taken several days to a week to scramble back up to the trail, or down to Dharamsala. Not fifteen minutes later we crossed the runout zone of an old avalanche. I could see the Forest Rest House through a faint, damp haze, precipitously perched just off the trail in the distance.

Built of rocks, timbers and a corrugated metal roof, it was a crude, but secure, mountain shelter built and maintained by the Government of India. We took shelter a while, even though we didn't need to, then continued onward. Until I came to my senses and stopped.

I'll never forget finding myself standing in three feet of snow on a steep slope in the Himalayas, looking up into a sea of white. I was dressed for a spring day hike with no extra provisions or warm clothes – and maybe a candy bar and some water left in my daypack. Reality, and good sense, finally hit. I sucked in the beauty that surrounded me for 360 degrees – again and again. Then I turned around and headed back for Dharamsala. This time, the German followed me.

THE AUDIENCE

The Dalai Lama's Private Secretary and I talked for almost an hour. He spoke fluent English. And I remember he expressed to me his greatest regret: that Tibet did not establish its credentials as an independent nation to the satisfaction of the world community prior to the brutal Red Chinese invasion in 1949 – and the suppression in 1959 when the Dalai Lama successfully fled to India. After we finished our conversation, he gave me a time to return the next day for a 15-minute private audience with the Dalai Lama. I was in blissful shock.

The outer perimeter of security for the Dalai Lama was provided by the Government of India. The inner perimeter, more stringent, was provided by trusted Tibetans. I had no set topic or agenda. It was better that way – I could relax and let the audience unfold. I was ushered into the reception room and offered a seat.

I remembered as a kid in the late 1950s reading about the Dalai Lama – the "god-king" of Tibet. Now here I was in India and I'd be meeting him privately in a matter of minutes. There was a quiet commotion at a corner door, and in walked the Dalai Lama. He filled the room with an aura of compassion and spirituality that is difficult to put into words. I was ready.

I stood up with the kata in my hands. The kata is a white ceremonial scarf that is mutually and respectfully exchanged when meeting a high Tibetan political or spiritual official. I had picked up a generic white kata at a shop in upper Dharamsala, but when I mentioned it was for a meeting with the Dalai Lama, the merchant immediately suggested upgrading to a more appropriate (and more expensive) higher quality silk kata. I went for it, without hesitation or regret.

I placed the kata on the Dalai Lama's out-stretched forearms and he placed his around my neck. Wow, I thought, this beats receiving a diploma at high school or college graduation a thousand-fold. But later, I wondered…a kata blessed and received by the Dalai Lama is a spiritual gift to be treasured and revered and passed on to the kids and grandkids. But what about all the katas the Dalai Lama receives? I wouldn't blame him one iota if he recycled them. After all, they'd be doubly blessed – once when he received them on his forearms and again when he presented them to his next guest. The whale and wildlife-loving Dalai Lama is one of the world's greatest environmentalists, but the Indian Union of Kata Merchants might have a legitimate grievance.

The Dalai Lama and I talked about the extraordinary changes unfolding in former Soviet-oppressed Mongolia and the newly broken up Soviet Union, especially the Russian province of Buryatia (Buryatia and Mongolia heavily subscribe to Tibetan Buddhism). I suggested I could best help Tibet by not going to Tibet, but by focusing my attention on Mongolia and Russia. Surround China, if you will. The Dalai Lama agreed and I had my mission.

The Dalai Lama then joked how Buddhism, which was born in India and headed north through Tibet, China, Mongolia and into southern Siberia was maybe now poised to make a U-turn at its northern terminus in Russia and re-flourish in Mongolia, China, Tibet, and maybe India.

When my fifteen minutes with Anchorage mayor Tom Fink were up after a scheduled meeting a loud buzzer went off on his desk, immediately followed by the no-nonsense voice of his secretary saying, "Your next appointment is here." I found that jarring. I liked the Dalai Lama's approach. Adopting a playful smile and facial expression, he turned to me and asked: "Well, did you bring your camera?"

I had brought my camera, but in my excitement and nervousness I left it in the anteroom. His Private Secretary retrieved it, and the Dalai Lama and I posed for photos. Mindful of how busy his schedule must be, I tried to make an exit. He presented me with a small gift-pack, and then proceeded to open it. It contained a commemorative Tibetan coin and note and also a small pamphlet he authored on World Peace. The pamphlet was printed on thick, glossy white paper. Halfway to the exit, His Holiness sat down at a small coffee table, opened the pamphlet, and proceeded to write an inscription (in Tibetan cursive) to me, followed by his signature.

The Dalai Lama knew that if you write on glossy paper with a felt-tip pen it takes time to dry. Had he closed the pamphlet it would have smeared. So he blew on it gently, then held it up to the light (if it glistens, it's still not dry). Standing over the Dalai Lama, I remember thinking at the time that here is one of the greatest and most respected spiritual leaders on earth. I knew that in the previous two weeks he had met with British Prime Minister John Major and U.S. President George H. W. Bush. But here he was giving me his full attention. And I knew that, since time immemorial, spiritual beings like the Dalai Lama could make time stop by living to the fullest in the present moment. Blow gently. Hold up to the light at an angle. Repeat as necessary…

It was the longest, and most spiritually refreshing, two minutes of my life. Finally, the pamphlet could be closed. One last gentle clasping of hands, and I was off across the peaceful, secluded garden, out the main gate and back into the delightful Tibetan/Indian chaos of Dharamsala.

A Rhesus Macaque, McLeod Ganj, Dharamsala, India. February 1992

Forest Rest House on the trail to Triund, uphill from Dharamsala,
India. February 1992

My first meeting with the Dalai Lama in Dharamsala, India. February
1992

Tibetan Children's Village, Dharamsala, India. February, 1992

CHAPTER 10
THE DALAI LAMA, SECOND MEETING: A TIBETAN-GYPSY DIALOGUE

A TIBETAN-GYPSY DIALOGUE (MARCH 2003)

I picked up a book by Isabel Fonseca many years ago entitled: *Bury Me Standing*. A book about the Gypsies, the title is the first half of the Gypsy proverb: "Bury me standing, I've been on my knees all my life." Although the term 'Gypsy' is universally understood and recognized, it has become a negative and debasing stereotype. The correct word to describe this ethnic group is Roma.

One of the most tightly-knit and persecuted peoples, the Roma are the second-largest transnational ethnic group in the world, after the Kurds. Numbering today between 14 and 16 million, they began a one-way dispersion from northern India some 1,000 years ago, taking more than 400 years to reach the outskirts of Europe. Their long journey can be traced in reverse by studying their language. Stopping for generations in various countries along the way and practicing their trades, they incorporated practical terms from the local language into their own Romani. For example, there are numerous Persian words in the Romani language and words referring to ironsmithing, but only one Mongolian word.

Fonseca's book makes many references to Dr. Ian Hancock, a Roma professor of English and Linguistics at the University of Texas in Austin, who almost singlehandedly secured representation for the Roma at the United Nations. He was also appointed by President Bill Clinton to represent the Roma on the Holocaust Memorial Council – only the second Roma to serve on the Council (the first, Minnesota musician

Bill Duda, was appointed by President Reagan.) I tracked down Ian and invited him to Anchorage to speak to the Alaska World Affairs Council about the persecution of the Roma.

I went to Anchorage International Airport to meet Dr. Hancock the night of his arrival. Neither of us had any idea what the other looked like, so I held up a large cardboard sign with the word *gadjo*. *Gadjo* is a Romani word that means "outsider" or "non-Gypsy". Non-gypsies were unclean, or *mahrime*. That was me. It was, of course, a condescending term, but helped explain their survival as an ethnic group. So it was kind of like me going to the airport to meet the Reverend Al Sharpton or Jesse Jackson and holding up a sign that said "honky". I was certain Ian Hancock would be the only one getting off that Delta flight who recognized the word *gadjo*. I just hoped he had a sense of humor.

Then I saw Brian Davies, who I knew socially. Brian was the retired Vice President of BP Alaska. A member of the Alaska World Affairs Council, Brian and his wife would be hosting Dr. Hancock at their Anchorage home. We chatted a bit before I told Brian in no uncertain terms that I did not want him standing within ten feet of me. It had nothing to do with me being a Sierra Club environmentalist tree-hugger and him being one of the "Big Oil" guys. It was just that, as I explained, *gadjo* is masculine singular, and if he stood next to me I would have had to change the word to the plural *gadje*, and I did not have a Magic Marker on me and did not want to be grammatically incorrect. Brian understood and graciously stepped well off to the side. Ian arrived and thankfully got my sense of humor.

Ian Hancock may be best known for his international activism on behalf of his people, but his academic forte is studying the various Creole languages. He was once drawn to a locale in western Africa to study a remote Creole dialect. He was concerned that if the locals knew he spoke English, they would resort to English as the medium to teach him, distorting or polluting the Creole in the process. So he passed himself off as a French sailor who spoke no English and, in short order, mastered the dialect and its grammatical structure.

I knew Ian's work had taken him before the United Nations, the European Parliament and several heads of state. And he had an ongoing dialogue with then German Chancellor Helmut Kohl. Sitting in my idling car in Brian Davies' driveway, I asked Ian if he had ever met the Dalai Lama. His face lit up warmly at the mention of the name. No, he hadn't, but he sure would like to. "Well," I said, "I'll see what I can do."

My first audience with His Holiness the Dalai Lama in February 1992 took 24 hours to set up. This one would take over two years, involve multiple e-mails, phone calls and letters, as well as meetings in Anchorage, Portland and New York City. But it became more than just an "audience request" as the idea of a "Tibetan – Roma Dialogue" took hold. The Roma are widely scattered geographically and politically after a 1,000-year diaspora. They have no homeland, no leader, and no epic. Yet, they maintain their language and culture almost to a person. The Tibetans, on the other hand, have been in diaspora 60 years since the Communist Chinese invasion of their country. They are worried and struggling to preserve their own language and culture, but they have a revered leader in the person of the Dalai Lama and the richness of their Tibetan Buddhist tradition to help guide and sustain them.

I envisioned a dialogue where the Roma could share their incredible language and cultural survival skills with the Tibetans, and the Tibetans could share their culture and heritage, especially the Tibetan Buddhist ideals of compassion and non-violence, with the Roma. And there was no doubt that recognition by a revered spiritual figure like the Dalai Lama would be very uplifting to a beaten-down people like the Roma. The Roma have no single, internationally recognized leader, although there is a self-proclaimed "King of the Gypsies" somewhere in Romania. Looked like Ian would be unofficially representing the Roma before the Dalai Lama.

On August 8, 2002 I was forwarded an e-mail from the "Office of H.H. the Dalai Lama". Known as the "Private Office", it is located at the Dalai Lama's residence in Dharamsala, India. This was where all final decisions were made. Our request was granted and His Holiness would see us the following March 14, 2003. Plenty of time to prepare. The date was later moved up to March 12 so the Dalai Lama could accommodate a former Indian Prime Minister in Hyderabad.

Coordinating our schedules, I took off from Nome, Alaska and Ian took off from Austin, Texas and we met in Taiwan and continued on to New Delhi after a stop in Kuala Lumpur. We had given ourselves plenty of time to figure out how we would get to Dharamsala, at the base of the Himalayas. India was its usual chaotic and delightful self. The hotel I planned to stay at was closed, so we prevailed upon the taxi driver to find us an alternate. They get commissions for this, so he was happy to oblige and took us to the Rajdoot Hotel. It was around midnight. We had a couple beers at the bar to celebrate our safe arrival and watched a Hindu dancing girl up on stage whose act was so tame that Ward and June Cleaver wouldn't have batted an eye if Wally and the Beav had been with us (provided the boys drank Cokes, of course).

The following morning, having booked our rooms for another night and under no time constraints, we plunged into the Indian sunshine and grabbed a motorcycle rickshaw across town. I wanted to look up a Delhi cop I knew. Walking through the Lodhi Colony neighborhood of New Delhi, I suddenly got a sinking feeling in my stomach.

"Ian," I asked calmly, "do you remember the name of the hotel where we are staying?"

"No," he replied.

"Do you remember the name of the street it is on?"

"No," again.

"Did you happen to pick up their business card on the way out?"

"No."

"Did you leave your room key at the front desk like you were supposed to?"

"Yes." The sinking feeling in my stomach progressed to a pre-panic because my own answers to the first three questions were the same.

I took a few calming breaths with Ian now curious at my line of questioning. Then, with a prayer on my lips, I slipped my hand into my pocket and my fingers caressed a large, round coin. There was a key attached. I was so happy it might as well have been a Spanish doubloon. I pulled it out. On it was written the word "Rajdoot" and a telephone number. I shuddered to think how, in this sprawling city of over 10 million, we could have possibly found our way back to our hotel (and belongings) without knowing the name of the hotel, the street it was on, or even which part of the city it was located in.

As we headed toward the train station to inquire about tickets, the crowd got thicker and more chaotic. It became hard to even walk. Suddenly, it seemed, the crowd surged and a wave of humanity swept us away from the train station and eventually deposited us in front of the tiny cubicle office of a tour guide named Happy. It was almost providential. We decided to charter a jeep from Happy for the long drive north.

The first part of the journey, toward Punjab, was on the famed Grand Trunk Road. We shared the road with trucks, busses, motorcycles, bicycles, pedestrians, carts pulled by oxen and yes, even elephants and camels. After Chandigarh we started winding our way up into the mountains.

It was a long twelve-hour drive, but I couldn't have had a more interesting conversation partner. Ian was a renaissance man who could discuss everything from the fine points of Malaysian cooking to the differences in grammatical structure between the English–based and French–based creoles. But it was Holocaust politics that captured my attention. Ian and Elie Wiesel, I learned, had been butting heads for, well, maybe decades.

Elie Wiesel is the revered Holocaust survivor and Nobel Peace Prize Laureate (1986), author of some 57 books and recipient of the Congressional Gold Medal (1985) and Presidential Medal of Freedom, among other honors and awards too numerous to mention.

Wiesel has been criticized for promoting what has been called the "uniqueness doctrine". This holds that the Jewish Holocaust/genocide, being the "Horror of Horrors", is unique, towering above other genocides. It cannot be compared to or shared with any others. This doesn't go over well with the Armenians or the Roma. And probably not with the Rwandans.

Hitler specifically targeted only two ethnic groups for extermination in the Final Solution: Jews and Gypsies. Ian coined the term *porraimos* to describe the Gypsy Holocaust. From the Romani language, it means "the devouring." Yet, during his years of influence, Elie Wiesel resolutely refused to have any Roma representation on the Holocaust Memorial Council or at the Museum. It may be personal, as his father was supposedly betrayed by a Gypsy capo at one of the concentration camps. "I will never forgive those people (the Gypsies)", Wiesel reportedly once said. He was certainly aware there were also Jewish capos. As Solzhenitsyn once famously said: "The line separating good and evil runs through every human heart". And everyone has their breaking point.

Later, I asked Ian where the legendary Nazi hunter Simon Wiesenthal fits into all of this and the conversation turned to that interesting and little-discussed zone of overlap between Holocaust politics and Nobel

Peace Prize politics. Before long the snow-covered peaks of the Himalayan foothills came into view and we arrived in Dharamsala.

The Dalai Lama's private reception room hadn't changed much since I'd been there eleven years earlier. We sat down on the same sofa. Ian took the place of honor next to the chair the Dalai Lama would be sitting in. When he entered, His Holiness the Dalai Lama filled the small room with his spiritual aura and compassion (this time I noticed that his shoelaces were untied). Once I introduced Dr. Ian Hancock to the Dalai Lama my job was over and I sat down to listen.

The first-ever high-level Tibetan–Roma dialogue commenced: Dr. Ian Hancock in suit-and-tie wearing a ceremonial white silk kata (scarf) that had been draped over his neck by the Dalai Lama and a smiling, focused and humble maroon-robed Tibetan Buddhist monk. As their conversation began, the Dalai Lama reached down and tied his shoelaces. Relieved, I made a mental note - even Dalai Lamas have to tie their own shoelaces.

Dr. Hancock briefly outlined the long history of the Roma and their current isolation and persecution – mostly in Europe. The Dalai Lama offered concrete suggestions and stressed the importance of education. His Holiness also agreed to host a delegation from the Romani Parliament in Europe to travel to India to meet the Tibetan government-in-exile.

As the conversation wound down, it was now unspoken time to ex-change gifts and then pose for photos. I had two books for His Holiness – written by my late meditation teacher, Sri Eknath Easwaran, and personally inscribed to the Dalai Lama by his widow, Christine.

Sri Easwaran, as a young boy, received his spiritual education from his illiterate grandmother in Kerala, India, almost a century ago. (Literacy is not a pre-requisite for spirituality.) He went on to become an English Professor and Sanskrit scholar in India. Then he met Mahatma Gandhi, walked with him, and his life was changed forever. He came to the United States in 1959 as a Fulbright Scholar and in the 1960s founded the Blue Mountain Center of Meditation in California, which taught a very practical form of "passage" meditation.

Sri Easwaran was fascinated at the way Gandhi vanquished his ego and totally transformed himself. Many books had been written about Gandhi's life and accomplishments, but Easwaran focused on his "being" in *Gandhi the Man*.

The second book was *A Man to Match His Mountains* about the Badshah Khan. A devout Muslim and fierce Pathan warrior from the Khyber Pass region of what is now Afghanistan, the Badshah Khan's life changed completely after meeting Gandhi. He totally embraced ahimsa (non-violence) and brought it back to his violence-plagued homeland to cope with the British.

A book about the foremost Hindu apostle of non-violence and one about the foremost Muslim apostle of non-violence being presented to the foremost Buddhist apostle of non-violence. Only the Reverend Dr. Martin Luther King, Jr. was missing.

His Holiness perused the Gandhi book oblivious to everyone in the room. Aware that we were running late and concerned about getting pictures, it felt as if he spent half an hour leafing through the pages, although it was only a couple of minutes. But nobody tells the Dalai Lama to "shake a leg." He has a gift of seemingly suspending time by giving his full attention to what is at hand. Stephen Hawking, had he been with us, would have gotten some insight into the human dimension of time. After what seemed like an eternity to my western–conditioned time sense, the Dalai Lama slid the Gandhi book aside and stared into the face of the Badshah Khan.

Now, the Dalai Lama is probably the epitome of calmness, composure and equanimity. Yet suddenly his eyes widened, his face lit up and he clearly seemed either excited or agitated. I wasn't sure which, but I was worried I had committed some sort of transgression. After over twenty minutes of relaxed and fluent conversation, the Dalai Lama was suddenly at a loss for words – or at least English words. He turned to his long-time private secretary and began to speak in rapid-fire Tibetan.

Finally, after the Dalai Lama calmed down, his private secretary turned to me and calmly said: "His Holiness has met with the Badshah Khan. Unfortunately, His Holiness never met Gandhi."

After posing for photos in the small private garden, we walked through the security gate and found ourselves back in India. Our heads were still in the clouds and our feet were still about six inches above the ground. It would be about fifteen minutes until landfall. They seemed to know it. Yup, the little street urchins, in cahoots with the kiosk manager, scammed us. I should have expected it. It only set us back about $5.00 - a small price to pay.

Dalai Lama (reading Gandhi book), Ian Hancock, Bill Cox and Amy Huang. Dharamsala, India March 2003

CHAPTER 11
ASIAN TOILET TALES

Toilets. They're necessary, ubiquitous and, in North America, mostly staid. But in Asia things can get interesting.

JAPAN

The Japanese are very fastidious, formal, polite and ritualistic. So of course their toilets are squeaky clean. When you enter a Japanese home you always leave your shoes outside – there will be a pair of slippers for you to wear indoors. Slippers always come off before you walk on a *tatami* floor. And they come off before you enter the toilet. There will be a special pair of slippers – usually red plastic – for use in the toilet only. It should be mentioned that toilets in Asian homes usually do not share a room with a sink, tub and shower as they do in the USA. They are in a tiny closet unto themselves.

I was staying at a friend's home in southern Japan years ago when suddenly his little kids could not stop pointing at me and giggling. I was wandering the house wearing the red toilet slippers! Small faux pas.

The latest generation of Japanese toilets, I understand, come with more options than an iPhone: seat warmers, a button that plays a recording of a flushing toilet to mask the noise of flatulence, which is very popular with the women, and many more. I heard a story of an American diplomat who had a very unpleasant encounter with one of these high-tech marvels.

At a formal diplomatic gathering, the American had a sudden need to use the toilet. He left behind a rather sizable and malodorous deposit which he was anxious to flush quickly, as the little toilet room was shared by all the guests. But he turned around to face a panel of maybe a dozen buttons and knobs – all in Japanese. Calling in a translator, under the circumstances, was out of the question.

He pushed what looked like the obvious button and was relieved to hear the flushing sound, only nothing moved. He had hit the fake-flush-for-flatulence button. He tried again and was horrified to see jets of water go shooting across the room. He had hit the bidet button. Poor guy…

SINGAPORE

After clearing customs in Singapore I went straight to the airport men's room to take a leak. A bouquet of silk flowers was mounted above each urinal. Forewarned, I made sure I flushed. I was just going to give my hands a quick rinse, but a uniformed attendant insisted I use soap. While I washed, he stood next to me with a hand towel, blotting up every drop of water that I inadvertently splashed on the countertop.

In Singapore it was a $150 fine ($100 US) for not flushing a public toilet. (It was never clear how they enforced it, but now they have auto flush). If a drunk, or a toddler, urinates in a public elevator it is picked up by a sensitive ammonia detector and an alarm goes off in the nearest police station. Cops are on the scene in minutes.

The Japanese may be fastidious, but Singapore is downright anal. The whole place had the atmosphere of a Catholic Elementary School in the late 1950s. I was glad when my jet touched down in Bombay.

INDIA

There was shit everywhere in India. Cow shit. Human shit. But I was OK with that. At least I was no longer in Singapore.

Public toilets in India were, well, public. A tile wall with a shallow trough at the base on a sidewalk or in the middle of the public market. The only privacy shield was the tile wall you peed on. The crowds surged within feet of you. Obviously, it was just for men and stand-up only.

BURMA

Formal pit-stops were few and far between (and mostly closed) on the 12-hour overnight bus ride from Mandalay to Rangoon. But this had already been worked out by the Burmese. The bus would stop periodically in the darkness in the middle of nowhere. The men would all go to the side of the road and urinate. A group pee.

The women all congregated on the opposite side of the bus in the middle of the road. One would squat down and the others, facing outward, would back up into a tight privacy circle around her (like musk oxen protecting their young). When she finished, she would stand up and join the privacy circle while the next woman squatted down. I guess I've just admitted I was peeking, but my interest was purely cultural. And besides, the privacy circle was very tight and it was too dark to see anything anyway.

Yes, the Burmese had worked things out.

RUSSIA

Most of my toilet tales hail from Russia, the largest country in the world. And one I visited frequently.

Russia has a mix of Asian-style squat toilets and western-style sit-down toilets. Virtually every western toilet was missing its seat. I never found out why. Warm butt-cheek, meet cold, white porcelain. Well, it was seldom white but, this being Russia, it was almost always cold. One needed to either sit sideways or sit with one cheek on the cold porcelain and the other hovering unsupported over the center of the bowel. And one needed to be sure there was a newspaper or magazine on the floor. There is no toilet paper. All this before even getting started.

Once, in Khabarovsk, after getting positioned, I was delighted to discover a stack of pre-torn squares of newspaper thoughtfully left behind by a previous patron. I helped myself. After three or four I noticed each one had a brown stain in the middle. Yup, I was recycling an already recycled Russian newspaper - taking it from the discard bin. Live and learn.

Early one morning in the beautiful Altai National Park in western Siberia I wandered over to the facilities to take a leak. The "urinal" was a long, angled metal trough flushed by spigots every meter or so. Just like

I remembered from Boy Scout camp when I was a kid (there's a shorter version of the trough urinal at Anchorage's Chilkoot Charlie's). The place was empty, and as I zipped up and walked away a Russian camper came in and took my place - and started brushing his teeth where I had just peed. Strange, I thought, it's early, but he's a Russian and therefore probably already hit the vodka. I walked out through a different room – and passed a bunch of individual urinals on the wall. Yup, I'd just peed in the sink. Things aren't always what they seem.

Back in Khabarovsk, I paid a few rubles to use the public toilet at the marketplace. I got a couple squares of coarse toilet paper in return which, fortunately, I didn't need. Just as Russian western-style toilets were all missing their seats, the stalls housing the Asian squat-style toilets were all missing their doors. Several men could be seen squatting in full view.

It was the cleaning lady that caught my attention. Old, stooped, horrendously ugly and mostly toothless, she was right out of a 16th century London slum, albeit with Slavic facial features. She pushed a filthy broom over the filthy floor with the vigor of a Russian peasant woman plowing her field. And she pushed that broom right up to the feet and ankles of the men in the stalls, sadistically trying to knock them off balance as they squatted helplessly and precariously. It was probably one of her few remaining pleasures in life.

MONGOLIA

There is not much to say about Mongolian toilets because beyond Ulaanbaatar City limits there…aren't any. Just the vast steppe. I was told that when U.S. Secretary of State James Baker was in Mongolia during the First Gulf War, a helicopter had to ferry a hygienic porta-potty from stop to stop for his squeamish girlfriend.

Julia Roberts is a different ball of wax. When she was in Mongolia filming a movie about wild horses, some friends of mine were on the periphery of the set. Hankhuu told me how he once saw her wander off alone a respectable distance out on the steppe, squat down to do what needed to be done, then walk back to the set and return to work. A real trooper, that Julia. Way to go, Pretty Woman!

CHAPTER 12
ARCHBISHOP GABRIEL OF RANGOON, BURMA

Thai Airways flew me to Rangoon, Burma and I arrived after dark. Maung-Ko Ghaffari, who I had met when he came to Anchorage on a personal trip to see family, met me at the airport. I was happy and honored that he came to pick me up.

MR. GHAFFARI

Mr. Ghaffari was the de facto leader of Burma's small, but influential, Muslim minority. He published their newspaper. Widely known and respected, he nevertheless was forced to walk a tight-rope under the military junta that has ruled Burma (Myanmar) with a ruthless iron fist since 1962. He did so skillfully.

Mr. Ghaffari was one of the most educated and intelligent individuals I met in my Asian travels. He had a vast grasp of history and politics. He was fluent in Burmese, English, Arabic, Urdu (the language of Pakistan) and at least two other European languages (I've since forgotten which).

A passionate and devout Muslim with strong anti-Zionist views, Mr. Ghaffari espoused non-violence. This man went out of his way to become personally acquainted with every Israeli ambassador to Burma since Burma's independence from Britain in 1947. He even had a brief correspondence with the legendary David Ben-Gurion. He once said something to me I will never forget, something that should be blared from the mosques across the Middle East. Referring to Israel, Mr. Ghaffari said, "We need to talk and talk and talk. And if that doesn't produce results, we need to talk some more."

After clearing customs, Mr. Ghaffari and his friends took me to a hotel in Rangoon. A $25.00 a night hotel. I felt guilty staying at such an expensive place in such a poor country, but did not want to offend their hospitality. I could switch later.

I snuck across town on foot the next morning and booked a room at the Youth Hostel for $6.00 a night. Private room, ceiling fan, weak air-conditioner and cold shower. Unlike the Japanese, the Burmese were not into hot water – there was no need in their sub-tropical country.

A few days after I arrived, while driving around Rangoon, I pulled out the gift I had brought for Mr. Ghaffari, turned around and presented it. (Asians, in their infinite politeness, always deferred to my lengthy 6 foot 6 inch frame and insisted I sit in the front passenger seat.) It was a book (the same one that I would present three years later to the Dalai Lama) by my late meditation teacher, Sri Eknath Easwaran, who literally walked with Gandhi. It was entitled: *A Man to Match His Mountains* – about the Badshah Khan, the Pathan warrior from Afghanistan who converted to ahimsa (non-violence) after spending time with Gandhi. "Ahh," replied Mr. Ghaffari, "the Frontier Gandhi". He knew. I wasn't surprised.

THE ARCHBISHOP

On my second trek across town I passed an unusual building – St. Mary's Cathedral. A Catholic Church seemed out of place in an overwhelmingly Buddhist country like Burma. I stopped to talk to a woman washing dishes in an outdoor sink and she volunteered that the bishop lived there. I asked if I could meet him. She politely asked me to wait as she dried her hands before disappearing into the rectory. I didn't know at the time that the bishop she was referring to was the Roman Catholic Archbishop of Rangoon.

I was ushered inside and given a seat at a long table in a room with walls paneled in dark wood. It was elegant, but not overdone. A cup of hot, British-style milk tea and some crackers were set before me by a housekeeper. After waiting a bit, I assumed I was supposed to enjoy the tea and crackers alone.

Finally, a small man walked into the room wearing a sweaty white T-shirt, sandals and a traditional Burmese longyii. (The Burmese longyii is a type of dress, also worn by men. It resembles a patterned bed sheet that is wrapped around and cinched at the waist.) He had a non-Burmese face and I assumed he was probably an ethnic Karen. I pushed my empty teacup and cracker wrappers across the table toward him. The small man smiled in a gentle and understanding way and said to me in perfect English: "I know I don't look like an Archbishop but really, I am the Archbishop." Oops. Big faux pas. We talked a bit and he invited me to come back later that evening.

Evenings in Burma were warm and still. I stopped by the Archbishop's after dinner. He kept a large bottle of whiskey and one of vodka in the refrigerator. He poured me a whiskey and we talked. Burma being so isolated and repressive, he was clearly starved for company and conversation. All his mail arrived and was sent out through a trusted courier in Bangkok. The junta couldn't touch him, but neither could he provoke them. It was an uneasy and uncomfortable detente.

Conversation with Archbishop Gabriel was relaxed, pleasant and enjoyable. There was no ice, but the whiskey was pleasingly cool and he kept my glass full. I reflected for an instant on how I'd only been in Burma less than 48 hours and already I'd met the country's top Muslim leader and now I was drinking whiskey with its highest Roman Catholic official. He'd been serving as Archbishop since July 1971. He told me to come back the next morning, as he wanted to take me on a drive to the river.

I arrived the next morning and was surprised to be greeted by Archbishop Gabriel Thohey Mahn-Gaby dressed in the long white robes, colored sash, head-piece and all the intricate and ceremonial paraphernalia befitting an Archbishop of the Roman Catholic Church. Wow, I thought, nobody's gonna be pushing any empty teacups his way. But he was not being ostentatious or trying to impress me. He was being entirely practical, as I would later find out. His uniformed driver arrived in a spotless white van and opened the door for me. I hopped in the back seat and we took off.

I thought we were only going to drive out to the Rangoon River at the edge of town, but we drove across a good chunk of the Texas-sized country to the great Irrawaddy River – Burma's Mississippi.

About fifty kilometers north of Rangoon we were approaching the famous military roadblock that had once stopped Aung San Suu Kyi, the Burmese opposition leader and head of the National League for Democracy as well as Nobel Peace Prize Laureate. Archbishop Gabriel stated to me matter-of-factly: "When we get there, they will pull us over. When they see I am the Archbishop they will leave me alone. They will escort you to their post, check your passport and visa and ask you where you are going. Your answer will be that we are going to see the bridge."

When we were a few kilometers from the roadblock Archbishop Gabriel explained how a long bridge had been built across the wide expanse of the lower Irrawaddy River. It was considered by the government to be a masterpiece of Burmese socialist engineering and they were eager to show it off to foreigners. Burmese socialist engineering, I wondered, what a concept.

Everything came to pass as the Archbishop predicted. We were pulled over. Dressed as he was, he was allowed to stay in the van. I was escorted by armed soldiers to a small bamboo hut where my papers were checked and questions were politely asked. I followed the script and we were soon on our way. And the bridge? Nothing Ayn Rand would have raved about. Photos were strictly forbidden, which didn't make much sense – probably just junta paranoia. I took one anyway.

PANTANAW

U Thant, the former Burmese Secretary-General of the United Nations, is revered in Burma (U is an "honorific" in Burmese, like Don in Spanish, La in Tibetan or San in Japanese.) The eldest of four sons, he was born and raised in the village of Pantanaw in lower Burma, where he attended the National High School. He later returned to teach at the very same school. He became the third Secretary-General of the UN after the death of Dag Hammarskjöld, and he served from 1961-1971. The Archbishop's van pulled into the village of Pantanaw.

Many villagers seemed to know the Archbishop and he stopped to talk with people at their homes. We dropped by the boyhood home of U Thant, where his descendants still lived. U Thant was a devout Buddhist, but it didn't matter, as there was virtually no inter-religious fighting in Burma. (I saw my first Torah at a synagogue in Rangoon.) Later, standing on the bank of a small river at the edge of the small town of Pantanaw, Archbishop Gabriel confided to me that I was the first

Westerner to visit the boyhood home of U Thant (apparently, it lies in a region closed to foreigners). I was honored.

Upon my return to Anchorage I was able to get Archbishop Gabriel and Anchorage Archbishop Francis Hurley in contact (via the Bangkok courier.) Turns out they were both born within a year or two of each other in San Francisco.

Left: Bill Cox and Maung-ko Ghaffari (de facto leader of Burmese Muslims) Rangoon, Burma November 2000

Right: Roman Catholic Archbishop Gabriel of Rangoon, Burma November 2000

Drinking with the bicycle rickshaw drivers on a sidewalk in Mandalay, Burma November 2000

CHAPTER 13

TRAVELS IN LAOS WITH UDA AND KEIKO (OCTOBER/NOVEMBER 1998)

A chorus of birds would break into song in the pre-dawn darkness, gently nudging me toward the lighter stages of sleep. Yet it was the loud cock-a-doodle-doo of the neighborhood rooster that would jolt me awake. By then it would be nearly sun-up and the first motor scooter of the day could be heard through my open bedroom window. I was staying at a $15 a night guesthouse on a dirt road in Vientiane, Laos – just blocks from downtown and the Mekong River.

This landlocked Southeast Asian country was still a backwater paradise in the 1990s, largely untouched by the economic growth frenzy and rampant materialism that has surged through its neighbors like a conflagration over the past two decades, gobbling up land and culture and spitting out skyscraper hotels and manufactured goods. A six-story joint venture hotel going up in Vientiane (it would be the tallest building in all of Laos) indicates its immunity may be limited.

The capital and largest city, Vientiane can be covered by bicycle in a day – from the Presidential Palace to the Great Sacred Stupa to the National Parliament and Morning Market. Traffic is sparse, many streets are unpaved, life is slow and the people are friendly.

It was time to head north. Best to fly, since there were still some Hmong insurgents who rendered portions of the single highway unsafe. Lao Aviation had a French plane and a Chinese plane that flew to Luang Prabang, the old royal capital. The US State Department, I was told, urged Americans not to fly on the Chinese plane. Not only was it unmaintained, but if you got too close a piece could fall off and hurt you. Found that out later. Ignorance is bliss.

Lao Aviation was delightful and nostalgic. They were not computerized and intracountry calls were problematic, so they could not confirm your return reservation. You flew on faith (especially if you took the Chinese plane).

Faith worked for me in Luang Prabang and on a later trip to Pakse. When it's time to return you simply go to the airport one or two days early and are sent to an office in an adjacent building. A spartan white, cement office with a single mahogany desk, a Lao Aviation calendar adorning the otherwise bare walls, and, yes, the incandescent bulb hanging by a wire from a hole in the cement ceiling. A uniformed officer eventually arrives.

Sa bai dee (hello) you say and hand him your ticket. He pulls out a dog-eared manifest with a long list of names and numbers scribbled in pencil. He erases and scribbles and erases and scribbles some more. Then he makes a sweeping illegible mark on your ticket and tells you what time to show up at the airport the next day. *Kawp jai lai lai* (thank you very much) you say.

TO LUANG PRABANG

Arriving in Luang Prabang, I stepped out of Lao Aviation's aging Chinese turboprop to a panorama of forested hills that spanned the horizon a full 360 degrees. The beauty of northern Laos struck me at once from all directions. I walked in slow circles across the tarmac to the minibusses waiting to haul travelers into town. Tired of the incessant decision-making forced on the solo traveler, I opted to follow a Japanese couple I met on the plane to a hotel they had chosen from their guidebook. $3.50 a night at the low-budget Viengkeo Hotel bought an 8 foot by 10 foot partitioned cubicle in a large wooden building set back in the trees. A mattress on a plywood bunk, some wobbly wooden furniture and a single light bulb hanging by a wire from the ceiling filled out the little room. First order of business, since I had opted to forego malaria prophylaxis this trip, was to get out needle and thread and repair the tears in my mosquito netting.

My two companions were not your ordinary Japanese travelers. Uda, a dark-skinned, whiskey-drinking, unemployed roadworker, had soloed most of South America before heading to Southeast Asia. He clearly fell near the bottom of Japan's invisible, yet pervasive and oppressive, caste system, yet retained those timeless Japanese traits of respect, honesty and politeness. I trusted him instantly and implicitly. Keiko, a Japanese woman in her late 20s with an infectious sense of humor, had wandered much of the planet herself between jobs. They were to become my traveling companions for the next four days and we became good friends.

THE WATERFALL

We set off early the next morning in a chartered tuk-tuk on the 29 kilometer trip to the World Heritage Kuang Si Waterfall. The winding dirt road passed through Hmong villages nestled in the jungle-covered mountains. We stopped and handed out popcorn to happy but raggedy-looking children and posed for photos with the older village women in their traditional dress.

Rounding a bend, I spotted a grizzled old man nearly knee-deep in mud struggling with a wooden plow behind a pair of oxen, plowing furrows in a wet rice field. I had to take a photo, so I asked the driver to stop. As I approached the shoulder of the road with my camera the old man reached down into the muck and pulled out what looked like a congealed lump of wet clay. He tossed it up onto the road where it landed at my feet. Upon closer inspection, it turned out to be a drowned rat.

From an incident at the marketplace the previous day I knew Keiko was deathly afraid of rats, though in a self-deprecating sort of way. So I picked it up by its tail, walked up behind her, and tapped her on the shoulder. She turned, let out a piercing scream and bolted into Uda's arms with such force it nearly sent the two of them sprawling onto the dusty road. A troop of schoolgirls standing in the shade of a nearby tree broke into a chorus of giggles. And the old man behind the plow had long since dropped the reins and was standing there watching, grinning from ear to ear.

Kuang Si falls spills out of the mountains in multiple cataracts grouped into at least three tiers that disappear upwards into the thickly jungled slopes. Its beauty was striking. We followed a trail on the right up to the second tier where there was supposed to be a nice pool for swimming. Climbing steeply through dense green foliage the trail soon leveled off and rapidly deteriorated. The last ten yards or so was little more than a four-foot wide ledge between two successive waterfalls. My Japanese friends plunged ahead fearlessly. I hesitated a bit, tied my shoes around my neck, and stepped into the swirling water.

Almost knee-deep in places, the water surged across the narrow ledge, trying to sweep me over the edge where it spilled onto the rocks more than fifty feet below with a deafening roar. With nothing to hold onto for support save a jumble of wet rocks and loose woody debris, I hugged the rock wall on the upstream side, away from the edge, getting thoroughly soaked by the water pouring down from above.

We had a nice swim in the pool, a picnic lunch, and explored a small cave under one of the cataracts on the far side of the lake. Then, after consulting the guidebook, we descended along the recommended trail on the left.

BACK TO LUANG PRABANG

The Japanese occupation of Southeast Asia leading up to the Second World War was marked by a brutality that seared itself on a generation. Their treatment of the Laotians was no exception. After a brief respite, the Americans, as an adjunct to the Vietnam War, began their saturation bombing of Laos. When they were done, more bombs had been dropped on Laos than in all of World War II, making Laos the most heavily bombed country, per capita, in the history of warfare. Air America, compelled to fulfill its seemingly endless quotas, unloaded its bombs wherever its pilots detected any sign of life. There is a well-documented story of a farmer in eastern Laos who wanted a fish pond. He hung out some clothes on a line, built a smudge fire and retreated before the predictable afternoon bombing run. He had his fish ponds that very evening.

So I might have been justifiably a little nervous when we pulled off the road at a thatched refreshment stand and were introduced as Japanese and an American to a small group of young, well-educated Lao students hanging out in the shade. They were sure to know their country's history. Yet they welcomed us, poured us shots of lao-lao (a strong, homemade rice liquor) and toasted us! This was to be a common occurrence in Laos. For unlike the Balkans and the Middle East, where grudges and hatreds are passed from generation to generation, the gentle Lao people seem to have a forgiving let's-get-on-with-life approach that is most refreshing.

Later that evening found us sitting around in the small hotel lobby drinking Mekong whiskey - me, Uda, Keiko and Reinhard. Reinhard was an Austrian who was biking through Laos and crashing in police stations at night when he had nowhere else to sleep. He seemed to be having quite the adventure. Reinhard's composition, though, was slanted a bit more toward testosterone and muscle and a bit light on the "little gray cells" that Hercule Poirot always boasted about. Therefore, he hovered quietly at the periphery of the conversation, although he spoke English well. Finally, when the conversation turned toward religions, he asked his first question to Uda: "What do the Japanese worship?" Uda laughed, and replied without hesitation, "The Japanese worship the yen." Bingo, I thought, I like this guy Uda.

So I decided to ask Uda a question I never asked a Japanese person before. "Tell me about the burakumin, the eta," I inquired politely. His eyes widened with surprise and curiosity as he related that this was the first time a foreigner ever asked him about what he referred to as the "dark side" of Japanese society. And he explained without hesitation or apology.

Physically indistinguishable from other Japanese, a burakumin (or eta, as they're more derogatively referred to) is one whose ancestors - generations, even centuries earlier - worked in what was then considered a demeaning or polluting occupation such as leatherwork or butchery, or could be traced to the vanquished in some long-ago feudal war. The stigma is often ferreted out in status-conscious Japan by sleuthing investigators hired by the families of a prospective bride or groom. The results have been more tragic than simply broken engagements. There have been some widely publicized suicides over these disclosures.

Uda shared his thoughts and knowledge freely and with the same quiet indignation I would have shown, say, discussing discrimination in America against Blacks and Natives.

MEKONG EVENINGS

Evenings in Luang Prabang were spent watching the sun set while drinking cold Beer Lao at one of the many outdoor cafes that dotted the Mekong River. The falling sun became a glowing orange orb in the tropical haze, splashing yellow across the soft ripples on the Mekong and illuminating the gently rocking wooden riverboats of the villagers one last time before dropping behind the smoky blue mountains. At our table there was Pitr, a late-middle-aged and somewhat heavyset Dutchman with a pronounced limp who was an on-again, off-again expat in Laos since before the 1975 revolution. He had a near-encyclopedic knowledge of the country and its people, culture and economy. And he could speak Lao fluently. He offered to take us to a Hmong village in the hills and introduce us to the fine art of smoking opium. "Where there are Hmong there is opium", he said with the reassuring smile of one who speaks from experience. He talked about the experience in some detail. "Libido is the first thing to go," I remember him saying. The next day, though, he met a French woman at the Dala Market and they went down the river together, so we were unable to take him up on his offer.

At the far end of the table Gonzalo, a Cuban-born spotter pilot from Cordova, Alaska, lapses into Spanish with a pretty classics student from Madison, Wisconsin. Meanwhile, Keiko tells me of Japan and her brother's friend who is head of the *Yakuza* (the Japanese mafia) for northern Honshu. She realized something was up early on when they always managed to get tickets for sold-out concerts and other events. We made plans for me to meet one of her mobster friends in Roppongi (Tokyo's entertainment district) on my next trip to Japan.

FAREWELL

My last night in Laos I sat drinking beer at the outdoor café surrounding the water fountain in downtown Vientiane. A party of Germans at the table next to me was starting to get a little loud. Off in the darkness, beyond the illumination of the fountain and away from the flow of pedestrian traffic, sat a lone Lao selling dried squid from a wooden pushcart. Sitting there, against all odds, with that infinite Asian patience. My mind drifted off to central Siberia, that old woman in Irkutsk sitting on a wooden crate before a small pile of matches and waiting, waiting with the same infinite patience. Even as the dark clouds rolled in from Lake Baikal and big raindrops began to splatter on the sidewalk, she was the last to leave.

The well-dressed Germans drinking their beer with Hofbrauhaus camaraderie caused me to feel somewhat disconnected. I left. In the darkness near the squid peddler I nearly tripped over an old woman beggar. I walked quickly over to a nearby shop and returned with a carton of cold soy milk. Her hands were trembling so badly there was no way she could have pierced the tiny foil seal with the pointed edge of the skinny plastic straw. I squatted down in the darkness beside her and managed to get the straw into the carton. As I left she was sipping the cool soy milk.

I felt good about myself, then immediately felt bad for feeling good about myself. Then I felt confused as I walked down the darkened streets back to the guesthouse. Of one thing I was certain, though. I would someday return to Laos.

Bill Cox with kids in Hmong village along the road to Luang Prabang, Laos January 1997

Plowing the field along the road to Luang Prabang, Laos January 1997

Uda (front row center), Bill Cox (back row left) and Lao friends along the road to Luang Prabang, Laos January 1997

The trail to Kuang Si Falls is a bit wet and slippery. Near Luang Prabang, Laos January 1997

CHAPTER 14

FATHER JOE MAIER, BANGKOK SLUM PRIEST

When folks with a selfless determination to right a wrong, correct a social injustice or just do pure good, march forward and literally put their lives on the line, they are usually armed with something positive. Often a strong religious conviction, a life-altering experience or tragedy, or maybe a tainted multimillion dollar inheritance - the guilt of which burrowed under their skin. Roman Catholic priest Father Joe Maier, on the other hand, walked into the horrific slums of Bangkok's Klong Touey with nothing. "No hope, no judgment," he would later explain. And Father Joe kept walking.

Joseph H. Maier was born and grew up in Washington State. Stricken with polio at the age of twelve, he demonstrated his resilience at that young age by recovering nearly completely after two years. Ordained a Redemptorist Catholic priest in 1965, he interned in a poor section of St. Louis, Missouri before being sent to Thailand.

After studying Thai for a year in Bangkok he was off to Thailand's rural northeast – and a short stint in Laos - before returning to Bangkok in 1971. And there he remains to this day, having founded and still directing the Human Development Centre.

I first learned of Father Joe from an article in "Parade Magazine" on March 25, 1990. I read about a priest who set up shop, permanently, after walking into the slaughterhouse section of Bangkok's Klong Touey slum. It was a neighborhood of suffering, poverty, disease, drugs and filth. But Roman Catholic priests can't just go where they want. They answer to their unelected, autocratic bosses at the Vatican. Father Joe's raison de etre, his legitimacy for being there, was the slaughterhouse.

Pork, after rice, is everywhere in Thai (and Southeast Asian/Chinese) cuisine. But in many areas, like Klong Touey, refrigeration is lacking. The butchering must be done in the cooler hours of the late evening, night, and very early morning so the meat can be shipped to the wholesalers, retailers and restaurants before spoilage. It was a system that worked. But there was an ecclesiastical reason for the slaughterhouse and Father Joe having become entwined.

Father Joe's parish was, obviously, never demographically defined or "perimeterized". But it was reported in the "Parade" article to be about 98% Buddhist and maybe 2% Christian. Buddhists do not slaughter animals. The slaughterhouse was run by the 2% Christians. Were they Catholic, or any one of a number of possible Protestant denominations? Didn't seem to matter to Father Joe, who said to me once on one of my visits, "These people don't know the Pope from Rambo."

I was impressed enough that Sunday in March 1990 reading about a Roman Catholic priest whose parish is 98% Buddhist and who is not into converting people, but rather teaching Buddhists to be good Buddhists and Christians to be good Christians. Two phone calls led me to a priest in Homer, Alaska who knew him. All I now needed to do was to get to Bangkok – which I did on two separate occasions.

THE SLAUGHTERHOUSE

I only saw it from the outside in broad Thai daylight, when it was locked up. Scattered piles of garbage and puddles of putrid, stagnant water dotted the parking lot. But as darkness falls, a scene out of Dante's Inferno unfolds.

Tattooed, sinewy young men, clad only in shorts and sandals against the stifling indoor heat and humidity, begin the night's work as the pigs arrive. Pigs that died in transit from the heat are slaughtered first. The rest are herded, clubbed into submission with iron poles and summarily slaughtered. Amid a cacophony of pathetic squealing and shouted Thai, the porcine horror continues through the night. The worker's wives and children try to sleep nearby, or even in squalid apartments above the slaughterhouse pens.

It was hard for me to imagine these were the same folks, gentle and cleanly dressed, who attended mass in the quaint little slum church at the edge of Klong Touey. Like Father Joe, I reserved judgment.

FATHER JOE BUYS A YOUNG GIRL

Most priests would not appreciate a story written about them with the above subtitle. But Father Joe is not your ordinary priest.

The little towheaded eight-year-old girl was very cute. Yes, it was the faintly reddish hair and the precocious Amerasian facial features, Father Joe explained. He knew kids and he knew the slum. Cute to this extent at her age equaled sexy in the slum economy and she was a potential cash-cow in Bangkok's often brutal sex trade. Her mother was a prostitute, so it was only a matter of time, maybe only a couple of years, if that, before she could get started. It would have been a lucrative maybe two decades before she died miserably of AIDS or drugs. And she and her family would have reaped little or none of the profits.

But Father Joe couldn't just snatch her away and protect her. He had to follow the rules. No, not the rules of the Vatican which, in Bangkok, didn't amount to a hill of beans (or, in Klong Touey, a pile of pig carcasses). He had to follow the rules of the slum. The only way he could assure her protection till adulthood was to literally buy her. It would set him back 800 US dollars.

And the word went out. American expats, well off in Bangkok, quickly ponied up. The poor, who had next-to-nothing, gave half that. And, I am told, in the seediest bars in Bangkok the same ruthless pimps who would have gladly exploited this little girl dropped their Bahts in the hat. It was because they trusted and respected Father Joe. The cash was raised and the transaction concluded.

I met the girl, briefly, on my follow-up visit with Father Joe. She was a pre-teen and thriving as a student at the Human Development Centre. She was still allowed to visit her mother. "I will not teach her that prostitutes are bad," Father Joe said to me. I recall similar sentiments from Jesus.

CREAMY GREEN TWATS

Unless you want to see Father Joe become incensed and launch into a tirade, don't bring up the issue of creamy green twats. I would never have thought to bring it up. Father Joe did. He possessed quite a lexicon of vivid and vulgar slum gutterisms and they could flow freely – much to my surprise and delight. Apparently, one does not semantically dance-around-the-bush in a place like Klong Touey.

Father Joe knew that sexually-transmitted disease (STD) was rife in his parish, but it was HIV/AIDS that was the real killer. And that women with pre-existing STDs are far more likely to contract and transmit HIV/AIDS. And that the "creamy green" symptoms of these vaginal infections, so unpleasantly obvious, were blithely ignored by so many girls and women. It almost made him want to tear out what hair he had left on his head.

There was only so much he could do as a Catholic priest. But Father Joe was an unapologetic condomophile. Much to the consternation, I'm sure, of Joe Ratzinger and his head-in-the-sand Vatican minions, he openly displayed, flaunted and gave away condoms like Ronald Reagan did his jelly beans.

And then he picked up the pieces. Father Joe had a soft spot in his heart for AIDS kids. He embraced them where he found them and took them in, no matter how hopeless or terminal their situation. Move over, Karol Wojytila (aka John Paul II), this guy is the real saint.

SANDWICHES AND BEER WITH SPIRITUAL GIANTS

My first trip to Father Joe's was in the relative safety of the backseat of a Bangkok cab with my Scottish friend Basil McCall, an executive with the Amari Rincome hotel chain in Thailand. Basil was a friend I met in Calcutta who, at the time, was supporting British farmer–turned-doctor Jack Preger - Calcutta's street doctor.

On my second visit to Father Joe's I took advantage of the newly introduced motorcycle taxi service, supposedly regulated by the Municipality of Bangkok. I should have known better. Bored-looking kids, teenagers at best, leaned against their motorbikes on the corner of Soi 33 and Sukhumvit Blvd. They all wore sleeveless vests with numbers on them, which sort of gave them a veneer of legitimacy. I negotiated a ride to Father Joe's.

It was hair-raising to say the least. High-speed on the back of a motorbike, sans helmet, weaving in and out of traffic and playing chicken with oncoming vehicles of all sizes and shapes. We arrived safely. Who to thank? Probably the reckless but skillful kid.

Father Joe's friend, Father Denys Rackley, was in town and we ended up driving back to nearly where I had set out from, albeit with a more careful driver behind the wheel – Father Joe himself.

Father Denys was a Carthusian priest, one of few Americans to join this austere and silent order. He was studying vipassana meditation at a Buddhist monastery in Rangoon, Burma. There was no contradiction here, he later shared with me. He said mass every night in his monastic cell.

It was the famous Trappist monk Thomas Merton himself, author of multiple books and widely published inspirational writing, including The Seven Storey Mountain, who urged Father Denys to become a Carthusian. Thomas Merton traveled widely in Southeast Asia after slipping away from the confines of his strict monastic order and was very much influenced by the intense spirituality of the Eastern religions.

Father Joe pulled up to the small supermarket on Sukhumvit Blvd., just kitty-corner from the Iranian Embassy. I knew them well. Yes, both the Iranian Embassy (which I visited once) and the little supermarket, where I'd been to multiple times, including once after being fleeced by a clever bar-maid who relieved my front left pocket of about twenty dollars in Thai Baht. She didn't get my vitals (passport, credit cards, big US cash, etc. in a money belt under my shirt and over my kidneys). I had enough residual loose Baht to get a sandwich at the little supermarket to relieve my post 2 am munchies after a night out on the town with my friend and mentor Al, a former US military guy and longtime Bangkok expat.

Father Joe sent me into the supermarket with a short list. We would be having lunch together. He asked Father Denys if there was anything he wanted. "A fresh onion," he replied, apparently liberated from silence. "There's nothing like a slice of fresh onion on a sandwich," Father Denys volunteered. Wow, I thought, this American Carthusian priest knows a thing or two about sandwiches. I went inside while they waited for me.

And I came back out with everything on the list, including a fresh onion for Father Denys and a six-pack of beer for Father Joe. I apologized to Father Joe that they would not allow me to split the 6-pack. Too much for lunch, I thought. Father Joe gave me that stern look of his and said "Don't worry, it will be drunk." I could tell he meant it. We headed off to lunch.

We drove off to the basement of a building somewhere in the vicinity, made sandwiches, drank beer and talked. I didn't take notes or record. I wasn't a reporter. And I would later be assured, from Father Thomas Merton's writings, that it was not the words that were important.

I did ask Father Joe about born-again right-wing Christian fundamentalism, something I was dealing with at the time, and inadvertently pushed a "hot button" (if creamy green twats was a red, this one was at least a bright orange). "They just wanna keep sucking on mother's tits," exploded Father Joe, before launching into a mini-tirade, "and they don't want to let go." I relished it. He'd obviously dealt with this issue before.

And I asked Father Denys how they dealt with the authoritarian Vatican, which must certainly disapprove of much of what they are doing, saying and promoting. And I got a wordless answer from Father Denys, perhaps out of respect to the silent Trappist tradition – an answer that would have made his colleague from Gethsemani, Thomas Merton, proud. Father Denys folded his hands gently into a perfect Thai *wai*, turned toward Rome and bowed lightly. Then he turned 180 degrees, lifted his head and unraveled the Thai *wai* by rapidly rolling his wrists. I understood, and his eyes confirmed it: kowtow to Rome, then turn around and do what needs to be done.

THE GIANT WAFER

Mass was about to begin at the small Roman Catholic Church in Klong Touey. A barefoot Father Joe officiated, proceeding in fluent Thai. Father Denys and I sat in a back row. I don't know how much he understood, but I comprehended zip. When it was time for communion to be served, decorum was observed.

I remembered Humane Vitae in 1968, when I took my first timid steps to leaving the Roman Catholic Church. Sadistic nuns physically and psychologically abusing and terrorizing my first-grade classmates at Holy Spirit School in Pequannock, New Jersey in the late 1950s. The fall of 1959, when my courageous father did the unprecedented and unthinkable at the time: he drove over to the Nuns' Convent, adjacent to the Rectory and the Church, barged in, berated and cussed out the sadistic penguins and summarily yanked me out of Sister Marie's second grade class after only two months. He had already rescued my younger brother, and I always felt that it was my mother's constant cooking for the nuns that spared me from that sadistic monster, Sister "Saddam" Christine, my first grade teacher. I settled in well with Mrs. Kolms's second grade class at the public school. It was a good move. Thanks, Dad!

As I was in the back row with Father Denys, he was the last to go up to receive communion. Then, after everyone was seated, Father Joe walked directly toward me with a wafer. Back when I was a kid, they were the size of a quarter, but this baby was the size of an IHOP (International House of Pancakes) silver dollar pancake, though still paper thin.

I stammered… "I don't think I'm still a Catholic…it's been decades… and I didn't go to confession yesterday." The look on Father Joe's face clearly said, "I'm not going to stand here all day." Then he finally asked me, "Do you want the thing or not?" I figured he knew the rules, so I let him place it in my mouth.

EPILOGUE:

Thomas Merton died in 1968 of an accidental electrocution in a Bangkok hotel. Father Denys Rackley died in 1998 in a hotel in Rangoon, Burma at the age of 76. He had been studying Buddhist meditation. Father Joe is still going strong, doing his good work as director of the Human Development Centre in the Klong Touey neighborhood of Bangkok.

And only Father Joe would organize a fundraising carwash in Bangkok where, after the cars were sufficiently soaped and scrubbed, Thai elephants would dip their trunks in clean water and spray the cars clean. Father Joe cares about his kids.

Father Joe's kids in the slaughterhouse slum, Khlong Touey, Bangkok, Thailand April 1994

Father Joe Maier making the rounds in the Khlong Touey slum,
Bangkok, Thailand April 1994

Chapter 15

President Lee Teng-hui (June 2005)

Among Asian politicians, Lee Teng-hui is a colossus. After the death of Chiang Ching-Kuo, the authoritarian son of the brutal Dictator-President Chiang Kai-shek, Lee assumed the authoritarian reins of power as President of the Republic of China (Taiwan). And he continued on as Chairman of the Kuomintang (KMT, or Chinese Nationalist Party). The KMT has the reputation of being probably the wealthiest, and one of the most corrupt, political parties in the world. During his twelve years in power, the wily former professor slowly turned the tables on his own political party and ushered in Taiwan's democracy. When he stepped down in 2000 a direct presidential election brought to power an opposition candidate, Chen Shui-bian, for the first time in Taiwan's history. Yes, President Lee was one of the good guys. And I wanted to meet this great man.

Lee Teng-hui was born in 1923 to a rural Hakka family in Taipei County, northern Taiwan. He never learned his native Hakkanese dialect, but did learn Taiwanese. And like many at the time (including my wife's father) he developed an affinity for Japan and its culture. Taiwan was under Japanese rule until 1945. Much of Taiwan's infrastructure and educational system was set up by Japan. His brother served and died in the Imperial Japanese Navy. Lee received a scholarship to Kyoto University and graduated, despite the crisis of the Pacific War, in 1946.

The Republic of China took over Taiwan after World War II. Lee received a bachelor's degree in agricultural science from the National Taiwan University in 1948, a master's degree in agricultural economics from Iowa State University in 1953 and a PhD in agricultural economics from Cornell in 1968. His doctoral dissertation won high honors.

After returning to Taiwan in 1971 Lee joined the KMT. In 1978 he was appointed Mayor of Taipei. In 1984 he was appointed Vice President of the ROC (Taiwan).

There was some opposition when Lee ascended to the Presidency in January 1988 - mostly from the *waisheng ren* (mainland Chinese who came to Taiwan after 1949 and their descendants). A master political puppeteer, Lee allowed his rivals to occupy positions of influence as he gradually replaced them with U.S. educated *bensheng ren* (residents of Taiwan before 1949 and their descendants) technocrats.

Two years into his presidency, in 1990, the Wild Lily student movement hit Taiwan, demanding full democracy. Over 300,000 staged a sit-in in Taipei. Chiang Kai-shek, like Communist China's Li Peng, would have ordered his army to slaughter them and drag the survivors off to vile, off-shore island prisons. President Lee Teng-hui welcomed several students into the presidential office for discussion and pledged his support for their goals and full democracy in Taiwan. It was one of his finest moments, and the finest moment for true democracy in Asia.

Lee followed up, dismantling the obstacles to democracy in Taiwan. In 1996 he became the first popularly elected president. He stepped down in 2000, honoring the term limits he helped enact and an opposition candidate, Chen Shui-bian, won the presidency for the first time in Taiwan's history. And in 2004 Lee campaigned for President Chen when he ran for re-election! President Lee had completed a remarkable transformation - a phenomenal, calculated, political about-face.

I really wanted to meet this guy and I thought of a way that would benefit more than just myself.

Alaska's two-term governor Tony Knowles had been out of office less than a year when I called him at home in 2003. I told him I was heading to Taiwan in a couple weeks and suggested maybe he could write a letter to former President Lee recalling their brief meeting in 1995 when Lee's plane stopped in Anchorage to refuel on its way to Syracuse, NY. (Tony was Alaska governor and Lee was President of Taiwan at the time). "Just recall your meeting, reminisce, inquire about his health and the like," I suggested. "He'll appreciate being remembered and I'll hand-carry the letter to his office". Tony said he'd start working on the letter.

I stopped at Tony's home a few days before leaving for Taiwan and, over coffee, we put the finishing touches on his letter, as well as a cover letter explaining who I was and my support for President Lee and his policies.

Our hotel in Tamsui, on the far edge of vast, sprawling Taipei, turned out by happenstance to be just across the street from President Lee's office. It was auspicious, I felt. We politely and persistently penetrated through the previous president's outer perimeter and were assured Governor Knowles's letter would be delivered to him. And I learned, several weeks after I got back, that a letter from President Lee had arrived in Tony's Anchorage mailbox.

Prior to my return to Taiwan in June 2005 I made inquiries, requesting an audience with President Lee. My wife, Hsiu-Yuan Huang (Amy), and I were shielding ourselves from the rain and dodging gushing street water in the Taipei suburb of Jung Li when her cell phone rang. It was President Lee's office. He would welcome us the following day.

Knowing President Lee spoke the native Taiwanese, and was proud of it, Amy (who is fluent in three Chinese dialects: Mandarin, Taiwanese and Hakkanese) gave me a mini-crash course and intensive one-on-one coaching until I could master a short two-sentence Taiwanese introduction to President Lee,

Just like I forgot everything I learned in skydiving school when I plunged out of that small Cessna 3,000 feet up on my first parachute jump, I forgot every word of Taiwanese that Amy taught me as we were ushered in to meet President Lee. In the presence of that great man all I could manage was "President Lee", followed by a deep bow. President Lee's assistant, Chow Mei-li, accompanied us. She was married, incidentally, to the Dalai Lama's nephew. These were, indeed, my kind of people.

I wasn't a reporter or lobbyist. I had no agenda. I simply wanted to meet Asia's greatest living politician, thank him for his visionary and selfless accomplishments and hear what he had to say. Still, I was nervous enough to run into the toilet for at least three pees in the thirty minutes we waited before being ushered into the sitting room outside President Lee's office. (Yes, I'll admit it was the same with the Dalai Lama, only the infrastructure in Dharamsala was more primitive. In a pre-audience panic I had to exit the building and jog down a forested trail until I found a secluded rock to pee on. After I zipped up I saw a group of Tibetan pilgrims hike up the trail and stop to pay homage to the rock

I had just watered. Holy shit, I thought, as I quickly scurried back up the trail. It must have been a sacred rock stupa. I expected the following audience with the Dalai Lama would automatically absolve me. And I assume it did.)

Our talk with President Lee was most relaxed. Before I even had a chance to take my first sip of the hot green tea that was sitting beside me, he asked: "So, how is my good friend Frank Murkowski?" I admitted I didn't know, but promised I would find out. Our conversation ranged from the incredible variety of fruits and vegetables available in Taiwan to the authoritarian one-party "democracy" of Singapore presided over (in perpetuity, even if it necessitates a future return from the grave) by Lee Kuan Yew. It was quite clear that Taiwan's Lee does not consider the "pseudo-democracy" of Singapore's Lee a true democracy at all.

What I enjoyed most, however, was sitting back, sipping the green tea and watching my wife and President Lee converse, bouncing between Mandarin and Taiwanese. Amy grew up dirt poor in a hardworking rice farming family in north Taiwan and walked barefoot two miles each way to elementary school (her only pair of shoes, several sizes too big, were draped over her neck – a budget purchase by her frugal parents with the future in mind so she could grow into them). Relaxed and confidant, she was now talking with the former president of her country like he was one of her old schoolteachers.

Amy and President Lee would be chatting away until suddenly they would both become silent, turn toward me, and start laughing. I was OK with that. I found out later that President Lee asked her how we met and Amy told him that what endeared her to me most was that, when I found out she was Taiwanese, I said that Chiang Kai-shek was a dictator. (I usually eschew politics when I'm one-on-one, but fortunately President Lee did not hold Chiang Kai-shek in high esteem.) And when the golf-playing former Taiwan president wanted to invite me to play a dozen or so holes, Amy volunteered that I was not the typical golf-playing American doctor.

After our talk we sauntered over into his private 37th floor office with a 180 degree view. He quietly reminisced on the many changes that had taken place in Taipei over his long life.

After we parted I noted to his assistant, Chow Mei-li, that President Lee was such a nice man. So honest and so gentle. Not the attributes one would expect to be applied to one of Asia's greatest, most enigmatic and wily politicians.

My wife and I with Taiwan President Lee Teng-hui (1988-2000)
Taipei, Taiwan June 2005

Chapter 16
A-bian's Mother (October 2011)

After the marriage of our niece, A-Chai, to Kevin in Jung-Li City in north Taiwan, my wife and I took off south along Taiwan's heavily populated west coast. It was a route Amy and I had previously not taken, having always opted to plunge inland on the precarious, cross-island mountain highways. I suggested, half-seriously, that if we were headed south maybe we could stop in Guantian, the hometown of former President Chen Shui-bian (A-bian, as he is affectionately known to those endeared to him) and meet his mother.

The Drive South

We stopped first at the salt museum, detailing the history of salt extraction in western Taiwan. It was still an active industry. Water from the shallow Taiwan Strait was pumped uphill into shallow, increasingly concentrated, evaporation ponds. Women in rubber boots wearing straw peasant hats and pushing brooms constructed from bamboo would rake the salt into conical piles in the center of the shallow brine pits. I grabbed a broom and tried it. We dropped into the salt museum, which sold all kinds of salt-laced delicacies. Warning: not recommended for hypertensives.

We next visited the highly touted "Snake Village" in Tainan County. It was a weekday and we were the only visitors. The Taiwanese usually tour en-masse, on weekends or holidays. So we had time to meet and talk with the ethically-challenged big boss/owner. (He had bred a lion and a tiger resulting in a stillborn "liger" in violation of Taiwan government regulations). A flamboyant showman, he once recklessly snuck up behind an adult cobra, its neck cape flaring, and kissed it on the back of its neck for the news media. The photo of this act was visibly displayed on the wall. A reckless fool, I thought.

An assistant reached into a cardboard box full of squirming baby Taiwanese cobras and pulled one out. I was surprised. It coiled around his hand and wrist. He offered to let me hold the baby cobra. "Don't worry," he said, "if it should bite, it doesn't have much venom. You will just get some swelling about your wrist and fingers." I declined. Next, he showed me the cage housing the most aggressive venomous snake in the world – the notorious African black mamba. It sat there as if frozen, poised and elevated, ready to strike. He joked how once a week he would drop a mouse into the cage while wearing a padded glove, then quickly shut the top of the cage. There was no black mamba anti-venin in Taiwan, so a bite by this snake would be 100% fatal. Reckless fool number two, I thought.

We settled for stir-fried cobra and snake soup in their small restaurant. Then it was on to the oyster farms.

Wanggong was all about oysters. Restaurants offered them in every way, shape and form. Oysters were being shucked on every other street corner, their shells piling up. It reminded me of a joke which I tried to share with my Taiwanese wife. "Amy," I asked as we parked our car near the harbor, "what is the difference between an epileptic oyster shucker and a prostitute with diarrhea?" As expected, she had no answer. "The epileptic oyster shucker shucks between fits," I explained, ready for us to burst into shared laughter. But I was met with a puzzled look. No amount of explanation could translate this into Mandarin Chinese, so we settled on a restaurant where we could chow down on cooked oysters.

Continuing our drive south, we were soon surrounded by water fields. We had left the oysters behind and had entered water chestnut country. We were getting closer to A-bian's hometown.

Trapa bispinosa, known by its common name as the water caltrop, or water chestnut, grows in water-logged fields, like rice. In Chinese, it is called *lingjiao*. An annual, aquatic plant, its fruit is anchor-shaped with three points and kind of resembles a steer's horn. They are harvested in late summer/early fall. Boiled, then split to make them easier to peel and eat, they are sold roadside by the bag full. They are quite tasty and make a healthy snack. Note: *Trapa bispinosa* is not to be confused with the unrelated *Eleocharis dulcis*, also known as the Chinese water chestnut and found in Chinese restaurant food all over the United States.

I was snacking on these guys and tossing the husks out the window when Amy pulled over next to a small building surrounded by short trees and bordering on the water chestnut fields. A village woman squatted on the sidewalk across the street selling, of course, water chestnuts.

PRESIDENT CHEN SHUI-BIAN

Chen Shui-bian was a human rights lawyer from the more traditional and Taiwanese-speaking south of Taiwan. He defended the courageous pro-democracy activists of the "Kaohsiung Incident": Annette Lu, who would later serve as his vice president for eight years; Mr. Lin Yi-hsiong, founder of the DPP (Democratic Progressive Party), which was Taiwan's first opposition party; and Chen Ju, currently mayor of Kaohsiung, Taiwan's second largest city, among many others. After he lost a local election for county magistrate in Tainan in 1985 Chen's wife, Wu Shu-Chen, was struck twice by a truck under suspicious circumstances and left paralyzed from the waist down.

Chen Shui-bian served as mayor of Taipei from 1994 to 1998. In 2000, Chen became the first opposition candidate to win the presidency. As a progressive he put Taiwan first, declaring from the outset that Taiwan's sovereignty rested with its people. And he was not cowed by China. While he was a major thorn in the side of Beijing with his pro-independence sentiment, he was probably a greater and more piercing thorn in the side of Taiwan's authoritarian and corrupt Chinese Nationalist Party, or Kuomintang (KMT), who felt they alone had the right to rule Taiwan indefinitely. When Chen won re-election in 2004 it was like throwing salt into the KMT's still open wounds. In 2008, having reached the constitutional two term limit, he relinquished power peacefully.

A poorly defined and poorly regulated large sum of money was available at Taiwanese presidential discretion for soft-power diplomacy and lobbying with Taiwan's existing diplomatic supporters (23 at last count). It was prone to perennial abuse. And it appears that President Chen's disabled wife, and possibly some dysfunctional family members, were busy wiring some of these funds to overseas accounts. I and others have always felt that President Chen, admittedly guilt-ridden for failing to protect his wife and family when he actively entered politics, was more negligent than complicit. To be otherwise would be totally out of character to his performance during his eight years of the presidency.

But it didn't matter. When the KMT's boyishly handsome, pseu-do-reformer Ma Ying-jeou became president, the KMT pounced like a suddenly freed caged panther. Chen was vigorously prosecuted and thrown in jail. It seemed a lot like political retribution. When a judge wanted to let Chen out on bail KMT legislators threatened to im-peach the judge. President Ma even had lunch with a wavering judge in Chen's trial.

What is more clear than Chen's guilt or innocence is that he did not receive a fair trial. He was initially given the outrageous sentence of life in prison, which was later reduced to 17 years. The appeals continued. For the world's wealthiest and most corrupt political party to jump on Chen Shui-bian the way they did is like, well, 10,000 pots calling one kettle black.

I was still concerned enough about President Chen in July 2010 that I pulled his vice president of eight years aside after she spoke to the Alaska World Affairs Council in Anchorage, Alaska. I asked her to convey my concern and support to him. She told me she had recently visited him in jail.

Abian's Mother

The old woman in Guantian still sat before her huge bag of boiled and split *lingjiao*. An equally old man jumped up and volunteered to escort us to the home of President Chen, where his elderly mother still resided. We followed him up a narrow, cobblestone street.

The old man called out the name of A-bian's mother in the local Taiwanese. He tapped on her window, then knocked on her door. It was late afternoon. I felt a little embarrassed, as we had arrived unannounced.

The inner door opened and an old woman stood behind the screened outer door. It was so dark in the house I could barely make out any features. But I could see her gently waving to us. We both bowed to her. It was A-bian's mother.

Amy addressed her in the native Taiwanese, using the respectful term "old aunt". She had apparently been napping, so Amy apologized for bothering her and urged her to take a good rest. She continued to wave to us during the short conversation. We bowed again, then retreated back down the narrow road to our parked car

A-bian's mother misses her son, the jailed former president, and wants him back home.

WE FINALLY MEET A-BIAN (PRESIDENT CHEN SHUI-BIAN)

As mentioned, the KMT's "show trial" of President Chen began very soon after he peacefully left office, honoring term limits. His only real crime, as far as the KMT was concerned, was his winning the presidency in a free, democratic election as an opposition candidate and ending the authoritarian KMT's unbroken rule of Taiwan. And an unfair trial and poor prison conditions quickly caught the attention of freedom and democracy supporters overseas, particularly in the United States and Europe.

Alaska's former Governor Frank Murkowski, a longtime supporter of Taiwan and its democracy, weighed in early. Senator Lisa Murkowski forwarded my letter of concern to the U.S. State Department, who got back to her. The Tom Lantos Human Rights Commission of the U.S House of Representatives sent a medical team. Senator Sherrod Brown got involved and Representative Steve Chabot visited President Chen in a prison hospital.

KMT apologists churned out lengthy English language pamphlets trying to show how President Chen was receiving such good care while trying to make the case that he was not a political prisoner, but a criminal. They gloss over his serious medical issues, including severe depression and are conveniently silent about President Chen being given anti-depressive medication without his knowledge or consent. Nor do they address Exhibit 2, a copy of which I have in my President Chen folder. It shows the room where President Chen was confined at least 23 hours a day – little more than a 58-square foot tiled bathroom with a toilet and some racks for hanging laundry, where President Chen was forced to eat, sleep and write on the tiled floor.

Frank Murkowski's friend Mr. Wu, who was also senior advisor to Taiwan President Tsai, was kind enough to arrange an audience with President Chen for my wife and me in Kaohsiung, where President Chen was on medical parole at his home. We took the train down to Kaohsiung in March 2018. After going through a security check on the ground floor we were escorted to one of the upper floors in the multi-story condominium complex and given a seat in a small waiting room.

After maybe ten minutes or so President Chen was escorted in to see us. He was much smaller than I expected, frail and seemed somewhat pained, walking with a cane. But I could see, maybe feel, some kind of indomitable strength radiating from him beyond the physical. It seemed clear he had not been vanquished by his brutal authoritarian jailers, but maybe even strengthened. Human rights activists like President Chen pay a high price the world over for standing up to dictatorial power. We all sat down and talked.

Or I should say President Chen and my wife talked, as President Chen spoke virtually no English. And Amy, who grew up dirt poor in a northern Taiwan rice farming village, chatted away with the former president of her country like he was one of her old school teachers – the same as she did with Taiwan President Lee when we met with him thirteen years earlier.

I made it a point to thank President Chen for the responses I got from his office to every letter I wrote him during his presidency from 2000-2008. He recalled Representative Steve Chabot's visit and then surprised me by wishing me a happy birthday! Yes, it was my birthday. We posed for a photo and then parted, but not before renewing our commitment to continue working to support and protect Taiwan's freedom, democracy, rule of law and respect for human rights.

My wife and I with Taiwan President Chen Shui-bian (2000-2008)
Kaohsiung, Taiwan March 13, 2018

CHAPTER 17

YOSHIO

My train pulled into Osaka station one early evening in May 1991 and the gray, oppressive megalopolis of Osaka, Japan's second largest city, confronted me. I'd seen the Michael Douglas movie "Black Rain" about the ruthless *yakuza* (Japanese mafia) in Osaka. And I'd heard about the famous Japanese "capsule hotels." The coffin–like "rooms" in these hotels provide just enough space to sleep and sit up – literally. But they do come with a small packet of toiletries and a flimsy towel in a sealed plastic bag.

It would have been interesting to watch a *yakuza* slice off the distal half of his pinky finger or initiate a new recruit by slowly inserting a knife into his butt cheek and daring him to wince. But I deemed that a bit risky, so early the following morning I went off looking for a "capsule hotel" and I found one.

They wouldn't let me in to gawk unless I wanted to rent a room. (Unlike the famous bullet train this, apparently, was not something Japan was proud of and wanted to showcase to the world). I doubt they had capsules that would have accommodated a 6'7" American, but I never found out and just then I stumbled into Yoshio. He had just checked out and the course of the day changed.

Osaka did not seem a likely home for a sensitive, big-hearted Japanese bohemian philosopher "salaryman" named Yoshio. Also surprisingly, for a blue-collar working man, he spoke excellent English.

This is my tribute to Yoshio:

YOSHIO AND THE NERVOUS
PIGEONS OF OSAKA STATION

Yoshio
my friend of one hour,
unkempt-looking, ill-at-ease
anonymous Japanese salaryman
I met in the lobby
of an Osaka capsule hotel.
Osaka – gray, overwhelming, incomprehensible.
I just wasn't sure.

Yoshio
my friend of two hours,
after coffee we walked,
bucking the morning rush hour human tide
in the massive train terminal.
The two pigeons swooped over us
low and fast, in formation
like two jet fighters,
then banked and turned
as they flew out the main entrance.
It was Yoshio who made the observation
that the pigeons here were skittish,
or nervous,
because they don't get enough rest
with the lights on till 11 pm,
long after the other birds
have gone to sleep for the night.

Yoshio
my friend of three hours,
was rising fast in my estimation.

This Japanese salaryman philosopher
with the keen mind and big heart.
He related the history
of Osaka's tallest buildings
in sequence
over the past 26 years.
And he talked of Japan and the Japanese people,
of litter and decaying morals
and oppressive, impersonal Osaka.

Yoshio
my friend of four hours,
saw me to my train
at Shin–Osaka station.
My last sight of him
was through the train window
as he tried to tell me something,
gesticulating with his hands.
But I didn't understand him
and the train pulled out too fast
and Osaka swallowed him,
reclaimed him.

CHAPTER 18

A FRIENDSHIP CLIMB UP JAPAN'S MT. FUJI

It was not yet 4 am and I was leaning against my hiking stick, panting in the thin air at 12,000 feet. The wind was howling and the predawn darkness, combined with the blowing fog, reduced visibility to less than 15 yards. Bobbing headlamps on the trail ahead of me disappeared into the swirling mist toward the summit of Mount Fuji, Japan's highest and most sacred peak. I trudged on up the steep volcanic slope toward an unseen goal.

A cone-shaped volcano rising to 12,388 feet above sea level, Fuji-san ("san" is an honorific term; the Japanese never say Fujiyama) is only about 75 miles southwest of Tokyo. It last erupted in 1707. It has been venerated within the Japanese "mountain religion" heritage since at least the eighth century.

EUROPE 1972

This story actually begins in Luxembourg back in the summer of 1972. I was a college student bumming through Europe on a shoestring budget and was just informed that the youth hostel was full. What to do? Shinichi Haraguchi, a Japanese medical student, was standing quietly in line behind me. He was obviously in the same predicament. We decided to split a room at a cheap hotel for the night.

Eating out was too expensive, so we each bought some food and shared a meal in our room. He taught me some Japanese and we talked. It was a little awkward sharing the one double bed in the small room – something we would joke about in later years. The next morning, after exchanging addresses and posing for pictures on the street, we went our separate ways. But we kept in touch.

And a whole quarter-century rolled by. We both became doctors. Got married. Had kids. We visited each other in Japan and America. In a Christmas card I proposed that in 1997 we celebrate 25 years of friendship by climbing Mount Fuji together. Shinichi made all the ground arrangements and on July 13, 1997 I hopped a plane for Japan.

JAPAN 1997

Shinichi and I were to meet in Tokyo a day after my arrival in Japan, landing in Narita. With a day to myself, I went exploring.

I was exhausted and drenched with sweat by the time I stumbled into the Kirinoya Ryokan in the little town of Narita. I'd been there twice before and Mr. Katsumata remembered me. This was a friendly, family-run Japanese-style inn – where hot green tea and rice crackers on a small lacquered table greeted you when you entered your room and a futon was laid out on the tatami-covered floor for sleeping. The inn dated to about 1902 but Mr. Katsumata's family, descended from the old samurai class, had been in the hotel business for at least 1,000 years. He proudly showed me a genealogy to prove it.

Narita is a pleasant town to spend a day or two resting and recovering from jet lag before flying off farther into Asia or tackling the Tokyo Metro. Behind the Shingon Buddhist Temple and its various shrines lies a sprawling park where you can stroll along a winding path lined by stone lanterns and shaded by tall pines. In the center of the park is a series of small ponds filled with large goldfish and lined by neatly sculpted shrubs. Once I followed the faint smell of incense down a dark trail to a small wooden hut where monks could be heard chanting inside. Just beyond the hut the trail ended in a small rocky grotto where a narrow waterfall spilled over a fern-choked cliff into a small pool. Narita-san always sets the mood for Japan.

The next day Shinichi and I met in Tokyo. After a night at the Ginza Dai Ichi Hotel downtown we made our way by train and bus to the fifth station at the 7,000-foot level on the broadly sloping lower flank of Fuji-san. It was cool and breezy at this elevation – a welcome respite from the heat and humidity of Tokyo.

We walked beneath a large wooden torii and followed a wide gravel trail along the side of the mountain for a kilometer or so before it turned and began switchbacking up the steeper slopes. Looking up we could see streaky gray clouds racing across the distant summit, which seemed to thrust itself up into the evening sky like a clenched black fist. The clouds soon coalesced into a fog that rolled down and enveloped us about the same time as darkness fell. Gusts of wind blew fine volcanic ash into my eyes, forcing me to don my sunglasses despite the poor visibility.

A series of primitive huts line the trail up Fuji-san all the way to the summit. Food and drink are available but pricey. We finally reached the Fuji-san Hotel, a wood and stone hut at about 10,000 feet elevation, where we had reservations to spend the night. The accommodations were very basic. Dinner was curried rice and Kirin Beer. I was happy enough as we all sat around a low table with a group of Japanese who stopped in for a meal before heading farther up the trail. I didn't understand the Japanese, and Shinichi was too tired to translate, but I enjoyed the camaraderie.

Around 10 pm one of the attendants led us up a narrow stairway to our sleeping quarters. Folded blankets lay on two tiers of wooden planks that stretched from one end of a long room to another. There was enough shoulder-to-shoulder sleeping space for at least 150 people in that one room! I suspected the blankets had seen many travelers and were only seasonally laundered. But it was mighty chilly, so I crawled underneath a thick layer and drifted off into a strange sort of hypoxic sleep.

The purpose of climbing Fuji-san is to greet the sunrise from the summit, which meant a wake-up call at the ungodly hour of 2:30 am. There were far more bodies under those blankets than it seemed like when we had gone to bed and they soon were all up and dressed, filling the hut to overflowing. Shinichi and I shared a can of Pocari Sweat (a kind of Japanese Gatorade) for breakfast and were out the door before 3 am. The fog had thinned some and we could see a long line of bobbing headlamps stretching up and down the mountain while an almost unbroken line of people marched by the hut. It was a dazzling sight, a mystical procession, made all the more emotional by the early hour and the mild hypoxic euphoria I was feeling. I waited for a gap in the procession and jumped in, becoming a part of it.

About 5 am we passed under another torii and the trail leveled off as some large wooden buildings came into view. The summit, therefore, was a bit anticlimactic, though not disappointing. Fierce wind and wet fog obscured any view and drove most people into the shelters. We joined them and rested on a long wooden bench. It was crowded. People dozed, drank beer, ate, smoked and took hits of oxygen from portable canisters.

I figured I might have some profound thoughts or say some sort of prayer at the summit, perhaps influenced by exhaustion and hypoxic euphoria. I had no idea what would come to mind, but as I sat on that hard bench cradling a hot can of coffee in my hands I simply reveled in being alive, thanking God for the simple, yet profound gift of life. In all its craziness and uncertainty, there is nothing like being alive, savoring the present moment to its fullest, sucking it dry. There was no other place I wanted to be than where I was at that moment.

Preparing for the descent, Shinichi and I teamed up with an American soldier from a nearby military base and his young wife. I noticed how underdressed they were, especially the woman, for conditions on the summit of Fuji. I had passed her on the way up and gave her an extra hat from my pack and told her to look for me on the summit. The four of us exited the shelter and started down the trail. Brutal wind, rain and cold forced us to abort after a scant hundred meters or so and sent us scurrying back to the shelter to regroup.

Back in the shelter the poor lightly dressed woman was frantic and crying. No way was she going back out that door. Until I reached into my pack and pulled out an extra pair of rugged rain pants and a rain jacket with a hood and handed them to her. I might as well have been handing her a winning lottery ticket from the look of relief and happiness on her face. We regrouped as a foursome and headed out into the horrific weather… and kept going.

A ways down the mountain we reached a fork in the trail where the military couple had to go left and Shinichi and I had to go right. The weather had improved considerably, so I gently indicated that she could probably hand me back the extra rain gear. Her look of pleading tinged with fear told me she did not want to part with it yet, so I gave them my name and address and told them to mail it back to me later. And some weeks later a clean and neatly folded rain suit arrived in my Anchorage mailbox via military mail.

The remaining descent was otherwise uneventful, trudging through loose cinder down the backside of the mountain. The last mile was a beautiful hike through a forest of stunted, twisted birch starting to transition to tall pines as we finally reached the trailhead. By then it was raining pretty heavily. We had a hot bowl of udon noodles at a nearby shelter and talked with an 87-year-old man who was starting his 18th climb of Fuji-san. He sort of hinted to us that it beat hanging around the house with his wife.

That evening found us soaking in a hot tub the size of a hotel swimming pool at a Japanese spa Shinichi had thoughtfully booked for us in the Hakone resort area. Then, perhaps remembering the meager meal we shared in that cheap hotel in Luxembourg 25 years ago, he arranged for us to share another meal together in our room that night. We dined on a five-course Japanese feast served by a kimono-clad waitress at the small table in the center of our tatami-covered floor. The sashimi came in a delicate, clear bowl made of pure ice. The beer was cold and there was more food than we could possibly eat. We slept well that night. The following afternoon we shook hands and said goodbye in a Tokyo subway station.

Aristotle, Francis Bacon and others have written essays analyzing friendship. But I suspect the great Zen Masters of Japan, if asked what is friendship, would simply reply, "If it's real, you'll know" Well, this friendship of 25 years is real. I know.

Bill Cox and Shinichi Haraguchi begin our climb up Fuji-san. July 1997

Menu at the Mt. Fuji rest house. July 1997

Mt. Fuji rest house - on the trail to the summit. July 1997

Summit of Mt. Fuji, Japan - elevation 3776 meters. July 1997

CHAPTER 19

GENNADI AND PAVEL

Siberia 1998: Secret passwords, spilled blood and the Russian criminal mafia.

It was the spring of 1998 and I was itching to get back to Russia. It had been two years since my previous visit and something about the place resonated with me. I just missed Russia. I had no official reason to go but I knew if I got an invitation, a visa and a plane ticket and put out the word that I was going the reasons and requests would follow. That was how it worked in Anchorage back then in the 1990s. I put in a call to my friends at the University. Weeks later the phone started ringing.

Misha pulled into my Anchorage driveway in a late-model SUV one warm afternoon in June. Misha was one of those nouveaux Russians resident in Anchorage at the time. Entrepreneurs of glasnost and perestroika. The latest model cell phone dangled from his belt. Dressed in casual slacks and an expensive-looking silk shirt open at the collar, he had the confident air of the new generation of young Russian businessmen.

The friend of a friend, Misha had a contact who was going to pick me up at the airport in Khabarovsk when I arrived. The plane got in around midnight and taxis were very few and far between. Would I take some cash over to his friend, Misha asked? No problem, I thought; I'd taken small amounts of cash into Russia before, as well as various gifts and parcels, including a small box of Miracle-Gro for a Magadan telecommunication guru's potatoes. The guy in Magadan thanked me by pushing a beige-colored phone across a giant desk in his giant office and told me I could call anywhere in the world, which was a big deal in the Russian Far East back then.

"How much cash do you want me to take?" I asked Misha. "Four Thousand," he replied. I hesitated, suggesting this was a large amount of money and might be trouble. "No problem," replied Misha, "just declare it to Russian Customs. It's perfectly legal". He went on to tell me he's carried as much as US $100,000 in cash in an attaché case to Moscow several times and there was no problem. I did not find that reassuring and wondered what kind of business Misha was involved in.

"OK, four thousand," I agreed, "but we need a secure password so I give the money to the right person." I thought for a second and suggested: *obleypikha, cheryawmykha, smorodina*. Three Russian berries. Misha indulged me, looking bored, then pulled out a small camera. "How about I just take your picture, scan it and send it to my friend so he recognizes you?" he asked. Misha is no fun, I remember thinking. If I was going to hand off a big wad of cash to a stranger in a Russian airport I wanted some drama. And that meant secret passwords. We agreed: photo and passwords.

It was nearly midnight when I cleared customs at the airport in Khabarovsk and wandered into the main lobby. I turned up my collar and cast furtive glances about the lobby, looking for a Slav with cold steely eyes staring at me over the upturned pages of a copy of Komsomolskaya Pravda he was pretending to read. I discerned nothing suspicious. Then a young man came up to me and said in English, "You must be Bill." Misha's friend, I thought, somewhat disappointed. These guys are just not going to play along and indulge me. "The password," I insisted. Smo… Smo… – come on, you can do it, I thought, giving him the first syllable – *Smorodina*! Cher… Cher… We got through two berries. I felt dumb conducting a post-midnight game of charades in a Siberian airport and could tell he was just humoring me. I handed over the four grand and he gave me a ride to Nellie's.

Not being a Russian, I never had a *babushka*. So I adopted Nellie. She was the mother of a translator I knew from Magadan. I loved that dear old woman. Married to her second husband Volodya, who retired involuntarily after almost forty years of working at a local factory, they were poor pensioners living in a tiny flat in a northern district of Khabarovsk. Volodya, who liked to ice-fish on the Amur River, showed me some of the most beautifully handcrafted pieces of wooden ice-fishing equipment I'd ever seen.

They had no phone so I could not give them advance notice of my arrival. I just showed up and banged on their door at 1 am. And then it was all I could do to dissuade Nellie from frying up a batch of potatoes for me in the wee hours. God Bless the Russian people!

The next morning, with Nellie's grandson Seryozha in tow, we headed downtown via tram and bus for my first "assignment."

Andrei worked for one of those new and politically sensitive "independent radio stations." But, as I came to find out, he covered his bases. Little Seryozha was impressed by all of the fancy electronic equipment at the station. Then we all headed over to the airport where Andrei's mother was awaiting us.

The Russian wife of a Seattle-area physician had myelofibrosis and would probably need a bone marrow transplant in the not-too-distant future. Her nephew Andrei and her sister (Andrei's mother) were judged to be the best possible candidates for a bone-marrow donation. I had a box full of test tubes that needed to be filled with blood – courtesy of Providence Hospital's "Angel of Mercy" Esther Petrie. And 48 hours to get the blood samples to Virginia Mason in Seattle via Alaska Airlines from Khabarovsk. God Bless Esther Petrie!

As a radiologist I didn't draw blood regularly, but drawing blood is like riding a bicycle. It comes back quickly. Andrei's veins were a "piece of cake" and I filled the requisite seven or eight tubes in no time. But his mom, unfortunately, turned out to be the "phlebotomist's nightmare."

Heavy-set women were always a bit of a challenge to me, but I knew there was more blood going down a larger extremity and that same blood had to come back up. Almost always I could sense the hidden big vein, poke it and strike red gold. Not that day. I worked my way down her forearm and into her wrist, poking away. Suddenly the room felt about twenty degrees warmer. The pilot was calling in from the Alaska Airlines jet on the runway telling me, in no uncertain terms, to hurry up. And then I remembered the advice of my former mentor in Detroit, the great trauma surgeon Dr. Charles Lucas. "If you're having trouble drawing blood or starting an IV," he counseled us, "go wash your face." Apparently, it helps you reset. I followed his advice using cold water from a nearby sink.

Chasing collapsing veins down to the base of her fingers, I managed to coax enough blood to fill about 5 & 1/2 test tubes. Olga, the station manager, was most patient. Her desktop, where I had set up shop, was covered with splotches of blood. The Alaska Airlines pilot was revving his engines. I was relieved to find out, weeks later, that the samples were sufficient for a complete type and cross-match. And some years later I ran into Olga at Carrs on Dimond in Anchorage and apologized for the bloody mess I made on her desk that day.

Andrei wanted to thank me for my service by taking me out drinking. Vodka lubricates most social, family and business encounters in Russia. It is always shared with others and served with food. A multi-course meal filled with laughter and conversation and punctuated with multiple vodka or cognac toasts will go on for hours until tea and a sweet dessert is finally served.

So far it was just Andrei and me in the apartment he shared with his mother, and she happily served us. I cringed with embarrassment when I saw the many pieces of gauze, cotton swabs and band-aids still pasted to both her forearms. She just smiled and was most thankful.

We ate, drank and talked. Like many Russians Andrei had a very fluid, or nuanced, approach to the law. He was comfortable on both sides. Dictators like Stalin and Brezhnev did not inspire fidelity to the Rule of Law, although they might be supported by the people out of nationalistic pride, or fear. I once met a wonderful and hospitable peasant woman in the Altai who told me how she cried when Stalin died in 1953. She cried because her newborn son would never have a chance to meet him. It's complex. And for many Russians it's just a matter of physical survival. I couldn't pretend to understand but at least I was here, on-site, and on a learning curve. I credit the counsel of Pythagoras again: "Check your prejudices at every port of entry."

The times they were a–changing, though I doubt Bob Dylan had any clue about Russia. Andrei explained to me that there were now three mafias to be dealt with: 1) the government mafia – out to do the government's work, 2) the businessmen's mafia, probably spawned during the chaotic Yeltsin years when state assets made their way into private hands and 3) the criminal mafia – its reputation for crime and brutality undiminished.

The three mafias usually operated independently, he explained, although occasionally the criminal mafia would be invited to join the government or businessmen's mafia on a project. I tried to explain this arrangement once in a letter to George W. Bush's lapdog, Tony Blair, after ex-KGB agent Alexander Litvinenko was poisoned to death with polonium-210 in Great Britain in November 2006. I don't know if he ever understood, although #10 Downing Street did acknowledge receipt of my letter.

Andrei suddenly decided to call a lady friend of his to join us, hoping she was in town. "Criminal Woman" is how he referred to her in English. Andrei spoke good English. He never mentioned her name, just "Criminal Woman", explaining that she did jobs for the mafia. He didn't say which of the mafias she worked for, but I could guess. He got her on the phone.

I was intrigued, envisioning a scowling and menacing version of Angelina Jolie dressed in black. They talked in Russian a while until Andrei hung up, disappointed. "She just got back from a job in Moscow," he explained. He didn't go into details. "She just wants to take a shower and sleep." Well, that just intrigued me more, but it was not to be. The night was young and Andrei had other friends he wanted me to meet.

Andrei and his friends had been helping Pavel hide out for the past year. Pavel was a member of, or at least worked for, the Russian criminal mafia. This is where trust came in. I followed Andrei to the "hiding place."

But first we needed to stop at a liquor store for a bottle of gin. It was raining heavily and muddy water was gushing over the surface of the poorly drained street, making for very slippery conditions. It was very dark and the vodka I consumed at Andrei's was probably starting to hit me. The combination of these three factors likely contributed to what happened next: I went down and gashed open my knee. Sheer machismo embarrassment propelled me back to an upright position. I hobbled after Andrei, we purchased the gin and finally arrived at the "hiding place."

First, a word needs to be said about "friendship" in Russia. In America, you meet someone on a bus or in a bar, chat about an interest you have in common, and you're "friends." Not in Russia. The Russians make a clear distinction between *druk* ("friend") and *znakawmie* ("acquaintance"). The difference is crucial. An acquaintance is just that: casual, probably honest, possibly fleeting. But true friendship, as I was beginning to understand, transcends family, political, legal, international and other boundaries. It implies trust and responsibility and probably other qualities only to be distilled from the extensive Russian lexicon of Pushkin. Pushkin, I am told, had a command of the Russian language greater than all other Russian authors. Which would eclipse my favorite, Anton Checkhov. Checkhov's stories were criticized for being all middle and no beginning or end. But he wrote about the common people – who lived and survived in the present. That's where I was and I was about to add some more *druks* to my life-long list.

Pavel didn't impress me as someone who was in hiding. He welcomed me into the typical, non-descript, small Soviet-style apartment he shared with a roommate, Gennadi. Gennadi was a police captain. Interesting arrangement, I thought. It certainly afforded Pavel an extra margin of safety if he was hiding from something. They were probably friends who went to their posts by day and returned to a shared apartment in the evening.

Before I could analyze the situation any further they popped open the gin, poured shots, and we all toasted. Then out came a guitar and the two roommates began to sing, with Andrei occasionally joining in. I sat back and reveled in the enjoyment of a mini-concert of Russian folk songs by a most unusual two-man band, barely noticing the blood trickling down my leg from a make-shift bandage on my knee.

Shortly after midnight it became time to leave. My arrangement with the University in Anchorage, for apparent business-related reasons, required me to spend a night at the Hotel Amur downtown. Police captain Gennadi had a car and offered to drive us back to town. Andrei and I finished off the gin in the back seat and I remember wondering if this was legal. Then I remember thinking that if anyone pulled us over, a police captain was behind the wheel and a member of the Russian criminal mafia was in the passenger seat. We had our bases covered. They escorted me safely to my room at the Hotel Amur.

I awoke early the next morning with a vicious thirst and an equally vicious hangover. Then I discovered I was locked in my room (the key would not open my door from the inside). And the phone did not work. I slaked my thirst with cold tap water and went back to sleep, hoping somehow this would all work itself out. I woke up again toward noon and nothing had changed, except I wasn't quite as thirsty.

I started counting the sheets, and measuring them, wondering if I could lower myself down from the 3rd floor when I heard a knock on the door. It was Sasha, a friend from Magadan now living in Khabarovsk, and her mother, both worried about me and, apparently, the company I'd been keeping. "*Klooch ne rabotayet*", I said ("the key doesn't work"). They summoned help and I was released before I had to start tying sheets together and breaking glass.

Seems like I was the only American on the 3rd floor. They all seemed to know me. The *dezhornaya*, or woman-in-charge-of-the-floor, offered me a shot of vodka in a very fancy crystal glass when she learned of my *prokhmelya*, or hangover. My head wanted it but my stomach reacted as if it was being twisted like a washrag. I felt bad declining her hospitality, but physically I had no choice. Her daughter, a drop-dead-gorgeous dancer named Nastia who had been working in Korea, gave me her address and phone number. Sometimes, Russia overwhelms. I followed Sasha and her mom back to their relatively spacious apartment where I spent the next few days until my flight back to Anchorage.

CHAPTER 20

VLADIMIR Z (AA TAKES HOLD IN THE SOVIET FAR EAST)

August 8 is a special day, I am told, for a small group of people in the Russian Far East. It was first celebrated, discreetly, by this same small group when the Russian Far East was still the Soviet Far East. August 8, according to my friend Vladimir Z, is the birthday of Alcoholics Anonymous (AA) in the Soviet Far East. It is the day he received the Russian language AA literature, which included the 12-step program, that I forwarded to him in Magadan, USSR after I received it from John Grant at the AA office in New York City. Upon receiving it Vladimir Z set about to work.

It had been a long journey from Anchorage to Magadan in March, 1990. Six days. I flew to Nome and then across the Bering Strait to Provideniya where I was stranded for three days by blizzards. A quick flight took us to Anadyr, where we were stranded again in white-out conditions for two days. Then finally to Magadan on an Aeroflot Tu-154. I thoroughly enjoyed every minute, every hour and every day of our delay. It was my first introduction to the wonderful Russian people. I was finally sitting in the Radiology Department at Magadan Regional Hospital where I had been invited to serve as consultant on the first CT scanner (a refurbished GE 8800) in the Soviet Far East. And in walks Vladimir Z, an alcoholic.

There were probably only a handful of Americans, or any westerners, in Magadan at that time. And it needs to be emphasized that there are two kinds of alcoholics: 1) alcoholics who drink and 2) alcoholics who have quit drinking and want to stay that way. Vladimir Z belonged to the second category. To their credit the Magadan Regional Hospital, my special and enduring friend (*druk*) Dr. Sasha Puzin (Chief of Radiology) and the Soviet system allowed Vladimir Z to approach me.

An unshaven, somewhat pained and uncomfortable-looking man was ushered in to see me. I was staring at an X-ray at the time, but there's nothing like seeing a real person once in a while. "I'm an alcoholic," Vladimir Z said to me, "and I need your help." 'Nuff said, I remember thinking, his sincerity having pierced my heart. You got it. After exchanging contact information, Vladimir Z was politely escorted out. I had a mission. And I would fulfill it.

AA, as practiced in the West, has been highly successful. To greatly simplify and summarize, you went to a meeting, usually in a room full of people you mostly didn't know. You stood up, gave only your first name and admitted you were an alcoholic – powerless over alcohol. A support group coalesced around you. You committed to follow the 12-step program. You could choose a voluntary sponsor available to you 24/7. A great program since the mid-1930s, thanks to surgeon Dr. Bob and stockbroker Bill W, it needed to be tweaked a bit, Vladimir Z explained, in the waning days of the Soviet Union.

Russian culture simply did not permit you to stand up and stigmatize yourself in front of anyone. And to call yourself an alcoholic was to stigmatize yourself. Even more importantly, with almost 70 years of oppressive and pervasive Soviet dictatorship weighing down upon your shoulders, you did not *ever* stand up and say *anything* in front of even one stranger – or even an acquaintance (*znakawmie*) you didn't fully trust. The KGB was everywhere and a midnight knock on the door, for no apparent reason, could be followed by a one-way trip to the Gulag Archipelago.

Vladimir would later explain that small groups of family and trusted friends had started meeting privately and built upon the literature I had forwarded to him. It was an auspicious start. And it was safe.

My second visit to Magadan took place while Russia was still part of the Soviet Union, although just barely. I wanted to meet with Vladimir Z and see how he was getting along. I got his address from a trusted friend. I stopped by one evening, unannounced, and knocked on his door. I knew what to expect.

Vladimir Z had the look of chronic suffering on his face when I first met him. When he answered the door I saw a look of acute fear super-imposed upon chronic suffering. The acute-fear aspect rapidly dissipated when he recognized me. He happily invited me inside and his wife prepared tea. Vladimir Z was a skilled amateur photographer and he shared his black-and-white photo prints with me in his cramped, Soviet-style kitchen.

The Magadan branch of the Gulag Archipelago was among the coldest, most brutal and notorious. Vladimir Z had some childhood memories, as his father was one of those incarcerated. I thought it might explain some of the lines of suffering on his face. He shared with me his photos.

I remember two photos: an undulating, weather-worn bleached wooden fence at a former Gulag site, listing ominously and a close-up photo of fiery Russian nationalist Vladimir Zhirinovsky, in Magadan, with his hand sliding under his suitcoat. The anti-Semitic misogynist Zhirinovsky once ran for President of Russia. "What was he reaching for?" I asked Vladimir Z. He didn't know. He was just the photographer. (Zhirinovsky's Siberian deputate from a past national election, an old KGB hand, is a friend of mine. I rescued him once from Anchorage International Airport when his flight to Russia was suddenly canceled. And I shall say no more).

Vladimir Z gave me a virtual tour of Magadan's Gulag. Much of it had been built over. But he remembered the sign: *Dobro pozhalovat* -"Welcome". It was the equivalent of *Arbeit Macht Frei* -"Work makes you free" - the now notorious sign that hung over the railway entrance to Auschwitz concentration camp. They both led to the same fate.

I haven't been back to Magadan since 1996 and sadly have lost touch with many friends there. But I trust that AA, established by Vladimir Z and nourished by the waters of need and desperation, continues to quietly grow.

CHAPTER 21

DMITRI AND FARIDA

ARRIVAL

It was a long, long way from Khabarovsk in the Russian Far East to Novosibirsk in Western Siberia. Siberia could probably swallow the continental USA at least twice. The Aeroflot jet made an unexpected landing in Irkutsk in south-central Siberia, probably to take on more fuel.

After coming to a stop a good distance from the terminal the passengers began disembarking. When it appeared I was about to be the only one left on the plane, I got off too. I had no idea what was going on.

People who know what is going on usually cluster in groups, I thought. So I followed the largest group, assuming they were transit passengers to Novosibirsk. Wrong move. I ended up on the street in front of the airport, surrounded by kiosks and hustlers and shouting cabbies. Wait a minute, I thought, I'm a transit passenger here. Gotta hustle and figure out the Russian system again. I finally found my way to a very non-descript transit passenger lounge and even recognized some of my fellow passengers. Soon we all reboarded and flew on to Novosibirsk.

Farida met me at the airport in Novosibirsk. She apologized that her boyfriend Dmitri wasn't with her. He was finishing up a business deal, she explained. He was selling someone a tank. No, not a water tank or a fuel tank, but a Soviet military tank! I knew right then I was going to like this guy.

NOVOSIBIRSK

Dmitri's BMW was parked under the tall pines lining the shore of the Ob Sea, a vast lake created by a 1950s-era dam on Siberia's mighty

Ob River. Towels spread over the hood were covered with food and drink – salami, cheese, bread, salted ferns, fresh tomatoes, onions and plenty of beer, cognac and vodka. And a large watermelon. I'd arrived in Novosibirsk, Siberia's largest city, a few hours earlier with nine hours of jet lag under my belt. I was tired but happy; I was back in Russia.

My plans for a canoe trip on one of Siberia's rivers were vague, so when Dmitri and Farida invited me to accompany them on a weeklong road trip through the Altai Mountains of Central Asia, I readily accepted. Farida was a member of a medical delegation that had visited Anchorage several years before. We ate and drank and they toasted my arrival. As the sun went down we swam in the cool waters of the Ob Sea, then built a fire on the beach and ate watermelon. It was a grand welcome.

ROAD DRINKING

Before heading off on the long drive south, we'd be spending a night at the family dacha on the outskirts of Novosibirsk. It was early afternoon when we hit the road in Dmitri's BMW. He reached down into a paper satchel on the floor, handed me a beer, and took one for himself. Those were the days before the ubiquitous cell phone, when drinking while driving was much less distracting.

We were driving down a busy boulevard when I saw a man sprawled on the sidewalk, the sparse crowd mostly walking around him, and some folks standing near him. "*Pyanoy* (drunk)?" I asked Dmitri, proud of my Russian as well as my keen observation skills. His matter-of-fact answer surprised me. "*Nyet*," he said, "*Oomer* (dead)." I took another quick look back as we drove by and it made sense. Drunks, apparently, will pass out and sprawl on the sidewalk in a different configuration than dead people.

We stopped briefly at the home of a relative on the outskirts of town and were given a jar of homemade pickles for our journey. And in no time we were out in the countryside dotted by fields, patches of forest and picturesque wooden homes. A young, very pretty woman was hitchhiking alone, just up ahead. Dmitri pulled over and she hopped in the back seat with Farida. They all talked, and Dmitri went a little out of his way to drop her off at her destination.

After we left her I remarked to my friends that in America a single young woman would be hesitant, even afraid, to get into a car full of strangers. I wondered if Russia was different, or safer? In his calm, unruffled tone Dmitri explained why the young woman wasn't the least bit afraid of getting into the car with us. "She had a gun," he said.

It was getting very dark by the time we got to dacha country. Streetlights were non-existent. I think we were on our last beer. Neither Dmitri nor I were prepared for what happened next: two soldiers with machine guns came from nowhere, jumped in front of us and forced us to stop.

Dmitri had somehow driven, unaware, onto a Russian military base. And there I was - an American with an open beer in my hand - sitting in the passenger seat. I avoided eye contact, looked straight ahead and tried my darndest to look like a Russian. Dmitri would have to talk his way out of this, I thought. And talk his way out he did, saving the day. As he would do many times during the ensuing week. When Russian friends got me (us) out of a fix, I didn't ask for explanations.

CONCERT ON THE KATUN

The rolling steppes of western Siberia spread out in all directions on the long drive south from Novosibirsk to Barnaul. I gazed out at rows of poplars, planted as windbreaks by communist youth groups, and I wondered under which ones my pilgrim friend George Walter took refuge as he passed through here on foot two years earlier on his long pilgrimage from Pennsylvania to Kerala, South India.

Late the following evening we pulled alongside the Katun River. This mighty river drains the glaciers and snowfields of the high Altai, a huge range that spills across the Russian borders with China, Mongolia and Kazakhstan. Its silty water lapped at our feet and forested mountains lined its banks as far as we could see. It merges with the Biya River to form the mighty Ob, which meanders northward over a thousand miles on its slow roll to the Kara Sea.

It was dark and drizzling when we pulled into a small clearing. A concert of folk music was about to begin. Toward midnight it became apparent that my Russian friends intended to party all night, so I settled in for a nap in the passenger seat of the car. "Bill, Bill!" Farida's voice suddenly cried through the car window, "Dmitri invited a man to come over and sing for us. His name is Vladimir and he can sing in Fenya."

136

I smiled to myself and rolled out of the car into the damp chill. It was 3:30 am.

Fenya, born of a gulag that spanned a continent and two generations, is a prison slang so extensive that it is almost a parallel language. Solzhenitsyn knew it well. Vodka went around again and Vladimir began his one-man show. It was so dark that we could barely see him, but he played his guitar and sang with a passion.

I could see he connected with my Russian friends, tapping into that elusive essence that for centuries has sustained and united the Russian people – the Russian soul. Dmitri whooped and whistled and jumped and hollered like a kid. A few paces behind us, barely visible in the darkness, a couple embraced and danced slowly in the mud. There was just enough ambient light to illuminate the mists swirling through the crowns of the tall pines and cedars.

At 6 am a young Russian crawled out of his tent with a bottle of vodka. He downed a shot and chased it with a long squirt of ketchup from a squeeze bottle, then passed it on. Sitting around the campfire singing and talking, these Russians had been going at it all night long. Their tents were pitched under the trees, just down the hill from the concert grounds.

Daybreak was sudden and by 8 am we were on the road again. Dmitri was more tired than drunk. I was trying to suggest that we stop and rest when the car swerved from the right side of the road to the left and I braced for the inevitable. Thoughts flashed through my mind as swiftly as the skinny trees scraped by the window. Briefly airborne, it was a rough ride for about fifty feet until we came to a crashing halt.

Once I realized no one was hurt, my relief turned to anger. Enough! I grabbed my duffel bag and pack from the trunk and ran off into the forest.

Crashing through the wet trees I pondered my options. I had time on my side and money in my pocket. Yet the deeper I got into the Siberian forest the more I began to feel like a very small fish in a very large pond. I finally reached the Katun and filled my canteen and drank.

I threw down my sleeping bag on the soft forest floor and, with sleep about to descend upon me, I shifted position one last time, rolling onto my left side. And there was Dmitri, squatting beside me, concern written on his face. He was a good man and capable, and he deserved a second chance, so I meekly followed him back to the car and we continued our journey. How he managed to get the car up a four-foot embankment onto the road and then find me in the forest before I even had a chance to fall asleep still amazes me.

A NIGHT ON THE URSUL

Dreamy peasant villages drifted past windows rolled up against the dust. These were lazy, midafternoon hours under the warm Altai sun. Each village, a haphazard array of weathered wooden homes and huts, was surrounded by green fields dotted with haystacks. Cattle roamed freely and thickly forested mountains formed a nearly continuous backdrop.

In the village of Ongudai I was greeted with the smell of rotting wood, muddy paths, strutting chickens and barking dogs. The smell of peasant Russia mingled with the clean mountain air but another scent, yeasty and homey, drifted across the road from a small log building. A sign on the door said, "Warm Bread."

I cradled two loaves, hot out of the oven, in the waist of my coat and the three of us hopped back in the car. The next stop was a small peasant shack where we bought a jar of fresh milk. A few miles farther down the winding gravel road we pulled off into a little wayside alongside the Ursul River.

More a gurgling brook than a river, the Ursul winds its way through the farming villages of the Altai countryside. Leaning up against the car, we ripped chunks from the warm loaves, doused them with Altai honey, and washed them down with milk. Then we went about building a fire and boiling potatoes for dinner.

The sun had just set and coolness settled over the land. We sat around the fire eating boiled potatoes, fresh onions and canned fish - all washed down with a strong Ukrainian wine. And we talked. Talked about our lives, about politics, culture, everything. We talked until the wine was gone and darkness settled upon us so thickly it threatened to smother the remaining embers.

Suddenly Dmitri's face lit up in the glare of headlights bouncing across the small field directly toward us. I looked into his squinting eyes for any sign of concern and saw none. The car veered off into the woods. Soon we could see another campfire blazing.

Bill Cox with Roman Catholic Bishop Werth. His parish, covering
nearly all of Siberia, is the largest in the world. Novosibirsk,
Russia August 1995

We threw some big logs on our fire so we could later find our way
back, then threaded our way through the trees to join the folks at the
other fire. Several forms jumped out of the shadows and grabbed us and
sat us down in the choice spots around the fire. Within minutes we were
drinking vodka and toasting our friendship while a tray of fried meat
was being passed around.

And then I noticed that the faces across the dancing flames were
not Russian faces, but more Mongoloid or Chinese. These were Altai
natives. Big-city Russians, Altai villagers and an American, strangers
only minutes before, were drinking vodka and exchanging addresses
and invitations around a blazing campfire under the starry Siberian sky.

Tucked in my sleeping bag on the soft grass under a riverbank willow
I slept like a log, lulled to sleep by the rushing water of the Ursul.
Awakening in midmorning, I stretched my arms toward the willow's
low limbs when I noticed, to my dismay, that due to a miscalculation
in the darkness, the foot of my sleeping bag was resting squarely on a
large and sloshy cow pie.

THE WATERFALL

It was well after dark when we arrived at the tourist camp on Teletskoye Lake in the heart of the Altai National Park, not far from the Mongolian border. The accommodations were basic, and the electricity conked out shortly after we hauled our gear into our room. But no matter; we enjoyed a late supper of canned fish, bread and watermelon washed down with gulps of vodka in the flickering light of my REI candle lantern.

And then Dmitri shared with me the news he had just learned from his friends: I was in the Altai illegally! Being an autonomous republic, Altai required a special visa that I was supposed to have gotten at the Russia/Altai Republic border. A big problem in today's Russia is that new laws and regulations are constantly being created but not publicized. I faced a fine of $600 a day if I got caught.

I awoke late the next morning to find there was no running water for coffee and no electricity to boil it anyway. I was headed outside to wash up in a clear puddle left over from the previous night's rain when Farida and Dmitri came by. We hiked down to a small stream where I washed my face and brushed my teeth. And then we looked out over the cold blue waters of Teletskoye Lake.

Dmitri had bottomed out his BMW on some especially rough road the night before. The stick shift wobbled loosely, engaging gears at random. It didn't look good, but being surrounded by such majestic natural beauty, and with confidence in my friends, I put the car problem out of my mind, along with my illegal status in the Altai. The day would be spent working on the car, so they put me on a boat heading down the lake. Finding a warm and windless spot over the engine, I sat back as we cruised down one of Russia's most beautiful lakes.

About two hours later we anchored at a remote beach and followed a boardwalk through the thick forest to a platform overlooking a huge waterfall. The view - the entire scene - was pristine and stunning. But soon the small platform was turned into an impromptu dressing room as two young Russian models changed into bathing suits, had their hair teased by their handlers, then scampered out onto the rocks dotting the pool at the base of the waterfall. They struck various seductive poses for a balding, middle-aged photographer. It turned out I had stumbled onto the filming of a Reebok advertisement. I sat back in the shade and watched, munching on cedar nuts I had scavenged from the forest floor.

After the photo session the film crew wanted to swim. The air was warm and still, and there was a narrow beach. One of the models, a tall blonde from St. Petersburg, chose to bathe in a most uninhibited manner. Grabbing a bar of soap I wandered down the beach and enjoyed my first bath in days, then floated out from shore on my back, admiring the beauty: mostly the mountains rising out of the clear water, with just an occasional glance at the model from St. Petersburg.

FAREWELL

In just a couple of hours I'd be leaving Novosibirsk on the overnight train to Krasnoyarsk. Farida had baked a fish pie and my farewell dinner was in full swing. Champagne and vodka flowed.

About an hour before the train was due to leave Dmitri hauled my duffel bag onto his back, Farida's mom plied me with food and a box of Russian chocolates, and we set off through the dark alleys that wind between the tall concrete apartment buildings. We stopped at a kiosk for more vodka.

We found the correct coach and got my gear stowed, then they – Dmitri and Farida, Farida's twin sister, her husband and their little daughter – dragged me off the train for one last round of drinks and toasts on the platform. I think I was the first to notice that the train had started inching its way to Krasnoyarsk. There was just enough time for a few handshakes, kisses and a heartfelt thank you and good-bye.

For some time I stared out the window as endless blocks of concrete high-rises swept by. The streetlights glistened on the wet rails beside us and the carriage rocked back and forth as we picked up speed in the city outskirts. I felt acutely aware of the increasing distance I was putting between myself and my dear friends.

I would face some challenges the next morning when I arrived alone in Krasnoyarsk, where I would be abandoned downtown with all my luggage by an irate cab driver and questioned in a small room by two intimidating uniformed women officials who were suspicious of my visa (they had good reason to be). But on the train from Novosibirsk I remember thinking that after a farewell like I had just received, I could handle anything this big country dished up for me. And then suddenly the lights outside disappeared and we slipped out of Novosibirsk and into the long, dark stretch of Siberian forest.

Young Russians strumming, singing and drinking about 6 am at their campsite along the bank of the Katun River, Western Siberia, Russia
August 1995

Dmitri, Farida and Vladimir (playing guitar) about 4 am in the forest along the Katun River, Western Siberia, Russia August 1995

With Dmitri at the family dacha outside Novosibirsk, Russia (I'm the one with the fake mustache) August 1995

Reebok models posing at Korby waterfall, Teletskoye Lake,
Altai National Park, Russia August 1995

CHAPTER 22
LEAVING MAGADAN, USSR (MARCH 1990)

The faint pink-orange blush on the horizon was the first sign of dawn. From 8,000 meters up, cruising along in our 1945 vintage Antonov-24 twin-engine turboprop, I could just begin to make out the snowy vastness of the Soviet Far East. It was 6 am. I'd been awake since the previous morning – and on the go since midnight. Traveling. I needed a cup of coffee. I wasn't optimistic, but I went to the back of the plane anyway. There was no food. The beverage service, in its entirety, consisted of a case and a half of sweet Russian soda pop stacked on the floor in the rear of the plane. It was self-service. The stewardess was busy filing her nails and ignoring the passengers. Better than nothing, I thought, so I grabbed a bottle. Using a puzzled facial expression and appropriate eye contact and body language, I conveyed to the stewardess my next question, which was: "Like, where's the can opener?" She twitched the corner of her mouth and shrugged her shoulders, which I took to be Russian for: "Like, this is Aeroflot. Surely you don't expect us to have can openers."

Not to worry, I thought, I'd been up against this very problem several times during my three weeks in the Soviet Far East. I wedged the bottle between my knees, like I'd seen the Russians do, and tried to pry off the cap with my nail clippers. But it was on too tight, and with the back of the plane bouncing up and down and swaying from side to side, I was having trouble keeping my balance. I looked around. Where the rear exit ladder folded up inside the plane was a lattice-work of metal tubing. I found a sharp edge where two were welded together and positioned the bottle. The stewardess grabbed ahold of the main bar, trying to steady the whole unit and keep it from rolling back and forth with each bounce of the plane. I hesitated for just a few seconds as I thought about the bizarre situations one sometimes finds oneself in. Then I jerked down sharply and the cap flew off. I looked at the stewardess. Her pretty Slavic face broke into a broad grin and she gave me the thumbs-up sign. I smiled too. And just then I felt the cool gush of sticky wet foam running down over my hands, wrists and lower arms. Now, my previous Aeroflot flight had running water but no toilet paper. This flight, of course, had toilet paper but no running water. I didn't bother trying to ask the stewardess if she might have a package of pre-moistened towelettes or Handiwipes.

Resigned to my fate I walked back to my seat, sticky hands around a bottle of sweet, fizzy soda. It was about 6:15 am. I sat down and watched the sun come up over the Soviet Far East.

ANADYR, USSR

I was looking forward to the short layover in Anadyr to rinse my hands and get something to eat. Hunger was starting to gnaw at me. I'd had nothing to eat since dinner the night before – which consisted of a dried fish - and I was lucky enough to get that! At the time there were six restaurants in the Anchorage–sized city of Magadan. Four were closed and the other two weren't open. Everything shut down at 8 pm. I had scurried to a food store around 7:30 pm and stood in a long, slow line until I got up to the front and pointed out the fish I wanted. All I got was a small scrap of paper with a price written on it and directions back to the cashier. Another long, slow line. Since I was only buying one item she didn't need to use the abacus, so she rang me up on an antiquated cash register. I paid and got a receipt. Then back to the end of the long, slow fish line. I finally gave the woman my receipt and got my fish. It was now closing time. Shopping, Soviet style.

The plane touched down in Anadyr around mid-morning. We were off-loaded onto an unheated bus that sat on the runway for the hour or so it took to refuel and prep the plane for the next segment of our flight. No food, drink or amenities. It still being winter in the Soviet Far East, it was bitterly cold. I wasn't angry like some of my fellow passengers because there was no malice or rudeness here. It was just matter-of-fact, the way they did things in Russia. And we were still in Russia. I'll admit my heart sank when I saw them loading aboard several more crates of sweet Russian soda pop - the same sticky stuff that still coated my arms halfway up to the elbows. Shortly after that we took off for Provideniya.

I didn't know it at the time but another plane, filled with a smorgasbord of Russian officials and security personnel, was also making a beeline to Provideniya. Seems a small group of enterprising hucksters in Magadan was selling Soviet military paraphernalia (uniform and clothing-related) to the American tourists. About the only Americans or tourists in Magadan at that time were me and the Rotarians now on our chartered Antonov-24. Someone must have tipped off the authorities - unless they were in on it from the beginning. It would cause us a 5-hour delay in Provideniya.

PROVIDENIYA, USSR

First thing I did after getting off the plane in Provideniya was to rinse the dried, sticky Russian soda pop off my arms. Then I looked around for food but there was none to be bought, or had by any other means, either. The hours went by. Finally, a kindly pastor from Anchorage named Rick showed some true Christian charity by sharing with me a cold chicken leg. I was most thankful.

As we milled about in the spartan terminal the official reason we were given for the delay was that they were awaiting clearance from the U.S. State Department before they could fly a Soviet plane into U.S. air space. About 10,000 feet above the Bering Sea, where US and Soviet airspace met, a "hole" would appear with mutual US-USSR agreement allowing planes to fly through. The "hole" did not remain open for very long.

I saw Mikhail strolling about in the terminal. We recognized each other from my brief stay in Provideniya when I had been grounded by blizzards for three days on my way to Magadan almost three weeks earlier. Dressed in a suit and tie, he had an air of authority about him and was probably the local KGB guy. He knew I was here at the invitation of the Far Eastern Minister of Health and gave me no cause for concern, but played his cards close by not volunteering any additional information. So I was curious, but not really worried, by what had been taking place at the door. Two Russian soldiers faced each other at attention at the exit door. Every ten or fifteen minutes they would escort one or two Americans through the door and they would not reappear. Finally, it was my turn.

I was ushered into a room and offered a seat in the middle of a long wooden table. Facing me from across the table was a phalanx of about eight to ten Russian officials. The ones in the center wore military officer-style uniforms with shoulder stripes and various medals on their chests. Flanking them on the periphery were the plainclothes suit-and-tie guys that had KGB written all over them. I avoided eye contact. Behind them on the window ledge was a pyramid of confiscated military paraphernalia - boots and scarves and hats and medals and epaulets and just about everything that had to do with Soviet military uniforms. Did I have anything to add to the pile, they asked me in no uncertain terms. "No", I said without thinking, knowing that I had a couple of CA (Soviet Army) shoulder epaulets buried in my backpack. Fortunately, I was not searched. I really wanted a photo of these guys with all the confiscated booty stacked up behind them. If they were smart they'd take it back to Magadan and resell it. But they were not a friendly bunch and I opted against asking. They led me out another door where I joined the other "desaparasidos" in a cold hallway.

After we were all finally assembled in the cold hallway it was time to reboard for Anchorage. Five hours after landing in Provideniya. And yes, I watched them load several more crates of Russian soda pop on the plane before we took off.

On the long flight to Anchorage a goofy-looking uniformed Russian with bad teeth would wander to the back of the plane every so often for a few bottles of that sickly sweet stuff to bring up to the cockpit. Probably explained his teeth. His name was Victor and he was the navigator. We were flying in pitch darkness somewhere over the wintry Bering Sea in an ancient, Russian-built twin-engine turboprop Antonov-24. "God Bless You, Victor", I remember thinking, with just a bit of unease in my heart.

When we finally landed in Anchorage the Rotarians ribbed Victor. "Good job, Victor. You found Anchorage!", they said. Victor smiled a goofy smile. Upon clearing Customs I headed straight for the food court. When my stomach was finally full all I remember thinking about was my next trip to Russia. Great people and a great country! I vowed to return and missed it already.

CHAPTER 23

PILGRIM GEORGE AND THE MONGOLIANS THREE – A BUDDHIST-CHRISTIAN REUNION

Ordained a Catholic deacon in the fall of 1966, George Florian Walter was uncertain of his commitment to the Roman Catholic priesthood and a life in the pulpit. Uncertainty for George, in retrospect, turned out to be a good thing, but it initially caused him to be swept into a maelstrom of bewilderment in the social, cultural and religious changes swirling through America, and the world, in the late 1960s. From Vatican II to Haight-Ashbury.

Like so many others in a similar predicament at the time, George opted for a radical new start by heading to California. He landed at the Los Angeles YMCA looking for work, then drifted to Sunset Boulevard. Always engaging with the sincere, but otherwise directionless, anti-Establishment youth, he delivered meals, passed out underground newspapers, and searched for life's meaning. He communed with the Laguna Beach artists and the eclectic folks at the Esalon Institute, but did not find his calling.

He made a short return visit to his home, family and parish in Pennsylvania, but was seen as so changed by his California experience that he quickly rebounded back out West. And this time he landed in the Colorado Rockies outside Boulder with a friendly group of "freaks" camped out awaiting the end of the world.

The apocalypse apparently rescheduled itself (as it has done many times), but George sucked in the pure nature and beauty of the Colorado Rockies. And finally realized that it was God he was seeking and it was God he met in the Colorado mountains. He now had his life's purpose which, according to his book, was to undertake a "journey back to the heart of the Father who made him in the first place."

George moved back East again, took a job as an orderly at a major urban hospital and lived in a cramped $50-a-month attic flat. When not working or sleeping he read the Bible. He realized he not only had to seek out the "heart of the Father", but also get to know the Son, Jesus Christ. The idea of a pilgrimage to Jerusalem began to take shape and it had to be the long way: tracing the spread of Christianity in reverse.

In February 1970 George Florian Walter hitchhiked to New Orleans to catch the slow boat to Spain and begin his pilgrimage to Jerusalem. He tells the story in *A Pilgrim Finds The Way*.

Twenty-two years later, during the winter of 1992-93, Pilgrim George was spotted on the streets of Anchorage, Alaska. He had walked here from his hometown parish in Pennsylvania – via Mexico City. Two decades later he was still into taking the long way. Roman Catholic Archbishop Francis Hurley allowed him to do his winter *poustinia* (meditation retreat) in a small room in the Holy Family Cathedral. *The Anchorage Daily News* picked up on it with a front page story (not too many pilgrims blow into town). Intrigued, I chased him down and invited him over to our home for dinner.

Pilgrim George was the real thing. India has its share of phony gurus and we have our Jim Bakkers and Benny Hinns. But I was always convinced that in the long 2,000 year flowing shadow of the Roman Catholic Church there were those who remained true to the teachings of Jesus: St. Francis of Asisi, St. Teresa of Lisieux, St. Nilus of Orthodox Russia…and numerous others, unnamed and mostly under the radar. One of them was now sitting at our dinner table.

George wore a long denim robe studded with patches. He held a wooden staff topped off with a cross and carried a Bible. A photo of St. Mary of Guadalupe hung around his neck. The sandals he wore that carried him on his long pilgrimages intrigued me. George explained how he made them from retreads. These fragmented strips of tires cast off by speeding rigs are ubiquitous along the world's highways and byways. George estimates he gets about 1,000 miles per pair of self-made sandals.

What struck me most about Pilgrim George was how calm, unrushed and content he was – bliss, joy and equanimity are terms that come to mind. He had evidently tapped into the *unio mystica* from the Roman

Catholic approach and was living it. George accepted whatever food and hospitality that was offered to him on his journeys but, other than the rare one-way bus or plane ticket, no money. He put all his trust in the Lord. It was the same Lord who, as the Gospel of Matthew pointed out, took care of the sparrows. His follower, George, is worthy of many, many sparrows

We talked at dinner about the continuation of Pilgrim George's current pilgrimage (the Pennsylvania to Anchorage via Mexico City segment already behind him). And the audacity of it made the previous Barcelona to Jerusalem pilgrimage seem like a walk in the park. In April 1993 he planned to hop a short flight across the Bering Sea to Magadan, in the Russian Far East. And from there to walk across the Russian Far East into the vast expanse of Siberia, make a left in Yakutia, and then head south to Kerala, South India. The southwest Indian state of Kerala is about one-third Christian and a Catholic Church there was awaiting him several years hence.

April in Anchorage, southcentral Alaska, is a shoulder month. Almost spring, break-up, could still snow, not quite there yet. About the same in Magadan, where Pilgrim George was heading. He chose to walk from the Holy Family Cathedral in downtown Anchorage to the Anchorage International Airport to board the Russian jet on a one-way trip to Magadan. A small crowd of his supporters accompanied him and I joined them about halfway. It was a happy and hopeful group. We arrived at a point on the periphery of the airport where George made it clear non-verbally that he now needed to proceed alone.

Pilgrim George offered his blessing to anyone in the small crowd who came up to him, and I joined several others. As he placed his hand on my head and said a short prayer I felt very moved and honored to have come to know him. I have not seen him since, but we have had a rich correspondence for many years. Pilgrim George waved to his Anchorage friends one last time, then turned and walked toward the big Russian jet which, after a four-hour flight, would deposit him at the edge of the Eastern Hemisphere to begin the second leg of his long pilgrimage.

After milling about for maybe a week or so in Magadan, George was ready to hit the road - the notorious Kolyma Highway, a gravel road which stretched for over 700 miles through the taiga toward distant Yakutsk, the capital of the Sakha Republic (Yakutia) in northcentral

Siberia. This was gold country and gulag country and the road was built and paid for by a generation of forced labor – prisoners who labored and died under the most brutal conditions.

I had taken a nice photo of Pilgrim George and my seven-year-old daughter in front of our fireplace, but unfortunately didn't get the roll of film developed until after he left for Russia. I really wanted him to have a copy. So I wrote a short note on the back, stuck it in an unsealed envelope and drove to the airport when the next plane was scheduled to fly to Magadan.

That's how it was done in Anchorage in 1993. Folks would show up with letters and small parcels with a name and a local Magadan telephone number written on them and find a random passenger willing to take them over. It was never a problem. Once in Magadan, they would call the local contact who would then come by to pick them up. Even the pilots were known to take a small packet or parcel and stick it behind their seat in the cockpit. It was relaxed and informal, with none of the post – 9/11 paranoia.

I approached a random passenger who agreed to take my envelope over, but my request was a bit more challenging, as George had already left Magadan. I showed him the photo of George and explained he was a Christian pilgrim currently walking west on the Kolyma Highway. Would my random passenger kindly give this photo to one of the truck drivers who regularly ply the Kolyma and ask the driver to keep an eye out for this pilgrim along the road and give him the photo if he sees him? Random passenger agreed without hesitation. Still, I put the odds somewhere beyond 1 in 10,000.

Some months later I received the first of many wonderful handwritten letters from George. They often contained a couple of small, dry-pressed wildflowers plucked from wherever he was passing through. A pilgrim needs to be weight and baggage conscious, so George would write on both sides of small, thin sheets of paper and, if necessary, save them until he could get to a post office or find a friend who could help. Many were mailed in Russia, others apparently by courier with a foreign stamp.

I learned from one letter, later sent from Irkutsk, that George had arrived in the remote town of Neryungri, Yakutia. (Yakutia is twice the size of Alaska, yet only one of the many republics that comprise Siberia and the Russian Far East.) It was July 25, George's birthday. And someone had stopped by and handed him my photo! It was the first piece of mail he'd gotten since he arrived in Russia.

Pilgrim George continued on foot on a southwest trajectory toward Irkutsk, the largest city in southcentral Siberia. He planned to overwinter in *poustinia* in the small Polish Catholic village of Vershina – about a hundred kilometers outside of Irkutsk in the vast Siberian forest.

THE MONGOLIANS THREE

In April 1993, about a month before Pilgrim George restarted his pilgrimage by heading west out of Magadan on the Kolyma Highway, three Mongolians set off, on foot, on a long pilgrimage from Ulaanbaatar, Mongolia's capital, to Seattle. Their mission, in the Mongolian Buddhist tradition of pilgrimages to holy shrines, was to pay homage and respect to their martial arts master, Bruce Lee, who is buried in Seattle.

The San Francisco-born Lee was not only an action movie star who became a pop icon, he was a bona fide martial arts master who transformed the ancient Kung Fu, incorporating psychological and spiritual elements, into what became known as Jeet Kune Do. He died under unexplained circumstances in his Hong Kong apartment in 1973, at the age of 32.

The leader of the Mongolian trio, 33-year old P. Batzorig, was a fourth-degree black belt as well as founder and head of the Mongolian Jeet Kune Do Federation. Also on his resume, he was martial arts instructor to the Mongolian Army. Batzorig's 20-year old student, Natsagniam, held a black belt also and joined his teacher on the pilgrimage. And finally, retired Dr. I. Dendev, former physician to the Mongolian Olympic wrestling team, rounded out the trio. Not a martial artist, Dr. Dendev was still tough as nails at the age of 59, moderately fluent in English and fluent in Russian. He came along as physician, advisor and translator.

With warm clothes, dried meat and little more than $300 among them, they set off. It was tough going.

Somewhere south of Yakutsk, as best as I could figure from a brief perusal of the Russian-language journal Dr. Dendev later shared with me in Anchorage, the Mongolians must have been sleeping in the forest on their journey north when Pilgrim George passed by, heading south. George was an early bird and they may have missed by only a hundred

153

feet. How do I know? Later that day the Mongolians encountered excited talk about how "Jesus" had just passed through and were peppered with questions about if they had seen him. Translation ambiguities aside, the pious and religious peasants of Siberia would have quickly identified with George, the pilgrim tradition and his likeness to the number two guy of the Trinity. Yes, a near miss and one I would later set out to correct.

For the Mongolians, it was a brutal four-month slog across Siberia and the Russian Far East - snowstorms, rain, raging rivers, voracious mosquitos, bears, dwindling supplies, and lastly, endless tundra. They finally reached Provideniya on the coast. Their trek would have ended there if Nome-based Bering Air (the same airline I took to Provideniya three years earlier) hadn't offered them a 3-for-1 special.

The Mongolians Three arrived in Nome, Alaska raring to hit the road to Anchorage, only to learn there wasn't any. It was made clear to them that slogging the 1,000 mile Iditarod trail to Anchorage off-season would have been virtually impossible. Bering Air came to their rescue again and flew them to Fairbanks. They walked and hitchhiked to Anchorage.

I only learned about the Mongolians and their journey after they arrived in Anchorage and rushed over to meet them. They were staying at a hostel in Spenard. The timing was perfect, because I was leaving on a three week trip to Mongolia in just a couple of days, so I carried letters and greetings from them to their families in Ulaanbaatar, where I met Dr. Dendev's new grandson before he did. I promised to follow up when I returned.

Canada refused the trio visas, so they ended up flying to Seattle on raised funds. Preserving the integrity of their mission, they opted to first walk from Seattle to San Diego to make up for the lost Canadian mileage. Then they took a bus back to Seattle.

In what must have been an emotional climax, they finally gathered at Bruce Lee's gravesite and paid their respects to their master. And they spoke by phone with Bruce Lee's widow. Many years later Batzorig shared photos of that gathering with me. One of the young men in the photos would later become Mongolia's Prime Minister.

When I caught up with the trio after returning from Mongolia, they were back at the Spenard youth hostel. First thing I did was give Dr. Dendev a photo of the grandson in Mongolia he had yet to meet. And then I learned they were flat broke. Mongolia's economy had crashed, their sponsors had dried up and they were financially stuck in Anchorage with no way back.

Dr. Dendev and Dr. Bill Cox hold a Mongolian flag at the summit of Wolverine Peak (elev. 4455 feet) during a January whiteout. Anchorage, Alaska January 1994

A MINI-EXPEDITION TO WHILE AWAY THE TIME

Running down the list of options to get our friends back to Mongolia, and striking out each time, was slow going. A couple of weeks went by. Dr. Dendev politely confided to me that they were (literally) trying to find a "slow boat to China". I urged just a little more patience (something the Asians, as opposed to Americans, had in abundance). It was early January in Alaska and I suspected they might be suffering a bit of cabin fever. Even in urban Alaska. I suggested a hike in the nearby mountains and they jumped at the opportunity.

I didn't mention that this would also be the first ever Mongolian-American expedition to the summit of Wolverine Peak – and in early January at that. (I'd been to the summit at least sixteen times, but never in January.) With the summit at 4455 feet and a round-trip of eleven miles from the Prospect Heights Parking Lot at the entrance to Chugach State Park, it was no small hike.

They showed up rather lightly dressed, I thought. Cotton sweats. One had no hat. I had brought extra clothing in my pack, which Batzorig proceeded to grab from me and sling over his shoulder next to his own pack. And then he took off with the enthusiasm of a husky hitting the frozen trail after being chained up all summer.

Bitter cold and blowing snow made for challenging conditions and visibility, several times forcing us to take shelter on the lee side of a small rocky outcropping. But we reached the top.

On the summit, in howling winds and near white-out conditions, Dr. Dendev and I sat and held aloft a small Mongolian flag, thereby nullifying a declaration made several years earlier by my brother Bob, who stood on the same summit (on a warm summer day) and laid claim to the entire mountain on behalf of the Great State of New Jersey. Well, sorry New Jersey. Viva la Mongolia!

Lee Leinen, who was very active with the Roman Catholic Archdiocese of Anchorage, had been serving as liaison between Pilgrim George (wherever he was in the world) and George's family and parish back in Pennsylvania. Archbishop Francis Hurley was very supportive as well. Lee also became involved with the plight of the stranded Mongolians, which didn't surprise me. If someone needed help, Lee was there. She was a very special person.

I finally looked at a map and figured the cheapest and easiest way to get the Mongolians home was for them to fly direct from Anchorage to Khabarovsk in the Russian Far East. There they should be able to get a cheap train ticket on the Trans-Siberian to Ulan-Ude, where they would hop the Trans-Mongolian to Ulaanbaatar. And then it hit me. I remembered it was January and George was about halfway through his long winter *poustinia* in Siberia. No time to slap myself for not thinking of it sooner. I had to call Lee pronto.

I explained to Lee the route back home for the Mongolians and how the biggest expense, by far, would be airfare: "Maybe if we could raise the funds to pay for their plane tickets, we could ask them to continue beyond Ulan-Ude to Irkutsk, take the bus to Vershina and deliver some letters and supplies to Pilgrim George," I suggested. "It will be a win-win." I suggested maybe a karate exhibition where each of the martial arts schools in Anchorage would demonstrate their particular style and the Mongolian trio would be the star attraction. We'd set up a table at the door asking for donations and explaining why. Lee was on it, and the next day I went to the airport with a friend who spoke better Russian than me and we negotiated a reduced fare for three one-way tickets to Khabarovsk with the local general manager of Aeroflot.

For someone who didn't know squat about karate, Lee Leinen organized an exhibition that filled the entire gym at Anchorage's East High. Our friend Dudum emceed. And there was a lot of excitement when some locals volunteered to spar with the Mongolians. All in all, we raised enough to cover the three tickets and Batzorig agreed, without hesitation, on a side trip to bring letters and supplies to Pilgrim George at his *poustinia* in Vershina.

I picked up the Mongolians Three at the youth hostel the evening of their departure. They were sitting there playing chess like it was just another evening. I was amazed and impressed at their calmness. A small crowd of friends and supporters had gathered at the airport to see them off. Lee arrived shortly after we did.

Lee brought her "packet" of letters and supplies for George. It consisted of a massive duffel bag, chained and pad-locked. Musta been at least half the size of Batzorig. She gave them a pencil–sketch of St. Stanislaus Church in Vershina, inside of which Batzorig could expect to find George. Batzorig didn't even blink an eye, and had no questions. I had no doubt that package would arrive at its destination.

Aeroflot's Illushin-62 got them safely to Khabarovsk six hours later, where they spent two days at the train station fighting off petty thieves and extortionist fees for their luggage. Finally, they boarded the Trans-Siberian. Arriving in Ulan-Ude, Dr. Dendev and Natsagniam stayed behind while Batzorig and the duffel bag continued overnight to Irkutsk, arriving very early in the morning. There he killed the day, awaiting the early evening bus to Vershina.

He finally arrived at the log cabin village of Vershina in the vast Siberian forest. Late January, it was the dead of winter, dark and about minus 20° F. With incredible dedication and fortitude, hauling that massive duffel bag and a pencil sketch of the church where George was expected to be residing, speaking only limited Russian, he single-mindedly zeroed in on his goal. I will let Pilgrim George, in his own words*, describe what happened next:

"Friday evening, about 8:30 pm, I am still up though I am usually in bed by 7:30 pm. I'm writing a letter to my niece… I hear this loud knocking on the side door of the Church and someone trying the door handle to get in. I don't like the sound of it – one learns to read a lot into little things like a knock. I think it's probably one of the local drunks (yes, we have that problem in Vershina, too), so I go on writing, then I hear knocking at the front door; still I do not respond, then I hear rapping on my window even though it's ten feet off the ground and a voice saying: "George, George, I from America." I just say "no, no" and go on writing for I've had my share of people…I don't take the bait and go on writing.

After a few minutes of silence, rapping on the window again and the voice "I have clothes and letters from America." "OK, OK" I say as finally I feel confident it must be a friend and not an enemy so I go to open the door. And there is Batzorig with this large green duffle bag with a pad lock keeping it secure. He said in broken English "I brought this to you from Lee Leinen in Alaska!" "What?" I said. How did you find me? How did you get here? How did you meet Lee?" Then he pulled out this crumbled piece of paper and showed me MY sketch of St. Stanislaus Church in Vershina. "Oh, this is too much," I thought. "Come in and have a cup of tea… "OK," he said, "but first let me open the box for you." So he proceeded to empty out everything, slitting open the sealed boxes and displaying the contents…"

*in a handwritten letter to Lee Leinen from Vershina, Russia, on January 24, 1994, and ultimately mailed from Mongolia

George brought Batzorig over to a small log cabin, started a fire and allowed him to get some rest. And early the next morning, when he went over to accompany him to the 7:30 am bus to Irkutsk, Batzorig was already up doing his exercises. He caught up with his two colleagues in Ulan-Ude and they walked to Mongolia, arriving in Ulaanbaatar as national heroes. Their wives and parents, per Mongolian tradition, presented them with silver cups filled to the brim with milk and draped them with the blue ceremonial Mongolian silk scarf, the *khatag*.

And after Batzorig left, George reveled in the gifts from across the world. Again, in his own words:

"My eyes were wet all day reading one letter and note after another (well over 30, I think)."

EPILOGUE I: PILGRIM GEORGE

Pilgrim George continued on foot to Novosibirsk, the largest city in western Siberia, and then on to Alma Ata, Kazakhstan for his next winter *poustinia*. From there, finally, to Kerala, India. Tension in Pakistan and India's heat, he shared with me in letters, were big challenges.

From Kerala he took a one-way flight to Italy, where he met with Pope John Paul II. Then a multi-year, zig-zagging pilgrimage through Europe, Ukraine, Ireland, England, Poland and on up to Norway. Plying the pilgrim's trade and enriching lives along the way until the ultimate goal: the Holy Land (Jerusalem) in the millennium year 2000.

I was honored to receive a detailed, hand-written letter and photos from George in Israel in 2000. My last letter from George is dated November 19, 2001 and from Pennsylvania. He concludes..."Know you are always in my heart and in my prayers. May Jesus, the Good Shepherd, lead you safely to the pastures of his Peace. I love you and bless you always. In Jesus, Mary and Joseph, Pilgrim George."

George is still out there pilgrimaging stateside, I believe. I have no doubt we will meet again (and maybe we can patent those amazing sandals).

EPILOGUE II: THE MONGOLIANS 3

Dr. Dendev: Dr. Dendev and I caught up in Mongolia some years after his triumphant return and we had a grand adventure (well, it was a grand adventure for me, but probably routine for him) driving off northeast into the Mongolian steppes to his ancestral village (see accompanying story). Sadly, he died some years ago of hepatitis – another innocent victim of an endemic disease that is a scourge in Central Asia.

Our friendship was passed off to his eldest son, Oyundelger "Ogi" Dendev. It has taken root and will continue to flourish.

Natsagniam: Natsagniam entered Mongolian politics and has been difficult to catch up with. I am told he has aligned himself with the right folks.

Batzorig: Batzorig later took off on another trek from Mongolia to India and wrote a small book. He was then planning a trek across the Australian Outback, but some time afterward, due to circumstances well beyond his control, he opted to immigrate to America. He took work as a painter and night watchman in San Francisco and I caught up with him in nearby Oakland. We met for dinner, took a long walk along the Bay from Fisherman's Wharf, and talked.

Later he ended up in the Seattle area. And after five years of separation, this dedicated husband and father brought his wife and six children to America. He continued to work as a painter, or whatever job he could get, to support himself and his family. We visited again at his apartment north of Seattle. I could see his family was thriving and slowly assimilating.

Shortly after our last visit, Batzorig bestowed upon me an honor that would seem to dwarf an invitation to a Mongolian marmot roast. He announced we were "brothers". From then on it was Brother Bill and Brother Batzorig. I was deeply moved. We continue to stay in touch.

EPILOGUE III

In 2016, after the passing of Anchorage Archbishop Emeritus Francis Hurley, I reconnected with Pilgrim George. I shared with him my two stories about him, which filled in some gaps and prompted him to write two stories from his own perspective. These he sent to me, along with a 2-page handwritten letter (a rarity these days) carefully written on two sides of a single thin, lined sheet. And more info about those amazing sandals! His last pair, made from a new rubber Bridgestone tire in Anchorage in 1993, lasted twenty years and over 30,000 miles (I smell a lucrative sponsorship deal here). The tie-downs came from the nylon straps truck drivers use to secure their loads and were secured by screws he picked up along the road. They did, however, require a new heel every 3,000 miles, which was made from discarded roadside retreads - and oh, once in Canada in 2001 a new sole.

160

In March 2020 I received in the mail an autographed copy of Pilgrim George's book: *The 40 Thousand Mile Man*. Pilgrim George has retired as a physical pilgrim, but at age 80 shows no signs of retiring as a spiritual pilgrim.

Pilgrim George and my daughter Colleen at our home in Anchorage, Alaska Winter 1992-93

Seeing off the Mongolians 3 at Anchorage International Airport (Lee Leinen in center back row) January 1994

CHAPTER 24

PILGRIM GEORGE II: THE FINAL ARRIVAL OF A CHURCH BELL. LATE SUMMER 1994

A small village of about 150 families, Vershina lies in the vast birch forests about a hundred kilometers north of Irkutsk, the largest city in southcentral Siberia. Originally farmed by Buryat Mongols, Polish settlers started arriving in 1910. The Czarist government of Russia at the time built a tiny log church to accommodate the religious needs of the Polish Catholics. In 1935 Stalin banned religious services and the small church soon fell into disrepair, frequented only by playing children and grazing animals. In 1941 the church bell was pulled down by some young people – probably taken to be melted down for munitions by the Soviet Army.

With glasnost and perestroika underway after Mikhail Gorbachev came to power, Polish Salvatorian priests were allowed back to restore and refurbish the church. On December 12, 1992 St. Stanislaus was re-dedicated and re-opened. The new building had everything a simple church needed – except a church bell.

The Sunday collection basket in this poor village netted between $1.00 and $1.50, so there was no way the local town folk could ever afford a church bell. After doing *poustinia* at the church for a long Siberian winter, Pilgrim George was looking for a way to thank the kind and hospitable town folk. It was a no-brainer! George's parish in Pennsylvania raised the necessary funds and commissioned a foundry in Ohio to construct a 519-pound church bell. And Pilot Air Freight of Oakdale, Pennsylvania was commissioned to get the bell to Vershina.

I was a full-time radiologist at Alaska Native Medical Center at the time. Lee Leinen would stop by my office about once a week to chat.

Lee, as mentioned previously, was very active in the Roman Catholic archdiocese of Anchorage and also the liaison between Pilgrim George (wherever in the world he was) and his family and parish in Pennsylvania. Lee would always mention something about problems with a church bell in Moscow but, being preoccupied, I only paid her scant attention.

I was experiencing the ennui that occasionally creeps up on professionals and it was starting to peak when Lee stopped by my office once again. I needed something fresh, a challenge, and this time I gave Lee my full attention. The church bell, it seems, had safely arrived in Moscow but went no farther. It had become ensnared in bureaucratic red tape for weeks now, perhaps going on a month. Every effort made to shake it loose seemed to ensnare it further. I had some contacts and a few cards to play and I vowed then and there that I would free that church bell and get it to Vershina where it belongs! And I would do it without leaving Anchorage! Thus began my long correspondence with Vicky Revtai of Pilot Air Freight.

Vicky had been in the air freight business about twenty years and never came up against a brick wall she couldn't break through or go around. Until now. The bell was too heavy to lift out of the plane. The plane door was too small. Some kind of problem with the local union. It went on and on. I made some fresh suggestions, made a few calls, but nothing seemed to work. After a couple more weeks Vicky seemed to have reached the limits of her patience and said: "I'm going to fly that bell to Beijing and have it trucked across China and Mongolia into Siberia". "Hold on just a bit", I pleaded, a fresh idea welling up, "we need to get that bell transferred to the Trans-Siberian where it can go by rail all the way to Irkutsk. Let me make one more call." When you are desperate to shake loose a 519-pound church bell mired in bureaucratic red tape in Moscow, who do you call? Why, the personal physician to the King of Swaziland, of course! I should have realized this sooner.

Dr. Jack Hickel split his time between Anchorage and Africa and did provide medical service to the Swazi King. Also, his Dad, Wally Hickel, happened to be Alaska's governor at the time. I rang up Jack.

"Jack," I said, "I really feel uncomfortable asking political favors, but I think we need your Dad's help. This is not for me. It is a good cause." Jack listened patiently as I explained the travails of the church bell and he responded, "You know, the person you really need to talk to about this is my Mom. I'll have her give you a call."

Ten minutes later the phone rang. It was Alaska's First Lady Ermalee Hickel. She listened with patience and concern while I repeated to her what I had just told Jack. "Ted Mala is the one who can help you. I'll talk to him and make sure he gets back to you," she said. I thanked her for her concern.

If Ronald Reagan is going to get the credit for bringing down the Berlin Wall and the Iron Curtain, Dr. Ted Mala of Anchorage darn well better be credited with melting the Ice Curtain. People forget that Alaska, USA and the former Soviet Union shared a common border. Dr. Mala made the first forays into the Soviet Far East and Siberia. He brought over the first Russian delegation to Alaska. He never quite got the credit and acclaim he deserved.

But Ted was a busy man at the time and often didn't return his phone calls promptly. Not so after hearing from Ermalee. He called me first thing the next morning. "Ermalee Hickel told me to call you", he explained, curious. I thanked Dr. Mala for calling and repeated the story I related the previous evening to Jack and his Mom. He said he would see what he could do. I was leaving the next day on a two-week trip to Japan and wouldn't be able to follow up. But I felt confident - Ted had his marching orders from Alaska's First Lady!

I don't know what Dr. Mala did, but I suspect he talked with the Russian ambassador in Washington, D.C. I later learned that in short order the bell was transferred to the Trans-Siberian and taken by rail to Irkutsk. The rest of the story I got from Father Ignatius Pawlus, the Polish Salvatorian priest in Irkutsk. Father Ignaty, as we called him.

When the bell arrived in Irkutsk, Father Ignaty later told me, Russian agents came from nowhere and swarmed upon the bell. It was the funniest thing he had ever seen, and just recalling the event made him laugh hard enough to set his belly jiggling. After realizing it was just a cast-iron church bell and did not contain drugs or plutonium, they released it. It was trucked to St. Stanislaus in Vershina and secured in the new bell tower. It was May 1994. Unfortunately, it arrived five days after Pilgrim George hit the road for Kazakhstan.

IRKUTSK, RUSSIA (AUG. 1994)

I was on my way back to Russia. My self-appointed mission, in addition to just getting back to Russia and seeing Lake Baikal, was to go to Vershina, photograph the church bell secured in the bell tower at St. Stanislaus, and send the photos back to Pilgrim George's family and parish in Pennsylvania and to Vicky Revtai and her crew at Pilot Air Freight.

We landed in Irkutsk. I knew no one and had no hotel reservation in this city of about one million people. I had Father Ignaty's address scribbled on a piece of paper by Lee Leinen. We had never met and he was not expecting me. Unfortunately, no one answered at his apartment on Ulitsa Lopatina.

What to do, I wondered. I couldn't afford to spend US$100 a night for a cold-water flat at the Inntourist Hotel. I asked the cabbie, in Russian, to take me to "*samaya deshawvaya gostinitsa v gorodye*" (the cheapest hotel in the city). This he did.

It was quite the dive. This was a hotel for Russians and non-Western foreigners (Central Asians and Eastern Europeans). I was very relieved when the woman behind the reception desk registered me (I was afraid of being forced over to Inntourist). I got my own private room (and key) for $4.00 a night. I was good-to-go for a week or more in Irkutsk until I figured things out.

The communal toilet (sans seat) at the end of the hallway was hygienically untouchable. But no problem. Foraging through a dumpster outside the hotel I found a piece of sturdy cardboard that had housed a small Israeli-made bookshelf. Using my penknife I cut out a toilet seat that I could carry back and forth from my room.

Room? Check. Toilet? Check. Now I needed to buy some rubles so I could eat. It was Sunday afternoon and I was getting hungry. I went back downstairs to the woman who checked me in. "Where can I change money", I asked her. The English term "change money" is one of the most universally understood terms on the planet, save for a few undiscovered tribes in the Brazilian Amazon.

Speaking Russian, she asked me to follow her. Up the stairs and down a long, dark hallway on the second floor. Strange place for an ATM that dispenses rubles, I remember thinking. She paused, then knocked on a door. It opened slowly. Three Armenians drinking vodka suddenly stood up. The one who first caught my attention was bare-chested and rather fierce-looking. He had scars on his torso, a chain around his neck and a shaved head. It turned out he had been a soldier in Nagorno-Karabakh, the Armenian enclave in Azerbaijan.

"Change your money here," the old lady says, closing the door behind her, "just be careful." Then … poof …she's gone… One of the Armenian traders pulled out a very thick wad of ruble notes and offered me a deal. A quick mental calculation told me it was a reasonable black market rate (I was certainly not in the most favorable bargaining position). I changed twenty bucks.

After I pocketed my rubles they motioned for me to take a seat and poured me a shot of vodka. We drank and started talking. They each spoke five or six languages, but none of them spoke English, so we conversed in Russian. A large glass jar of stewed tomatoes came down off a high shelf. A round loaf of Armenian flatbread was set on the coffee table before us. They started frying potatoes on an electric skillet and shared their food with me. Many shots of vodka were poured and consumed.

It became quickly clear that my new Armenian friends were very proud of their country, proud that Armenia was the first Christian country. I reveled in hearing such national pride. After over an hour of delightful conversation they stood up, announcing they had to go to the airport to meet some arrivals. I stood up too, hoping I could make it back to my room down the hallway and get the key in my door before falling flat on my face. I was ultimately successful.

After a few days I finally caught up with Father Ignaty and Father Darius. They kindly allowed me to crash in their 4th floor apartment. We drove the 25 miles from Irkutsk to Lake Baikal the following day.

The largest freshwater lake in the world, by volume, Baikal holds more water than all the Great Lakes combined. It is incredibly deep, reaching down over 6,000 feet. I remember reading a statistic that if Baikal suddenly evaporated and all the world's rivers were diverted to refill it (the Amazon, Yukon, Mississippi, etc.) it would take 25 years to top it off! I had no time for a swim, but cupped my hands and drank its pure waters at the shoreline.

The next day we began the hundred-kilometer drive to Vershina — the same road Batzorig took by bus through the dead of the previous Siberian winter. I sat in the back seat with a student from Poland, Father Ignaty and his driver/chauffeur in front. The two of them talked, joked, laughed and sang songs together in Russian. The driver, Anatoli, was a former KGB agent. Twenty years ago KGB agents killed Polish priests! I remember thinking how refreshing and delightful it was how times had changed. We soon arrived in Vershina.

It was a Russian peasant village right out of Chekhov. Smelled of damp logs, wood smoke and animals. More horses than cars. I was so thoroughly happy and relaxed to be there. And there was St. Stanislaus Roman Catholic Church, looking just like Pilgrim George's pencil sketch! I approached her reverently.

A flock of pigeons flew off suddenly as I climbed up into the bell tower. And there it was! The church bell! All 519 pounds of cast iron from the foundry in Ohio securely mounted. I took several photos from various angles which were later sent to Pennsylvania. Mission accomplished, I thought. And I learned many years later that the Vershina villagers named the bell "George".

Father Ignaty would be spending some days in Vershina, so I went back to Irkutsk with Anatoli, the ex-KGB guy. He spoke freely on the long ride back, but my Russian was only good enough to pick up about 50%. Through one open stretch of road he pointed out several farmhouses but, in Russian, seemed to be describing an airport. The phrase "fly to the United States" and the number "21" kept popping up. All I saw were pastoral fields and farmhouses.

Suddenly it hit me! SS-21, the Russian ICBM (Intercontinental Ballistic Missile). Nuclear missiles programmed to strike targets in the United States. My ears suddenly perked up, like Ross Perot's, and I refined my questions. Seems Anatoli had worked in the Special Forces building silos disguised as farmhouses. Looks like a farmhouse on the satellite image, but it's only an empty shell over a nuclear missile silo. And, I learned, these nuclear warheads were pulled out of their silos at night and trucked on long flat-bed trailers to different sites scattered around Lake Baikal. Get more bang for your buck, or ruble, I thought - within the treaty limitations. But why was he telling me this?

Suddenly he jerked the wheel to the left and we bounced roughly across an abandoned farm field, while I held on for dear life, until we came to a stop in front of a small pond. Shit, I thought, he spilled the beans about the ICBMs and now he's gonna off me! I'll be spending the next ten years or more decomposing at the bottom of this small Siberian pond.

Anatoli reached under the seat for what I was sure was a gun and pulled out… a … rag. Then he foraged in the trunk and pulled out … a … pail. He went to fill it with pond water and started cleaning Father Ignaty's car. Relieved, I jumped out and joined him. Between the two of us we got Father Ignaty's little red 4-seater squeaky clean. And drove back to Irkutsk uneventfully.

A church bell named George at St. Stanislaus in Vershina, Russia
August 1994

Father Ignaty (center) and friends, Listvyanka, Russia August 1994

St. Stanislaus Catholic Church, Vershina, Russia August 1994

Lake Baikal, Listvyanka, Russia August 1994

Armenian money-changer friends in hotel for non-Westerners. Irkutsk,
Russia August 1994

CHAPTER 25
VITALY MENSHIKOV

KAMCHATKA, RUSSIA (JULY 1993)

I secretly nicknamed him *Poshlee*. In Russian it means "let's go". *Vamanos* in Spanish. Vitaly was a man in a hurry and he used the phrase often. *Poshlee*.

I'd already been to the Russian Far East twice (actually, during those trips it was still, technically, the Soviet Far East). But never to Kamchatka. Then a letter arrived from an Igor Vostokov in Moscow, dated March 31, 1992. It was sent to the Alaska Chapter of the Sierra Club and forwarded to me, their International Committee chairman at the time. Mr. Vostokov was the President of the Sports and Tourism Union of Russia and mentioned his friend and representative in Kamchatka, Vitaly Menshikov. It would take off from there.

I got in touch with Vitaly, who does not speak English. He was President of the Tourist Club, President of the Ecological Conservation Fund of Kamchatka, Peoples' Deputy and a host of other titles I found out about after I arrived in Kamchatka. And he was getting funding from the Soros Foundation, which could only help. But he would later prove to have what it took to be effective on the ground: influence.

With what I was learning about Vitaly and Kamchatka, I became intrigued and started plotting a visit. I had contacts who could help, but I needed justification for a trip there. I was interested in doing something to support their conservation efforts, so I came up with the idea of somehow setting up a cooperative Alaska-Kamchatka environmental exchange.

Kamchatka is a California–sized peninsula that hangs down from the huge northeast extension of the Russian landmass toward Alaska. The

Kurile Islands dribble from its southern edge toward northern Japan's Hokkaido. And during the long Cold War years Kamchatka was highly militarized – the USSR's Pacific flank opposing the USA across the Big Water. It made strategic sense. And with Russian civilian in-migration kept at bay, Kamchatka's natural and pristine wonders got a reprieve.

Even in post-Gorbachev Russia in 1993 Kamchatka was still sensitive and semi-closed. I might need to enter through the back door. So I flew off to Magadan in the Russian Far East in July 1993 – my third visit. I carried a letter from Neil Johannsen, Alaska State Parks Director, to Vladimir Birukov, Governor of the vast Kamchatka Oblast (region, or province). I had asked Neil to write a letter to propose a cooperative exchange between the parks and environmental officials in Kamchatka and the Alaska Division of State Parks. I figured if I could get to Petropavlovsk, Kamchatka and chase down Vitaly, he could help me get the letter to Birukov and the high officials who could make such an exchange happen.

Anatoly Nicolayevich was the top radiologist for the Magadan Oblast, and by now we were good friends. He kindly contacted his counterpart for the Kamchatka Oblast and I soon had a legitimate medical invitation to Petropavlovsk. I agreed to give an X-ray presentation and lecture. No problem, I thought. I was now in-like-Flint.

I boarded the old Soviet-built Ilyushin-62 for the domestic (read: lower quality and standards than international) flight to Petropavlovsk. A word to the wise: if you're flying an Ilyushin-62 domestically, do NOT take a seat in the last row. For those old fliers who remember the configuration of the DC-9, with an engine on either side of the fuselage in the back of the plane, the unique Ilyushin-62 has two engines, in tandem, on either side. They are screamingly loud (well above OSHA standards, I was sure, but OSHA had no jurisdiction in Russia). And a second reason for not sitting in the last row was the toilet. The door swung open and closed during the flight and the toilet expelled an ammonia-laden scent of stale urine which wafted heavily over the back couple of rows. Fortunately, it was a short flight and we soon landed in Petropavlovsk.

As the jet slowed down gradually on a massive asphalt runway I could hear the sirens of a Russian ambulance getting louder and closer. Jesus H, I thought, someone onboard had a medical crisis and they called in ahead for EMS. But that was not it. The hospital had sent out an ambulance to pick me up. I cringed with embarrassment and tried to hide my face as I was let off the plane before the other passengers, down the steps and into the waiting ambulance. When I walked past the seated Canadians I had befriended on the flight I avoided eye contact.

On the way downtown I remember bonfires blocking the road and the ambulance diverting. Never figured that one out. I was dropped off at the not-uncommon "cold water flat" of a local hotel in Petropavlovsk. But it was more than just cold water that came out of the bathtub tap – it was ultracold and somewhat silty. Being from Alaska I suspected it was at least partly glacial, so all I could manage was a quick shampoo while leaning over the tub. I got my hair clean, but experienced an aneurysm popping extremely painful, but transient, post-shampoo headache. Vitaly Menshikov rescued me the following day and brought me over to the roomy flat of one of his friends to crash for the duration of my stay. I had my own couch to sleep on.

I gave my obligatory presentation entitled "Interesting X-Ray Cases" at the big hospital in Petropavlovsk. There was a good-sized crowd assembled, but one important person was missing – an interpreter. I would have to wing it with my very limited Russian for the thirty minute talk and questions.

A surgeon I had met only briefly sat in the front row. Using only hand and body language and facial expressions, with the occasional verbal interjection, he pulled me through. He was my rock, and I never forgot his kindness and support. Thank you, Doctor.

The only entity I can remember who was faster on his feet than *Poshlee* Vitaly Menshikov was the cartoon character Bugs Bunny. Or would that be Road Runner? Anyway, Vitaly swept me over to Kamchatka's equivalent of a combined White House and Congress. He banged on the door of Kamchatka Governor Birukov, waited maybe two seconds, then barged in. Birukov was not in. He then banged on the door of Kamchatka's second-highest political official, who was also not in. We finally sat down with the second-tier of Kamchatka's two highest officials. Vitaly excitedly presented them Neil's letter. I was hopeful.

Vitaly, as I had hoped, invited me along on a hike - actually, an overnight backpacking trip - into the mountains of Kamchatka. A dream come true. We took off late the following morning on a paved road in what seemed, to me, like an armored vehicle that carried troops to the frontline. And we were dropped off, sans AK-47s and M-16s, at the trailhead. Our goal: *Golubiya Ozyera* (the Blue Lakes). Our mission: enjoy the pristine natural wonders of Kamchatka. We set off down the trail – me, Vitaly and a mixed group of several teens, including one whose extra sleeping bag I would borrow and whose homemade sewn tent I would sleep in that night.

We hiked through a dark forest which soon broke out into a mustard–green meadow dappled with wildflowers. Off in the distance, Kamchatka's famed, snow-streaked volcanoes were visible. It was a scene so beautiful I half expected Julie Andrews to waltz through, belting out "The Hills are Alive, with the Sound of Music." We set up camp that night under some trees along a shallow, cold, gurgling brook. Vitaly built a fire from scavenged dead wood and potatoes were set to boil, which would soon be transformed into a delicious Russian soup.

I played impromptu volleyball with the Russian kids, who seemed so happy and content to be where they were. And I slept well, although the cold of the wee hours that July night in Kamchatka's mountains forced me to burrow as deeply as possible into my borrowed sleeping bag. But no matter, Vitaly's tea the next morning warmed my nocturnally chilled bones. After breakfast we set off and soon broke through timberline into the alpine tundra high-country. I slaked my thirst along the way from the pure, cold water of the shallow brook we were paralleling. And then we arrived at the Blue Lakes.

Fingered, peninsula–like snowfields reached into the Blue Lakes. There was, of course, more than one Blue Lake – at slightly different altitudes. Our team had been picking up the odd piece of garbage on the trail ever since we set out. And I watched a young Russian woman, clad only in half-a-bathing-suit, wander thigh-deep into Blue Lake to retrieve a discarded can. (I think it was a can…I wasn't concentrating so much on what she retrieved). Then we hiked uphill to the next highest Blue Lake, where the July snowfields were larger. There, Vitaly prepared a treat.

Squatting, he filled a small pail with fresh granular snow. A couple cans of sweetened condensed milk (available everywhere in Russia) were roughly opened with knives (no K-Mart can-openers in Kamchatka) and poured onto the collected snow. (I half-hoped he would toss one empty can into the water so I could witness another discarded can retrieval. But it was not to be - Vitaly was too serious and committed –so it went with the rest of the trash to be hauled back to town). Then mix, serve and enjoy. Voila! Kamchatka ice cream!

On our long hike back we stopped at one point, just above treeline, for tea. The view was expansive, and Russians need their afternoon tea. It was the perfect convergence. It looked to be a well-used fire pit. A horizontal spit, high enough to hang a teapot over flames, sat upon two forked uprights burrowed into the ground. And Vitaly lost no time in pointing out to me that it was all metal. The implication was obvious: Struggling alpine and subalpine trees don't need to be hacked down to create such a contraption every time a group of hikers wants to stop for tea. This was semi-permanent, and there was plenty of dead wood around to bring a pot of water to a quick boil. Russian tea: black tea, always served hot, with sugar as desired, but never milk.

I reveled in sipping that trail-brewed tea. Reveled in looking over my shoulder at the Blue Lakes we had just descended from, and the vast panorama of Kamchatka's mountains and forests that extended to the horizon. Reveled in the company of the environmentally respectful Vitaly and his young protégés.

Approaching the trailhead, Vitaly pointed out a small clearing under the trees to our left. It had formerly been a garbage dump left over by geologists. Vitaly and his crew had picked it clean and hauled all the trash off to town.

At a small ceremony in a very rustic, wooden building outside Petropavlovsk a couple nights later I was formally inducted into the Kamchatka Tourist Club by its President, Vitaly Menshikov. I was greatly honored and still have my certificate.

ALASKA STATE PARKS DIRECTOR GOES TO KAMCHATKA

I was more than happy to do the on-site legwork in Kamchatka for Alaska State Parks Director Neil Johannsen. An Alaska State Parks-Kamchatka cooperative exchange was my idea, after all, and Neil was patient enough to write that first letter. It lit the fuse in Kamchatka and I brought back letters and proposals for him to consider.

The politics of administering, and expanding, state parks in a state like Alaska with so many anti-park and anti-government stakeholders kept Neil's plate full. He could have easily put the Kamchatka thing on the back burner to fade away, but he charged ahead, firing off letters and beginning to organize (well, maybe he wanted to get away from that full plate for a while). Neil made the right call and earned my respect.

His three-member delegation originally included Russell Berry, Superintendent of Denali National Park. I remember talking with Russ on the phone. Unfortunately, Russ being a federal employee disqualified him, as federal employees were not allowed to fly on foreign air carriers. So it was down to Director Johannsen and his colleague at State Parks, Dave Stevens.

It was an early summer morning in Anchorage when the Director of Alaska State Parks bade a somber farewell to his wife, Hilary, before flying off to Kamchatka. As if he were going off to war. Neil had told me that he and Dave had vowed to absolutely support each other in not getting on board any Russian aircraft in Kamchatka they mutually deemed unsafe. And Neil admitted to me later that it was a vow that "went out the window" before they boarded the first of many helicopter flights to Kamchatka's natural wonders. Helicopter transport was pretty much the only way to reach Kamchatka's natural wonders.

Neil described a massive, metal behemoth of a Russian helicopter, riddled with bullet holes from action in the Soviet-Afghan war. And inside: dysfunctional seatbelts and puddles of oily water sloshing around on the floor. I got him into this and he got himself out – with the help of the underestimated, but incredibly skilled, Russians.

EPILOGUE I:

In a follow-up phone call Neil confided to me that this exchange resulted in the protection of an additional one million hectares of land in Kamchatka.

EPILOGUE II:

I'm sure Neil and Dave were helicoptered to *Dolena Geyzera* (the Valley of the Geysers). A UNESCO site, it is Kamchatka's premier natural and geologic attraction. I later read about the geologist/hydrologist and her team, sent by Stalin to survey the mostly unexplored Kamchatka who, quite by accident "discovered" this now-famous Valley. It was the year 1941 and a story in itself. Her name was Tatiana Ustinova. She stayed on until 1946 studying, exploring and documenting the region. Years later her book would be published. In 1987 she left to go live with her daughter in Vancouver, BC Canada. My wife and I were headed that way in September 2005.

I chased down Tatiana's family and got them on the phone. I explained who I was, how I'd been to Kamchatka and helped organize the Alaska State Parks-Kamchatka exchange. How I'd just like to meet this famous woman, if only for a few minutes. Her family's response? "Well, why don't you and your wife come over and join us for dinner?" The typical Russian hospitality I knew well from experience. Wherever in the world there are Russians, you will find this. We readily accepted.

Tatiana Ustinova was 92 years old, but joined us at the table in her family's tree-sheltered home in a rustic Vancouver neighborhood. Good food and good conversation, as per Russian tradition. As we prepared to leave I remember bending over, holding the hand of this dear, wheelchair-bound woman, and trying to thank her in my bungling Russian for who she was and her great discovery so long ago. I gave her a kiss on the cheek.

And I immediately earned myself bragging rights. Next time, sitting around a campfire in the Kamchatka wilderness, I could blurt out that I kissed the cheek of the woman who discovered the Valley of the Geysers in 1941. It could only bring Russians, Americans and all lovers of pure nature closer.

In 2009 Tatiana Ustinova passed away at the age of 96. The following year her ashes were interred at the official entrance to the Valley of the Geysers.

L to R - Bill Cox, Lena and Vitaly Menshikov preparing tea in the mountains of Kamchatka, Russian Far East July 1993

CHAPTER 26
VALENTIN RASPUTIN (AUGUST/SEPT. 1994)

Pushkin once said that Siberia is so vast that only the migrating birds know its boundaries. And I would say that Valentin Rasputin is one of the few who has the legitimacy, temerity and soul to stake a claim to speak on its behalf. Ask any Russian if they have heard of Valentin Rasputin and the answer will be an inevitable *Da*. In fact, I have yet to meet a single Russian anywhere in the world who has not heard of him. Even Mongolians are familiar with him. He is the most famous contemporary novelist in Siberia and, in all Russia, probably second only to the great Alexander Solzhenitsyn.

I remembered newspaper accounts of him in the early 1970s facing down the powerful Soviet Union trying to prevent increasing industrial pollution of Lake Baikal by the pulp mills. At the time, I was a student at Michigan Technological University in Michigan's Upper Peninsula - less than ten miles from Lake Superior, Baikal's North American sister. Although Superior has the larger surface area, Baikal holds far more freshwater – as much as all five of our Great Lakes combined. I would be heading for Irkutsk, Siberia, where Valentin Rasputin lived. I simply wanted to meet him and thank him. It didn't matter that Rasputin's lake was half a world away from my lake. I could feel for, respect and care for, both.

Rasputin is first and foremost a Siberian patriot and self-appointed keeper of the Russian folk/Siberian peasant vernacular. The difference between classical and modern Russian may not be clear to non-Russians, but to Rasputin it's critical. His writings of the human tragedy of Siberia are set against a vast background of natural beauty. He is a natural environmentalist. And he is unapologetic about using dialecticisms and phrases that have been slipping out of use. Let his readers look them up.

While he and Solzhenitsyn agree on their important literary forbears, including the unassailable and legendary Dostoyevsky, Rasputin also acknowledges 17th century Kiprian of Tomolsk, Siberia's first Orthodox Archbishop who, according to Rasputin, is Siberia's "first enlightener". During the Gorbachev years, Valentin Rasputin was one of two writers appointed to his inner Presidential Council.

Valentin Rasputin lived in Irkutsk because his ancestral and boyhood village on the bank of the Angara River had long since been submerged by the massive reservoir that backed up behind the huge Bratsk hydro-electric dam. Absent his drowned village, urban Irkutsk was the closest thing to a spiritual, cultural and professional home. Before flying off to Irkutsk in August 1994 I asked a Russian journalist friend from Magadan if he could sleuth out Rasputin's address for me. Victor came through. Rasputin lived on *Ulitsa Pyatoi-Armee* (Street of the 5th Army).

I was hanging out for a few days with the Polish Catholic priests on *Ulitsa Lopatina*. I presented my dilemma to Father Darius. "*Otyets Daryawsh*," I asked (Father Darius spoke good Russian), "I have the address of Siberia's most famous novelist, Valentin Rasputin. I have no phone number. How do I arrange for an appointment to meet him?"

The look on his face gently said, "What a silly question." And then he answered: "*Beel, eta Rossia. Vam nada tolko stoochat na evo dvyer.*" (Bill, this is Russia. You only need to knock on his door). As a former Catholic (baptized, first confession, holy communion and confirmation), I still trusted and respected the vast majority of the Church's front-line priests, despite the compromised and extremist folks like Karol Wojytila and Joe Ratzinger that kept getting appointed to the papacy. With the advice and blessing of Father Darius, I set off early the following morning to the apartment of Valentin Rasputin. It wasn't an easy find.

A maze of drab, multi-story, pre-fabricated concrete Soviet-style high-rise apartment blocks confronted me. (Now, let's give the Soviets their due. There just wasn't enough room in this city to house every-one in single-story, neo-Cossack style wooden homes. The Soviet-style apartments might be small, but they were private, heated, had running water – sometimes only cold – and provided insulation from extreme weather and extreme politics). I found Rasputin's apartment and, at 9 am, knocked on the door of Siberia's most famous author.

If Valentin Rasputin was surprised to see me, it didn't show on his face. He survived the era where an unexpected knock on the door could mean a one-way trip to the Gulag Archipelago. He could probably tell I wasn't FSB (the post-Soviet successor to the KGB). Without hesitation, he quietly invited me into his rather spacious and book-lined apartment.

As per traditional Russian hospitality, Valentin excused himself to go prepare tea. When he returned we sipped tea and talked. Our conversation pushed the limits of my Russian but, first and foremost, I thanked him for his efforts to protect Lake Baikal. We managed thirty minutes of unrushed conversation, then he pulled a copy of his book, *Povyestie* (stories), off a high shelf and inscribed it to me. I was honored. After I said goodbye I was acutely aware that I had just received another major insight into that elusive, difficult-to-define entity - the Russian Soul.

When I returned to Alaska I wrote a letter to Farley Mowat, famed Canadian author and "liberal extremist" banned from entry into the United States. Farley had met Rasputin when he visited Siberia in the late 1960s and mentions him in his book: *The Siberians*. I just wanted to pass along news of his old friend. And Canada's most famous author took the time to write me back.

A street in Russia named for Lennon. Why not. Graffiti in Irkutsk, Russia August 1994

Valentin Rasputin, Siberia's most famous novelist, in his apartment in
Irkutsk, Russia August 1994

CHAPTER 27
THE VENERABLE KUSHOK BAKULA
(AUG/SEPT 1994)

Kushok Bakula, or Bakula Rimbuche as he is known to the Mongolian people, was the most revered Buddhist lama in all of Mongolia. And Mongolia is 95% Tibetan Buddhist. Only His Holiness the Dalai Lama is more revered, but he lives in exile in Dharamsala, India. The Venerable Kushok Bakula was born into a noble family in Ladakh, India. He was recognized by the 13th Dalai Lama as a reincarnation of one of the Buddha's direct disciples - Bakula Arhat. (The 13th Dalai Lama died in 1933. The current 14th Dalai Lama was born in 1935). Since 1990 Bakula Rimbuche has been India's ambassador to Mongolia.

Bakula Rimbuche was a humble and celibate Buddhist monk whose life served as an example to others. He was dedicated to Buddhist teachings and caring for those in need. He helped preserve the Buddhist tradition in Ladakh during difficult times. And he was a member of the Indian Parliament and served as head of the Minorities Commission, dealing with the Scheduled Castes and Tribes – among India's poorest people. In 1986 the President of India bestowed upon him the nation's second highest honor, "Padma Bhushan." In 2001 the President of Mongolia awarded Bakula Rimbuche the country's highest honor, the "Polar Star."

Traveling on his diplomatic passport, Bakula Rimbuche helped re-ignite Buddhism where it had previously flourished in Russia and Mongolia. As India's ambassador in Ulaanbaatar, Mongolia's capital, he supervised the rebuilding and re-opening of Buddhist monasteries and centers of learning. I wanted to meet this great man.

It was September 1994 - my first visit to Mongolia. Mongolia was just awakening from seventy years of brutal communist oppression and times were tough. The flame of democracy had been lit and was flickering, but the disappearance of the once massive Soviet subsidies left the economy reeling.

The Indian Embassy at the time was located in a row house whose neatly kept façade overlooked the sparsely trafficked broad boulevard known by the Stalinist name of "Peace Avenue." I walked up the cement stairway and stood before two unnecessarily tall wooden doors. Embassies the world over all seem to have unusually tall doors at their entrance - perhaps to intimidate visitors and remind them of the power and importance of the diplomatic officials within. I gave the heavy bronze handle a tug. The doors were securely locked. Wouldn't even jiggle. A knock would never have penetrated the thick wood and sounded into the interior. Then I noticed the buzzer, a small white button off to the side, with a tiny sign neatly printed in English saying: "Do not push this button unless you have an appointment." I laughed to myself. A typical Indian Catch-22. I had to push the button to get someone's attention to secure an appointment so I could come back and push the button. I'd been to India and these Catch-22s were everywhere - impossibly confusing and/or contradictory instructions or situations. But that great laid-back Indian tolerance always triumphed. I took a deep breath and pushed the button.

2,500 years ago one of the greatest and most courageous religious leaders ever to walk the earth wandered and preached in northern India. His ministry began after he achieved enlightenment following a long meditation under a Pippala (poplar–fig) tree. "I am awake," he said, and the Buddha was born.

The simple message of the Shakyamuni Buddha diverged over the centuries after his death, and especially as it spread over the vast geography of Asia. It took almost 1,200 years to reach Tibet, where it took hold during the reign of the 7th century King Srong–tsan Gompo. Partly absorbing, partly displacing, but never entirely vanquishing the native Bon and Shamanist religion, Tibetan Buddhism grew and flourished in its own unique way. It is sometimes referred to as the "Diamond Vehicle" as distinguished from the original Hinayana "Lesser Vehicle" and Mahayana "Greater Vehicle" forms of Buddhism. In 1578 the Altan

Khan of Mongolia bestowed the title of Dalai Lama (ocean of wisdom) on the third abbot of the Gelukpa Sect of Tibetan Buddhism in Lhasa and the Dalai Lama lineage was born (the first two abbots became posthumous Dalai Lamas). And thus Mongolia absorbed Tibetan Buddhism.

A polite, English–speaking Ladakhi named Sonam Wangchuk responded to the buzzer. There was no admonishment for pushing the button. Catch-22s often evaporate upon respectful face-to-face contact. I explained that I'd met with His Holiness the Dalai Lama in Dharamsala three years earlier and wanted to follow up with Reverend Kushok Bakula. An appointment was set up for two days later.

I arrived back at the Indian Embassy at the appointed time, and did not hesitate to push "the button." I was ushered in and asked to please wait in a very ornate Victorian-style anteroom. Too excited to simply sit, I switched to my reading glasses and started perusing the black-and-white photos. The history of India since emancipation from Britain lined the walls. I spotted a photo of the man I was about to meet standing with Jawaharlal Nehru, India's first Prime Minister. I was about to step into a historical, as well as a spiritual, realm. I had no agenda other than to ask for guidance, so I had no real apprehension or concern.

After a short wait, I was ushered out the back door by Sonam Wangchuck. We walked toward a ceremonial yurt set up in a grassy courtyard behind the Indian Embassy. It was surrounded by the requisite high cement walls and barbed wire required of diplomatic compounds. Indians don't have yurts, so this was clearly a sign of respect and solidarity from India toward Mongolia.

I was ushered to a seat next to the Reverend Kushok Bakula. Indian milk tea and crackers were set before us. The thin, ascetic–appearing monk filled the room with his compassion, much as the Dalai Lama did at our first meeting in 1992.

The Dalai Lama had encouraged me to help Mongolia, where democracy had been kindled and Tibetan Buddhism was undergoing a renaissance. I explained to Bakula Rimbuche that I was seeking his guidance and counsel as to how best to implement my promise to the Dalai Lama. Without hesitation, he replied that the two elements that sustain a people are their health and their religion. Both had clearly suffered in Mongolia during some seventy years of Soviet oppression. (I noticed he did not say "economic development").

I certainly had something to offer in the field of health. And I had already brought over a cash donation from Washington, D.C. to Abbot Choijampts, head of the Gandan Monastery in Ulaanbaatar.

We shared a pleasant and wide-ranging conversation and touched on the challenges that a free and democratic Mongolia would face as Christian and other missionaries, long kept at bay, were now free to enter with their doctrines and conversion tactics.

I always remember a young woman in post–Soviet Russia who was historically and culturally Orthodox Christian, but practically, in her day-to-day life, atheist. The newly arrived Baptists were making some headway with her until the Mormons came along. Joseph Smith and the golden tablets made for difficult going, but no matter, the Jehovah's Witnesses soon arrived on her doorstep. The poor woman ended up thoroughly confused.

Sonam Wangchuck related an incident that occurred in rural Mongolia while traveling with Rimbuche. A small group of young children spied the incarnate lama and prepared to run into his arms. Bakula Rimbuche was prepared to receive them, but Christian missionaries held them back. It was clearly not for security reasons. Sonam sounded concerned and a bit angry.

Supremely grateful for the twenty minutes I'd just spent in a one-on-one conversation with one of the world's most spiritually developed human beings, I signaled that our conversation could soon finish. One does not shake hands, in the western sense, with the Dalai Lama or Bakula Rimbuche. Rather, you extend your hand and they hold it. The longer the better. They channel their compassion.

Sonam Wangchuck escorted me from the ceremonial yurt across the grassy courtyard and through the Victorian stateroom to the embassy's front door. I thanked him. Walking up Peace Avenue, I was aware that I had just spent time in the presence of an incarnation of one of Buddha's direct disciples. It would take some time to sink in.

Venerable Bakula Rimbuche passed away, shedding his earthly body, on November 4, 2003 in Delhi, India. He'll be back.

EPILOGUE

Mongolian President Nambaryn Enkhbayar and his entourage stopped in Anchorage in the fall of 2007. Speaking fluent English, he addressed the Alaska World Affairs Council and afterward took questions from the audience. My raised hand was acknowledged and I was passed the microphone. I mentioned my meeting with Bakula Rimbuche and inquired about the current status of religion in Mongolia. He responded without hesitation that Bakula Rimbuche was his guru and went on to make it clear that Mongolia enjoyed full freedom of religion.

After the program, while people still milled about, I was allowed through security to meet him. We shook hands and I gave President Enkhbayar the photo of me and Bakula Rimbuche in the ceremonial yurt behind the Indian Embassy. He received the photo with two hands, bowed his head, lifted up the photo and gently pressed it to his forehead. It was a gesture of honor and great respect to Rimbuche – the same as a Tibetan would do if given a photo of the Dalai Lama. I was very impressed.

With the Venerable Kushok Bakula in a ceremonial yurt in the courtyard of the Indian Embassy, Ulaanbaatar, Mongolia September 1993

Chapter 28
A Marmot Roast on Mongolia's Tuul River

It was August 2004 and my third trip to Mongolia, and the first for my Taiwanese wife of four months, Amy. Ogi Dendev and his friends picked us up at the airport in Ulaanbaatar when the Korean Airlines flight got in around 1 am. Ogi's father, Dr. Ichirinov Dendev, was a very special and dear friend who had been the doctor and translator on the famed "Badarchin" expedition of 1993. Sadly, he had passed on from liver disease and we were not able to reunite. In unspoken terms, our friendship was passed on to his son, Ogi. Ogi welcomed us into his spacious Soviet-style downtown apartment and his friends joined us for a late night-cap.

First order of business the next day was to change money. The best rates, of course, were to be found on the black market. *Na leva* or "on the left", as they say in Russia. Ogi's friend, Hankhuu, was driving. Hankhuu, who spoke virtually no English, was a Russian language teacher. He was relieved to learn that I could speak conversational Russian. As we drove, I was engaged in conversation with their Russian-speaking friend in the back seat, talking about the prostitutes in Ulaanbaatar – availability, cost, features, etc. I wasn't in the market for one – this was just requisite man–talk in many Asian cultures. I don't remember his name, only that he was a cop and the criminal investigator for the Ulaanbaatar Police Department. A good guy to have in the back seat, I remember thinking, in case our upcoming black market transaction went sour.

Suddenly I noticed we were in a seedier part of town, which reminded me of Mountain View in Anchorage. And there were the money changers. A tall woman wearing an oversized visor approached. She had a cheap, bulky calculator in one hand (probably one of Texas Instrument's first generation) and a massive wad of Mongolian tugriks in the other. Menacing-looking figures lurked in the shadows, obviously watching over her.

My wife Amy was an accountant who worked for many years as a bank teller and postal clerk in Taiwan. She knew money and could count it quickly. I decided to let her handle this one. (This decision had nothing to do with the menacing figures, or the cop in the back seat).

As the Brits would say, the transaction went "swimmingly". Or would that be the Aussies? No matter, we were now on our way to an *Airaq Bar*. But first, a word needs to be said about Mongolian currency.

There's an old and wise anecdote about how, if you're lost in the wilderness with a huge satchel full of paper money, it's only good for one thing – you can burn it to keep warm. The anecdote needs to be modified for Mongolia. You see, for generations mutton has been the Mongolian staple. It's rather greasy, and fastidious handwashing is not a Mongolian trait – water is just not that readily available. So the grease tends to be transferred, over time, to the national currency.

So, if you're lost in the Mongolian wilderness with a satchel full of paper tugriks, do the following: separate out the high-denomination notes, which circulate more slowly and tend to be cleaner. They can be used as tinder to start a dung fire. The lower denomination notes, if you hold them up to the sun at a slight angle, all have a mutton-grease sheen - some more than others. Toss them into some boiling water and you've got a weak mutton broth. Maybe a bit inky – and I doubt their currency ink is soy-based.

I never tried boiled tugrik broth. I prefer the national Mongolian drink, *airaq* – fermented mare's milk, or koumiss as it is known in Russia. Flush with tugriks from the black market (yes, many of them a bit greasy), we pulled up to Mongolia's first urban *Airaq Bar*. With respect to tradition, it was located in a yurt.

The mare is milked on a regular schedule during the milking season. I've seen Mongolian herders in the steppes sing to the mare as the young colt is brought to its mother to start the milking process, then abruptly yanked away. The collected mare's milk is then poured into a calf-skin bag with some residual "starter" *airaq*. It is then churned with a wooden plunger 10,000 times over the ensuing three days, as it is allowed to ferment at ambient temperature. Ladle it into a plastic bowl and Mongolia's national drink is ready to be consumed.

Imagine a bowl of milk sitting on the countertop that has already warmed to room temperature and started to sour. Add a half-shot of vinegar or lemon juice and a half-shot of vodka. Garnish with a few animal hairs and a pinch of dust. Voila. You've got *airaq*. They say it is an acquired taste and has to be eased into each season. To be honest, I love it and drank gallons over my three visits to Mongolia. I never refused a bowl of *airaq*, no matter how much "garnish" was floating on top.

Amy and I volunteered our arms to churn the next three days' worth of *airaq* at least a hundred times. We had no idea that the hunters had been afield and plans were underway for the next day's marmot roast on the Tuul River.

One of the highest honors Mongolians can bestow upon a guest is a marmot roast. We drove miles into the steppe before intercepting the Tuul River well upstream from Ulaanbaatar. (Think Montana is Big Sky Country? Think again). First order of business was to stop at a random yurt and buy some *airaq*. That was no problem. *Airaq* was everywhere. Amy contributed a bottle of 116 proof Taiwanese Kaolian liquor. That may have contributed to a … well…incident later.

Mongolian marmots are basically giant groundhogs. The two our hosts provided had been thoroughly gutted, with the entire skin left intact. The raw meat was mixed separately with onions and garlic. A fire was built and multiple small stones were heated. We drank *airaq* and enjoyed a stunningly beautiful pastoral setting. The Tuul River flowed quietly. Large trees lined and shaded its banks.

When the stones were as hot as they were going to get, they were picked up with tongs and dropped into the hollowed-out marmot carcass – alternating with layers of meat, onion and garlic. When fully stuffed, it was tied off at the neck and allowed to cook internally. Externally, a couple of young Mongolians helped accelerate the process with blowtorches. Darkness soon began to envelope the beautiful Mongolian countryside.

When the marmots were deemed fully cooked they were cut open. As the guests of honor, Amy and I were served first. Our mouths watering, we held out our hands and were each given…a rock. They were still very warm and coated in marmot grease, and we were told to cradle them in our cupped hands. It would bring us luck and good fortune. We were very honored by the gesture. Under the illumination of car headlights our party feasted on roasted marmot. Quite good – it tasted like…well, chicken? It was a grand moment in a grand country with great friends, who polished off Amy's 58% alcohol Kaolian.

Driving back to Ulaanbaatar, it was just our two small cars in an immense, dark and open landscape. That is, until sirens and flashing red lights appeared behind us. In the middle of nowhere, in the dark Mongolian steppes, cops. We pulled over.

I didn't understand the Mongolian, but it appeared the officers were asking a lot of questions and maybe conducting field sobriety tests. After about five or ten minutes one of our friends, Georgie, became annoyed and impatient. I never found out Georgie's occupation, or who he worked for, but Georgie pulled out his cell phone and placed a call to police headquarters in downtown Ulaanbaatar. Within minutes, the cops scurried back to their cruiser and beat a hasty retreat. Wow, I remember thinking, Georgie was a good person to have along on a marmot roast, especially if Taiwanese Kaolian is being consumed.

When it was time for Amy and me to leave Mongolia, Georgie showed up to meet us at Buyant Ukhaa Airport. He presented me with a beautiful full white wolf pelt. I thanked him profusely, but explained that U.S. Customs would confiscate it as soon as we arrived in Anchorage. It was better left in Mongolia. He understood.

As I recall, there were three levels of security we passed through as we prepared to fly out of Mongolia. First, ticket and baggage check; second, customs; and third, passport check, when our passports were officially stamped as having exited Mongolia. Beyond each one of these three security barriers a familiar and smiling face awaited us: Georgie.

I was getting curious and really starting to like this guy more and more, but a little concern was starting to creep in. Was he going to follow us on the plane to Seoul, Korea? We said another goodbye and walked down the gateway. One final barrier awaited us.

An X-ray screening detector for carry-on luggage was set up at the entrance to the jetway, only it was unmanned. Still, we put our bags through. Being a radiologist, I had a passing knowledge of X-rays, so I took a look at the image of our bags. They looked OK to me, so I waved my wife and myself through. Then, ever the cautious one, I paused, thinking I should give myself a pat-down just to be doubly sure. I decided against it, as it might attract undue attention. We boarded Korean Airlines, sans Georgie, for an uneventful overnight flight to Seoul.

Left: My wife and I with two Mongolian contortionists, Ulaanbaatar, Mongolia. August 2004

Right: My wife holding the about-to-be-roasted marmot, Tuul River shoreline, Mongolia. August 2004

First generation Mongolian cell phone, Ulaanbaatar,
Mongolia. August 2004

CHAPTER 29

MONGOLIA'S FIRST SHELTER FOR DOMESTIC AND WOMEN'S VIOLENCE

Fascinated and intrigued after two visits to the Soviet Far East, I had set my sights on Mongolia. But how to get there? I went to the Mongolian Barbecue in Anchorage to secure some contacts, but they just laughed at me. They were all Korean. Down, but not out, I called the Mongolian Embassy in Washington, D.C. and ended up talking with a Mr. N. Bavuu. Mr. Bavuu spoke fluent English and was the Embassy's "Trade and Economics Counselor". Turned out his son, Enkhjin, was a medical student in Mongolia, so when he learned I was a physician/radiologist, he responded that he would not only get me a visa for Mongolia, but would arrange for me to stay at his family's flat in Ulaanbaatar, Mongolia's capital. Wow, I thought, I'm "in like Flint". I didn't know who Flint was (still don't), but I was going to Mongolia.

Mongolia in September 1994 was still in a bit of a daze. Seventy years of Soviet domination had been lifted just a few years earlier. It was mostly bloodless, thanks to the courageous policies of *glasnost* and *perestroika* promulgated by USSR President and Communist Party General Secretary Mikhail Gorbachev. (Mr. Gorbachev, in my opinion, is long overdue for the Nobel Peace Prize, despite his big screw-up with Chernobyl.) But Mongolia's economy was reeling with the sudden evaporation of massive Soviet aid and subsidies. That's when I showed up in town.

There weren't too many 6' 6" Americans on the streets of Ulaanbaatar at the time. I got a lot of sob stories and personal requests which I had to summarily dismiss. But when a few women from a group called something like the "Women for Social Progress" or the "Socialist Women's

Brain Pool" approached me on the street, I had to stop and listen to their story.

It appeared that oppression and violence against women was long ingrained in Mongolian culture. Phrases like "Man is on woman like saddle is on horse" were common. It may have been tolerated under the seventy-year Soviet "occupation", but it now seemed poised, after the Soviet retreat, to finally come out of the closet. But I sensed, in addition to difficult economic times, there was another exacerbating influence: C_2H_5OH, or ethyl alcohol.

Traditionally, Mongolians drank *koumiss* (*airaq* in Mongolian), which is fermented mare's milk. It's approximately on par with Utah's "Mormon-approved" (or, Mormon-tolerated) 3.2 percent beer. As the great Edward Abbey noted, you become water-logged drinking the stuff before you become drunk. (I picture a poor waterlogged and semi-drunk Edward Abbey walking out of a Moab bar into bright sunlight.) Ed Abbey is one of my heroes, but I digress...

Mongolians, in their many yurts, have a contraption to distill *koumiss* into what they called *nermel arkhi* or *shimin arkhi* - a "vodka" with the consistency of a mild Japanese sake. It probably served them well over the centuries and was usually served in a culturally prescribed manner. But the strong Russian vodka had made inroads in the culture and likely inflamed domestic violence in deteriorating economic times.

A middle-aged Mongolian man lay flat on his back in a small over-grown grassy lot in front of a building in downtown Ulaanbaatar. Two small children, obviously his kids, sat beside him. They rubbed his face and lifted his arms – which flopped down lifelessly. Their father was passed-out drunk. *Koumiss* and *nermel arkhi* were mostly unavailable in urban centers like Ulaanbaatar. This guy had been hitting the strong, cheap Russian stuff. I paused.

He finally aroused and staggered across the street, his two little children in tow, and stumbled into an occupied parked car that wasn't his. The two occupants got out and proceeded to beat him with their fists. The children, horrified at seeing their father beaten, could only stand there and scream. Fortunately, there was a cop nearby and I directed him to intervene.

And the pummeled drunk? If he hadn't already beaten his wife (probably in front of the kids in their cramped, Soviet-style quarters) he would likely do so when he sobered up enough to throw a solid punch. And in that vast, Alaska-sized country there was nowhere for the battered wife and traumatized children to go.

For every abused woman there are often traumatized children. Mongolia needed help and I had every intention of doing all I could to help deliver it, but it would have to wait until I returned to Anchorage. I knew who I had to see. Heather Flynn.

Heather had served as Chairwoman of the Anchorage Assembly, but her full-time job and passion was director of AWAIC (Abused Women's Aid in Crisis). It was Alaska's largest domestic violence shelter, located in Anchorage. I set up an appointment with her after I got back to Anchorage.

I relayed my Mongolian experience and concerns to Heather, and I could see they took hold. She began packing and sending boxes of information to the contacts in Mongolia I provided. But I knew that would not be enough. Heather had to go to Mongolia. And then I became one of those people I detested: a lobbyist.

I lobbied Heather to go to Mongolia. Incessantly. And when I learned she would be attending an international women's conference in Beijing, China in 1995 (a short plane ride from Ulaanbaatar), I intensified my lobbying. Finally, as I like to tell the story, she threw up her arms and said, "OK, OK, I'll go to Mongolia." Now it was just a matter of logistics.

Heather grabbed a colleague who spoke Mandarin Chinese (not very helpful in Mongolia at the time) and off they went. Arriving in Ulaanbaatar, Heather Flynn was recognized as the "shelter lady" and they were whisked across town, under fences, and finally into an old non-descript building. She had arrived at "the shelter" – maybe five rooms, a bath and a hot plate, according to her account. The NCAV (National Center Against Violence) had just been established that year.

Prior to the establishment of the NCAV an abused woman in Mongolia literally had nowhere to go for physical safety. She had three choices: suicide, the streets or back to the abusive environment. Usually, she chose number three. And in the early days of the NCAV there was no support from the government or police, and abusive husbands would track down their wives and forcefully haul them back. NCAV was housed in an "undisclosed" location and they moved around frequently.

Heather and her companion, armed with a Mongolian-speaking translator, spent several days training the staff on what Heather referred to as the "thornier aspects of the business". And when it was time to leave they emptied their pockets and left them with everything except the "clothes on their backs". That included a couple hundred bucks, which kept them going. And their efforts paid off.

On a return trip to Mongolia in August 2004 I wanted to stop by the NCAV for a follow-up visit. My wife and I were given the winding ride through the back streets to a nondescript apartment building. It was still smart policy not to be too ostentatious. But under the surface much had progressed.

The staff remembered Heather's help. Madeleine Albright had stopped by. The Mongolian Parliament had unanimously passed a law criminalizing domestic violence, a law that was being vigorously implemented by NCAV and other women's groups. A second shelter house had been set up in the Gobi region, as well as eleven outreach centers scattered across the country offering counseling, financial and housing assistance, legal support, programs for men, and more. More than 2,000 women and children had passed through the shelter by the time of our visit.

What particularly struck me was a brochure from a recent four-nation conference on domestic violence they presented to me. Mongolia, clearly the elder sister, appeared to have been the mentor to its three neighboring, and predominately Muslim, Central Asian Republics: Kazakhstan, Kyrgyzstan and Tajikistan

I remembered the pleas of those women who approached me ten years earlier, like voices in the wilderness, voices in the swirling daze of what was then post-Soviet Mongolia. I called Heather Flynn in Galveston, Texas soon after I got back to the States and gave her an update.

Epilogue

I stay in touch with the NCAV. And I stay in touch with Heather (impossible not to – she still looms large in the small town of Anchorage). And AWAIC keeps me in the loop on the ongoing NCAV-AWAIC cooperative relationship, including the occasional fundraiser to assist NCAV interns to attend international women's shelter conferences.

I stumbled upon Mr. N. Bavuu on my second trip to Mongolia. We passed each other on the street in Ulaanbaatar. He had just been appointed Mongolia's Ambassador to Russia – a prestigious post. We talked a bit. Sadly, he died from cancer several years later. His physician son, Enkhjin, works as a government doctor on AIDS/HIV.

Staff at the NCAV (Madeleine Albright's photo on wall) Ulaanbaatar, Mongolia August 2004

Chapter 30

To Mongonmert and back in an old Czechoslovakian Škoda

Retired Mongolian surgeon Dr. Chultem's Czechoslovakian Škoda was clearly a product of the old Eastern European automotive industry. I don't know how it compared to the Soviet *Moskvitzch* or *Zaparozhets*, but it had a simplicity about it. And I don't remember if it had the classic 1289cc Škoda engine or not. But I really had no say in the matter either way. We were headed across the steppes to Mongonmert, Dr. Dendev's ancestral village.

Driving in a country with few roads is challenging. Mongolia was mostly rutted with parallel and arcing jeep tracks, and it was virtually impossible to drive at night. It took us 27 hours to cover 100 kilometers. But I get ahead of myself...

We got an early start - Dr. Chultem, Dr. Dendev and myself. I could soon see that Dr. Chultem had been nursing his Škoda years (maybe decades) beyond the point when it probably should have been crushed, compacted and sent to India for recycling. I found this refreshing and internally rejoiced. But it required constant maintenance – as in, hourly maintenance.

Just about every hour he would pull that Škoda off the faint jeep trail we were following and park in on the steppe – always facing into the wind, which I thought strange. Then it finally kicked in, duh, the radiator needed to cool down.

Later, the muffler started dragging. Drs. Chultem and Dendev scoured the immediate steppe and came up with some rusted wire. It was enough. Dr. Chultem crawled under the Škoda, made the necessary repairs, and we were off.

It had been raining and we soon got to a point where the road was washed out by what looked like a pretty good-sized and fast-moving river. We parked the car and waited. And it wasn't long before the inevitable Mongolian on horseback came by and my friends made a simple request. The horseman then crossed the "river" several times, back and forth, before Chultem waved him off. Odd, I thought, until I realized he was observing how high the water came up on the horse's legs so he could choose a safe crossing. We hopped back in the Škoda and plunged into the torrent.

Water poured through the poorly sealed door and I had to lift up my feet to stay above the rising tide on the back floor. I felt a pang of fear, imagining this lightweight Eastern European car flipping over or being swept downstream, but soon I felt us driving up an incline and then onto the opposite shore. We allowed the Škoda to drain a few minutes, and were then on our way.

Nightfall was nearly upon us and one does not drive at night on the Mongolian steppe, even with highbeams. Why? You can't see squat. We pulled up to a small home – friends of Dendev and Chultem. It appeared to have been constructed from the recycled remains of an adjacent, abandoned Soviet military base. We were welcomed for the night.

As we sat around talking I noticed a huge chunk of what must have come from a sheep boiling away in a large pot on a small portable stove on the floor. Despite other options, Mongolians like to boil their food. No baking, frying, broiling, poaching or braising. (The French need not feel threatened by Mongolian culinary skills). And the large mass continued to boil…and boil…and boil. Meanwhile, Dr. Chultem examined several folks with his stethoscope. I was impressed and happy sitting in that small home.

Dinner was served. Lifted from the pot, the blob was now the size of a small volleyball – meat, lots of fat, gristle, bone, intestine and veins. It was passed from person to person with greasy hands and a very sharp knife. With the sharp knife one sliced off a piece of the blob while holding it up to one's face and allowed it to slide (effortlessly) into the mouth. Chew, swallow and wait for the next round. I loved it.

I asked our host family if I could take their photo. After my request was translated into Mongolian they immediately disappeared, returning fifteen minutes later bedecked in their finest ceremonial Mongolian regalia. Impressed, I took two photos of the parents and their two children. I went to sleep that night thinking how much I loved this land and its people. Early the next morning we continued our journey to Mongonmert, arriving safely, albeit pushing darkness.

Mongonmert was another black-and-white log cabin village right out of "Gunsmoke", only I got to see it in color. There were no shootouts, as I was among friends and we were welcomed. There was one cop, I remember, identified only by the stripe on his pant leg. He was no Wyatt Earp or Bat Masterson, wasn't carrying a Colt, but he kept the peace.

In Mongonmert I was immersed in the life of the Mongolian country folk. Trays of *aruul* were set out to dry - dried curds about the size of a small cheese-doodle, only more solid and with a slightly sour cheese-like taste. And Dr. Chultem taught me how to catch grasshoppers to use for bait to catch fish in the Kherlen River. He caught one – it looked like a trout of some kind.

Surgeon Chultem, who would do early morning head-stands on the steppe, was one of a minority of land-locked Mongolians not afraid of the water. It was a hot day, so we stripped down to our underwear and plunged into the Kherlen River. Mostly clear, not too deep, the Kherlen moved along. We swam and drifted at a diagonal downstream to the opposite shore, then returned at a similar diagonal and hiked back to our starting point. The villagers cooked Chultem's fish for us that evening.

The next day we were out and about in a Russian jeep. Our driver was a Mongolian Paul Bunyan. Huge and tall. If he knew hoops and had practiced early on, he could possibly have bested the NBA's legendary Yao Ming from Shanghai. Yao, at over seven feet, mastered the basketball court. Our driver, just a bit shorter, appeared to have mastered the bottle. Over the course of the day he consumed enough vodka to have driven two or three successive Russians under the table. I was impressed. And he just kept going.

By now it was getting dark and we had gotten stuck for the umpteenth time. Our incredibly skilled vodka-consuming driver could not free us this time, hard as he tried. We were in the middle of the steppe and a long ways off from the rustic Mongonmert hotel. It looked like we'd be going nowhere soon.

It was about 9 pm and very dark. Storm clouds had coalesced and obscured any light from the sky. Squinting, I could barely see my fingers in front of me, but I thought I saw some flickering lights on the distant horizon. No one had a flashlight. Our heroic, vodka-logged driver grabbed an attractive young woman who had joined us in our crowded jeep and announced they were going for help. I just smiled tiredly. I would have probably done the same.

On the positive side, their departure into the wet, black oblivion allowed us to re-position ourselves inside the formerly overcrowded Russian jeep. Dr. Dendev, my hero from the 1993 Badarchin Expedition and great Mongolian friend, shifted over into the driver's seat. Sober and relaxed, he exuded a quiet confidence and matter-of-factness about our current predicament. His presence in the jeep was encouraging enough.

The hotel proprietress, a very large woman, was in the back seat with me along with maybe one other individual whose identity has since escaped my gray cells. I just remember that I felt squeezed.

But my gray cells don't fail me when it comes to the occupants of the front passenger seat. The young woman who took off for help with our driver had dropped her young daughter onto the lap of Mongonmert's mayor in the front passenger seat. The mayor, a portly man, was drunk. Very drunk. But his belly provided enough of a platform to keep that little girl balanced. He was a gentle, quiet drunk and I liked him.

Still, we had to let the mayor out for a pee every few hours. Fortunately, he was dressed in traditional Mongolian attire: del and sash. The sash was a wide ribbon-like belt around his waist securing the robe-like del. We had to hold on to the tightly secured sash from behind, as the mayor tended to pitch increasingly forward... and forward... while he peed. A face-plant on the wet steppe would have been an ignominious indignity and we would not allow it. And afterward the little girl would quietly resettle onto his ample, warm lap. An unspoiled child from the Mongolian countryside, she never uttered a peep.

Thunderclaps and lightning strikes periodically visited us during the long night. I jolted awake with each flash, as we were probably the highest elevation for many kilometers and seating arrangements had forced my head against an iron bar on the back right-hand side of the jeep. I feared electrocution, or at the least, permanent damage to my hitherto suave hairstyle.

I finally drifted off to sleep, only to be awakened by loud Mongolian voices. It was now 5 am and I barely recognized our Paul Bunyan driver through the faint dawn twilight. With him was a small army of Mongolian heavyweights. Nothing mechanical was available, so they all slogged through the wet night to free our jeep manually.

"Heave-ho, heave-ho", they chanted in Mongolian, or something to that effect. Soon we were free. Our amazing driver drove us back to our hotel. Don't know what happened to his friends, but I wasn't worried. They could take care of themselves. Last night's dinner, now cold, was still set for us. I devoured it and caught a few hours sleep.

Later that morning, in Chultem's Škoda, we began a relatively un-eventful drive back to Ulaanbaatar, but not before stopping at the posted border of Mongonmert. It was marked by large, ornate wooden poles driven into the ground. Boundary markers like these, understood by the Mongolian people, probably went back centuries or more.

The "Who's Who" of Mongonmert saw us off at the boundary where a final toast of vodka was passed around. Yes, our driver was there. And he imbibed enthusiastically.

I am thankful to all the good folks in that small village who touched my life, taught me, and made my stay both challenging and supremely enjoyable. It is my prayer that rural life and the Mongolian nomadic tradition will continue into the future.

Drs. Dendev and Chultem and the Skoda at an old Soviet Army base, Baganuur Tov, Mongolia. August 1994

Mongolian family along the Ulaanbaatar-Baganuur Road,
Mongolia. August 1994

Mongonmer't Mayor Rinchen Dorj (in white hat) and son at their
home in Mongonmer't, Mongolia. August 1994

An old lama in Mongonmer't who remembered the 13th Dalai Lama (The Great 13th died in 1933. The current 14th Dalai Lama was born in 1935) August 1994

Farewell at the border of Mongonmer't sum. L to R - the town cop, Dr. Dendev, Dr. Demberel, hotel owner, Dr. Chultem, our driver, unknown. August 1994

CHAPTER 31

THE LURE OF THE GOBI

IN THE GOBI

From an altitude of 8,000 meters, the dry desolation of southern Mongolia seemed to stretch on forever, broken only by a small cluster of white yurts around the occasional water hole or a faded jeep track arcing across the desert scrub.

We were flying from Ulan Bator, Mongolia's capital, to Dalanzadgad, capital of South Gobi Province, in one of Mongolian Airlines' aging but reliable Antonov-24s. These Russian-built workhorses have been getting people and supplies to the far reaches of Siberia and Central Asia for decades.

A sudden lurch in my stomach told me we were beginning our descent, so I pressed my face against the window and watched the desert rise up to meet the two nearly bald tires dangling from beneath the wing. A few bounces and a couple of jolts and we were … down on the sand. No asphalt runways here. We taxied up to an old concrete terminal that looked like it had weathered many years of sandstorms.

A crowd of Mongolian country folk right out of National Geographic swarmed around the plane. A horse pulling an old wooden cart carrying a few flattened sacks of mail trotted up to the fuselage. I broke free of the small crowd and jogged about ten paces, then stopped and took a deep breath as I tried to comprehend the scene around me.

Ah, the Gobi! Since I was old enough to read maps and atlases I knew where the Gobi was. From the perspective of my suburban New Jersey boyhood home in the late 1950s it was so far away it might as well have been on the moon. And now, here I was.

Later that night I poked my head out of my yurt at the Tourist Camp about 35 kilometers out of town. It was the end of the season and I was the only tourist. The generator-supplied electricity had long since been shut down for the night and silence reasserted its authority over the Gobi. Yet the darkness was broken by a million diamond-bright stars twinkling overhead with the great white swath of the Milky Way, like a strip of frosted glass, arcing across the sky. Not since a night on the Spanish Esplanade 21 years earlier had I seen such a display in the heavens.

BLUE SKY, RED SAND

At 7 am it was dark and cold. I was awakened by an old Mongolian woman, warmly clad in her traditional del, who came into my yurt and started a fire in the stove using small sticks. She smiled at me as I lay huddled under several blankets, then left. In about half an hour, when it was warm enough to get up, I threw off the covers, hurriedly dressed and wandered over to the dining hall. After a breakfast of mutton, rice, salad, bread and coffee, we set off to explore the desert.

First stop was Bayanzag, famous for the dinosaur eggs and nearly complete skeletons its sands have yielded over the years. I was more fascinated by the Kodachrome world of bright rusty-red sand hills and clear blue sky and the razor-sharp contrast where the two met. We poked around, looking at the plants and small trees and flowers that survived here.

The sand was alive with the tracks of camels, lizards and birds. I photographed, and the old woman gathered wild onions for our lunch. We then hiked over to where our van was parked – at the point where the red sand hills spilled out onto flat scrubland – and sat down on blankets for a lunch of mutton shish-kabob cooked over an open pit, boiled potatoes, fresh tomatoes grown in the small garden behind the Tovshin Tourist Camp, wild onions, bread and tea. The vast Gobi breathed its warm silence on us from all directions.

JEEP TRACKS

After lunch we headed for the saxaul forest, which looked like a plantation of shrubs on the horizon. I noticed that the character of the soil had changed from scrubby pasture to a more desert-like consistency. And out the back window of the van I could see our tire tracks now imprinted on the fragile soil, each tread visible. This disturbed me greatly and I tried to convey this concern, but no one seemed to understand.

I raised such a fuss that they finally stopped the van. I stepped out and pointed to the two trails of destruction we were leaving behind us and, now speaking my best Russian, explained that I loved the Gobi wilderness too much to want to cause this damage and would rather not see the saxaul forest if it meant leaving such tracks behind. To drive the point home I held out my arm and made two light parallel gashes on the soft skin of my forearm using the small nail file I carried in my pocket. They winced, and I knew they understood. We walked to the saxaul forest.

SAXAUL, DUNES AND
FERMENTED MARE'S MILK

Saxaul is a protected tree in the Gobi, growing from one to four feet high out of the sand. Its often gnarled trunk is thick, hard and grayish-white. Evergreen-like needles fill out the crown. It somewhat resembles a Japanese banzai, making it a beautiful but almost surreal experience to walk through such a forest in the middle of nowhere. Our solitude was suddenly intruded upon as someone approached on horseback. Anna, my guide, thought it might be a zaschitneek, or warden-protector, of the forest. I was glad to hear there were such people watching over this Lilliputian forest, but our intruder was only a boy looking for his lost camel. No, we told him, we hadn't seen any loose camels. We followed a steep-banked, dry creek bed back to our van, impressed by the torrential flow the creek must have carried earlier in the rainy season.

Farther on down the road we pulled up alongside some of the largest sand dunes in this part of the Gobi. I took off my shoes and scrambled up the highest dune to investigate what looked like the ruins of a small vehicle and was quite surprised when it turned out to be the skull of a camel. Bleached white, it lay on its side in the shifting sands, grinning lifelessly.

If the desert was playing tricks on my vision, it was also taking its toll on our old, Russian-built van. It wouldn't start when we were ready to leave. Eighty kilometers – almost fifty miles – of desert lay between us and camp. I swallowed hard and thought of thirst and survival. The engine finally started.

We drove along a rutted jeep track through the wide-open spaces. There was a slight undulation to the land. Dry mountains framed the horizon off to our right. Anna dozed. I watched a small herd of wild gazelles sprinting off in the distance. The old woman, sitting alone in the back seat, quietly sang a Mongolian song about camels. Her weathered face, her song, the animals and the dry scrub of the vast Gobi – all were one. She sang not for me, but rather as an expression of contentment and happiness, of her life and the Gobi, which were inseparable.

Pulling up to a yurt next to a small corral where goats and sheep were being loaded onto a truck, we got out and stretched our legs. The head of the family, a friend of our driver, invited us inside the yurt, which was the home to his extended family. These sturdy, traditional Mongolian homes are built of felt and canvas over a wooden frame. Kept warm in the winter by burning animal dung, they are a year-round home for many families.

Sitting upon small wooden stools, we exchanged snuff boxes according to Mongolian tradition and then drank airaq, or fermented mare's milk - Mongolia's national drink. Sour and tangy and not unpleasant, the airaq was ladled into bowls from a large pail and passed around.

We played some kind of a game I didn't understand – shooting out our fingers, pointing one finger at a time – to see who would drink. Kind of like a Mongolian rock-paper-scissors. I faked it as best as I could – I lost, I drank; I won, they drank. My English-speaking friend in Ulan Bator could explain the rules when I got back.

The sun was getting low and it was time to leave. We were putting miles behind us when the driver pulled off the narrow dirt road, stopped the van and opened up the engine cover. Clouds of steam hissed up from the radiator. Things didn't look promising this time.

I offered what was left of my drinking water and immediately regretted it. A sinking feeling filled my stomach as I watched that water disappear into the steaming radiator. What's done is done, I thought. So, feeling like I still wanted to help, I offered what I had in my bladder, which was now nearly full from all the airaq I drank back in the yurt. My offer brought a round of laughter, but no takers. From the way everyone was acting, it appeared the van wasn't going to be going anywhere soon.

KOVIASHUKTOK

Koviashuktok is my favorite Eskimo word. An arctic Eskimo term, it means: "full awareness of the present time and place, with great joy and without desire." And as we sat on the gravelly earth alongside the rutted jeep track eating jelly sandwiches and cold boiled potatoes, I felt enveloped in a cocoon of peace and desireless joy, not wishing to be anywhere else but where I was, fully savoring a ride on the crest of the present moment as it rolled slowly into the Gobi evening. Koviashuktok.

It wasn't long before four horsemen broke through the horizon and galloped toward us, pushing their flock ahead of them. Shouted greetings in Mongolian brought them over to us, and a woman in our group borrowed one of their horses and took off for assistance. In about thirty minutes a motorcycle came barreling across the plain. A huge Russian motorcycle. The teenage driver gave us rides back to camp, two passengers at a time. It wasn't really far, hidden by a small rise from where we were stranded. I held on tight as we bounced along the scrub, leaving a trail of dust behind us.

FAREWELL

I wandered up to the bar my last night in the Gobi for a beer and some reminiscing. The owner of the Tourist Camp sat down with me and out came a bottle of Chinggis Khan, a Mongolian vodka. We talked in Russian, a second language for both of us. There was a certain taciturn quality to his demeanor, beyond just any language difficulties. It was as if the boundless expanse of the Gobi, over the years, had etched its silence into the coarse features of his face, much as the North Atlantic has done to the brooding Connaught Irishman.

Still, we toasted Mongolia, we toasted the Gobi. It was the end of the tourist season and he was busy dismantling the camp and boarding things up before heading into Dalanzadgad for the winter. After three shots of Chinggis Khan it was time for me to dismantle myself from the table and call it a night. I walked through the darkness alone and paused at the door of my yurt. And I looked up at the sky. The stars seemed to be shining more brightly than ever.

Author checking out a 2-humped Bactrian camel in the South Gobi, Mongolia September 1993

Mongolian family in their yurt, South Gobi, Mongolia September 1993

CHAPTER 32

RESCUES ON FLATTOP MOUNTAIN

Flattop is the most frequently climbed mountain in Alaska. And, in terms of the total number of deaths and injuries, probably the most dangerous. It is a big mountain with some very steep slopes and it is located in Alaska – two red flags right there. Yet it is trifled with and taken for granted by far too many, by Alaskans and out-of-state visitors alike. I helped bring down one guy in a body bag and almost ended up in one myself. Yet my daughter climbed it with me at age four and made it to the top without incident, though she did cry a bit on the summit after the wind had picked up. (Being unprepared for drastic changes in temperature and weather is a classic rookie mistake. So is forgetting your hat. I forgave her, though. She was four, after all.)

With a total elevation gain of about 1,200 feet, a summit at 3,500 feet, a round-trip distance of 3 miles and a few hours on the trail, it makes a great hike. The trail has been considerably improved over the 25 years I've been climbing Flattop. Starting at the Glen Alps parking lot, the hike is in three sections. First, a wide gravel trail loops around a low mound called Blueberry Hill. Then a narrower and steeper trail makes a wide arc to the south and back, finally reaching a high saddle. Worst you could do on this section is sprain an ankle or get scratched up falling into the brush. At the saddle the fun, and potential danger, begins.

The trail switchbacks up a large, rocky face with spectacular views. Falling rocks are a concern. It finally reaches the tip of a ridge that reaches down from the summit like a huge, crooked finger. The safe way to go on is to the right of the ridge. People who veer off to the left have fallen to their deaths. People who try to descend the north side of the summit have also met tragic ends. People who venture into the broad massive gully that makes up the west/southwest face of Flattop have been killed in avalanches when the snowpack is unstable.

The Alaskan wilderness must never be underestimated, even when it's in your own backyard. Our nature, while breathtakingly beautiful, is raw, rugged, and unpredictable. Following are some stories of times when people forgot that. Some such tales end happily; others do not.

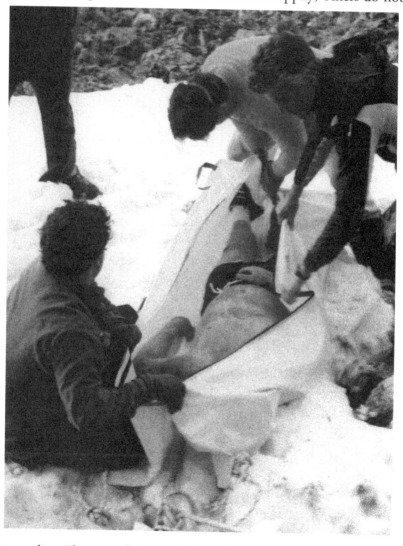

Descending Flattop off the marked trail, especially on the north side, can be fatal, as in this sad case.

CHAPTER 33

RESCUE #1:
THE CARRAGEENAN GUY AND HIS 2 KIDS

For experienced hikers, Flattop is an easy afternoon or evening stroll readily accessible in the beautiful Chugach Mountains. On a pleasant, early summer evening, I crested the summit for the umpteenth time. Wandering off to the left (north) to take in the view of the Campbell Creek Valley, I looked down to see a young man with his two young sons standing on a very steep slope, staring upward with a look of concern and puzzlement on his face. He had taken the highly treacherous left side of the final ridge and was less than ten feet away from where a 10-year old boy had fallen to his death a couple years earlier. He and his kids were in a world of potential hurt.

I yelled down and told him to stay where he was while I hiked down the safe trail and then scrambled up the dangerous left side of the ridge to where he was stranded. And then the seriousness of the situation struck me. There was absolutely no going back. The only option was to somehow go forward.

I saw the overhanging edge of a snowbank to my right and surmised, by its contour, that it led to the summit. It looked to be within reach and a few steps got me very close. But I was straddling a very steep and narrow ravine, trying to maintain a double foothold on the Chugach's famous wet and wobbly scree.

"Hand me the kid," I yelled to the father, and he handed me his 5-year old son as I tried to keep my balance. I reached up and placed him at the edge of the snowfield. This was one amazing kid, I remember thinking at the time. He had no gloves for crawling through snow, but didn't make a sound and followed instructions explicitly. "Crawl straight ahead, and I'll be right behind you," I told him. And using my fists to post-hole in the snow and my body as friction to keep from slipping, I followed right behind him.

I remember thinking at the time that I could only save one person in this situation and it was going to be this little boy. Dad and the 11-year old would somehow have to manage to follow. They did, and we all reached the summit safely.

We hung out together at the top and I was determined to follow them down to make sure they did things right. The younger kid and I had bonded, so we were best buds on the way down. We played a game where we had to tag every one of the white-slash trail markers. Sometimes we missed one and, laughing, had to scramble back up the trail to tag it. We talked about 5-year old guy stuff. It's a great age and children are precious.

The father and I got in a few words. He was an executive out on the East Coast with the company that manufactures carrageenan. Carrageenan is a thickening agent made from algae or seaweed that is used in a vast array of food products to give them texture, like non-dairy milk products. Every time I dump one of those into my coffee at a 7-Eleven, I think about him and his kids that evening on Flattop, thankful I was there when they were, and didn't read about their deaths or serious injuries in the *Anchorage Daily News* the next day.

CHAPTER 34

RESCUE #2: THE POWER OF A CANDY BAR (JULY 1996)

My brother and nephew were out from New Jersey and a Russian ornithologist had joined us for dinner. After we'd finished eating I suggested a hike up Flattop, as it would be light till nearly midnight. All agreed, and my 13-year old son joined us.

As we approached the final ridge, we passed a woman coaxing her tired and whining 5-year old niece, who had pretty much reached her limit. Little Taylor was making it quite clear that she'd had enough and it was time to turn around. I stopped and reached into my pack, as I had just what Taylor and her Aunt Jackie needed: a candy bar – and a rather sizeable one at that. I waved it in front of the tired little girl and her eyes widened. Then I cut it in half. She would get half now, but would not get the other half until she got to the summit. Nothing for Aunt Jackie, I'm afraid

It took effect rather quickly. We were all a team now and she needed only minimal collective coaxing to get her to the top. It was a pleasant evening and we all proceeded to the rock shelter for a group photo. I gave Taylor the other half of the candy bar.

Transformed and chatty, Taylor was now in her element on the summit of Flattop. It was soon time to descend, and that little girl held my hand nearly the entire way down the mountain as we talked non-stop (the sugar had definitely kicked in). We talked about Sesame Street, dolls, school... 5-year olds have a lot to talk about. Her Aunt Jackie, my son, brother, nephew and the Russian ornithologist were somewhere behind us.

Taylor and I were still chatting away when we arrived at the Glen Alps parking lot trailhead. The rest of the party soon caught up, and it was time to turn Taylor over to Aunt Jackie and thank them for their company on a fun hike.

CHAPTER 35

(ALMOST) RESCUE # 3: TO GLISSADE OR NOT TO GLISSADE (JUNE 2001)

I always enjoyed taking friends up Flattop in mid to late June. There might be a small, residual patch of snow to scramble across just before the summit, but it was quite safe. Then we would hike down the back side of the mountain where there would be multiple large snowfields. Several glissades would take us down almost to Upper DeArmoun Road where we would have parked a second vehicle.

Al and Steph Crease from Vermont came out to Anchorage in June 2001. Steph was running the Mayor's Midnight Sun Marathon. We were students together at one of Tom Brown, Jr.'s Tracker School survival courses in the New Jersey Pine Barrens. Tracker students bond. They contacted me and wanted to go hiking after the marathon. I was flying in from Nome that weekend and prepared to show them Alaska.

We summited Flattop without incident and began to descend the back side. I saw a large snowfield and ran over to size it up. I pulled out three heavy-duty trash compactor bags from my pack, cut the two lower corners at a diagonal, and showed Al and Steph how to step into them like an oversized plastic diaper. Pull them up and hold tightly, cinching them under your armpits. Viola! Ready to slide.

I knew from experience that snowfields like that one, when viewed from the top, can be visually deceptive. They are often convex, but it's difficult to detect. When you slide down and crest the apex of the convexity, you are suddenly sliding down a far steeper slope than you expected.

I also knew that, if you overshot, the runout from snowfield to soft tundra was not smooth. The snowfield melted back in a way that left

218

a trough, like a half-pipe, at the junction of snow and tundra. You did not hit a brick wall but you encountered a body-bruising "thud" before you went flying. Often there were loose rocks about.

I told them I would go first and make sure it was safe. I should have added: "Don't even think about launching until I reach the bottom, signal that it was OK and planted myself to be available in case something got out of hand." As fellow Tracker students, I assumed their Inner Vision (as Tom drilled into us) would prevail and guide them. But this was Alaska's Chugach Mountains and not New Jersey's Pine Barrens. My mistake.

Sure enough, it was convex, and I was soon going a bit faster than I would have liked. But I was in control – at least until I heard a woman's voice scream, "I can't stop!" It was Steph, closing in fast from behind and to my right. I turned to reach for her and missed. Just then something streaked past me on the left so quickly all I saw was a blur. It was Al, going frightfully fast. And he was eerily silent. Within seconds he slammed into the trough at the base of the snowfield and was airborne. Before I could see him land, I slammed into a small willow.

Of all the hikes and outdoor trips I'd led, I was sure Al was going to be my first fatality. My heart plummeted. Then I heard a groan in the distance. My heart lifted. Gravely injured is better than dead, I thought, especially if it's someone else. I'll just have to hike out and call in a chopper.

Steph was OK, and as soon as I disentangled myself from the willow we zeroed in on the groans, which were becoming more frequent. Al had landed in a crumpled heap and looked like a giant pretzel wearing clothes. He was moaning and fumbling about for his glasses.

Amazingly, Al was not seriously hurt. His wife and I went about the task of prying his limbs apart from each other and easing him into a standing position. We found his glasses. When Steph realized her husband was OK, she turned to me and shouted, "That was great!" before bursting into laughter. Al smiled meekly. We still had a bit of hiking, and more snowfields to cross, before we got to the car. We went more carefully. And every twenty minutes or so Steph would shout again, "That was great!" and start laughing uproariously. And Al would smile meekly.

I called them later that evening at their hotel in downtown Anchorage to see how they were doing. They had discovered a nasty gash on a part of Al that rarely, if ever, comes into public view. They both joked about taking a "battle scar" back to Vermont and were thankful for the hike. I was thankful, too, but obviously more for the preservation of life than just the hike.

CHAPTER 36
RESCUE #4: MY OWN

I signed up for a weekend winter mountaineering course with Genet Expeditions back in the late 80s. Genet Expeditions goes back to the legendary Ray Genet, who died at 27,000 feet on Mount Everest in October 1979 after passing his oxygen over to his tentmate. People who personally knew Ray all said the same thing: "That was Ray and that was what he would do." Ray Genet is also famous for being a member of the team that made the first winter ascent of Mt. McKinley in March 1967. They shared with me other stories:

Ray was a small man, but his arms were like steel springs. He would get into arm-wrestling contests at the bars in Talkeetna at $1,000 a pop - and always win. Once, Ray got a contract with the military at Elmendorf Air Force Base to replace the old refrigerators in their barracks. He arrived with lots of rope and webbing, but no dolly. Climbers like Ray knew their ropes and knots. He strapped the old refrigerators to his back, hauled them down the stairs and, similarly, hauled the new ones back up to their occupants. There's a section on Ray Genet at the small Mountaineering Museum in Talkeetna that is worth perusing.

Genet Expeditions, when I took their course, was led by Harry Johnson, a well-known Anchorage mountaineer who had been to the Himalayas (where many mountaineers go wrong). His weekday job was manager of a local title company. If I had to describe Harry in one word, it would be "narcissist". There was no doubt that Harry, from his conversations on that weekend course and previous newspaper accounts of his exploits, was really into himself.

We practiced the four styles of ice axe self-arrest: face downslope and face upslope (prone and supine) on the safe lower flanks of Flattop.

Later, roped up as a team, we crossed the steep west-southwest slope of Flattop near the summit. The snow was hard-packed and, in retrospect, only experienced mountaineers should have been where we were (or, perhaps, students under the supervision of experienced mountaineers?) We crossed to the north side without incident.

On the far side of the vast bowl, and under the supervision of instructor Ken B., I was allowed to glissade down. My nylon snow pants were like Teflon on the hard-packed snow and soon I was sliding uncomfortably fast. I tried to slow down by dragging my ice axe but I flipped over suddenly, and my ice axe (unfastened to my wrist by the attached webbing) was jerked away. I found myself shooting downslope at high-speed and totally out of control, my life flashing before my eyes. I dug in my heels and elbows and snow flew into my eyes. Way down below, I could make out some fellow students.

Jim Breun, who later summited Denali after knee surgery, saw me coming fast. Jim, a course student, had to make a split-second decision. And I'm forever grateful he made the one that he did. He abandoned his ice axe, jogged out several yards and implanted himself in my oncoming path. I plowed into him like a high-speed freight train. But we now had the laws of physics on our side – to some extent.

Jim was grounded at zero momentum when I smashed into him. So our total subsequent momentum was mine plus zero divided by two. It helped. So did the increased drag of two people desperately grabbing each other as we continued to slide. Farther downslope a third student jumped on top of us and we soon slowed to a crawl before finally coming to a stop. And none too soon. Sizeable rocks in the runout zone some fifty feet away would have made for some nasty soft tissue injuries, broken bones, or worse...

I fault Harry Johnson and his crew on three counts: 1) They should never have allowed me to begin a glissade so high up on that steep slope. 2) They should have checked to see that my ice axe was secured to my wrist. And 3) There should have been at least one instructor at the bottom prepared for such an emergency.

As for Jim Breun, I am indebted to him for saving my life or, at the very least, saving me from serious injuries. He earned himself a case of beer per year for life – his life, that is – although I should probably alter my will to ensure that the shipments continue in case I predecease him. Problem is, I lost track of Jim some decades ago and I consider my commitment retroactive. And I'll make good on it, so Jim, if you're out there somewhere, give me a shout when you read this!

CHAPTER 37
THE REVEREND CHIEF DAVID SALMON

I arrived in Anchorage, Alaska in July 1984 after leaving New Jersey in September of 1970. Well, I transited some thirteen years in Michigan, earning a B.S. in Biological Sciences with High Honors from Michigan Technological University in Houghton in the beautiful Upper Peninsula of Michigan. Four years at Wayne State University School of Medicine in Detroit got me an M.D. A year at SUNY at Buffalo, NY, as an intern in internal medicine was followed by four years as a resident/fellow in radiology at Oakwood Hospital in Dearborn, Michigan (Henry Ford's old stomping grounds just outside Detroit). With one year to go until Board Certification in Radiology, I was heading in the right direction – professionally and geographically. It was a long drive from Detroit to Anchorage in my Volkswagen Rabbit, but I had taken precautions.

"Rabbit Rental and Repair" was located in Taylor, Michigan, as I recall. Taylor–tucky, as it was known, filled with migrants from Kentucky who were probably stealing jobs but were otherwise not deportable (including a few Hatfields and McCoys who knew better than to cause trouble). The owner of the shop looked like Michael Parks from the television series "Then Came Bronson" and constantly picked at small scabs on his face. His assistant was a rather chunky kid. They were both honest and competent mechanics and I trusted them. I had them pad my gas tank underneath with thick rubber and place a chicken-wire shield to protect my headlights and windshield. I'd been listening to too many scare stories about monster, car-swallowing potholes on the Alaska Highway from overweight Michigan deer hunters who'd rarely, if ever, left the state (except maybe to Wisconsin) and whose only source of information was probably "Field and Stream Magazine".

It was a fun journey through some beautiful and wild country. When you arrive in Anchorage in July, summer goes by quickly. Late August frosts and creeping September darkness sneak up on you. I got settled into my job as a radiologist at the Alaska Native Medical Center on 3rd and Gambell, but I wanted to get to the bush, the real bush, the "deep cold of winter" bush.

Joe McGinniss' Going to Extremes and John McPhee's Coming into the Country were my inspiration before I set off. I later discovered Richard K. Nelson at the now-defunct Cook Inlet Book Store when I arrived in downtown Anchorage.

I settled on Chalkyitsik, where Richard K. Nelson had set up shop. How to get started? I needed contacts, so I went to the office of the eternal Congressman for all Alaskans, Don Young – a former teacher from Fort Yukon. It was now late fall, 1984.

I sat in the anteroom and watched people come in and out of his office. There was lots of laughter, hand-shaking, and a good deal of back-slapping. I didn't smell cigar smoke, but fleetingly wondered if Tammany Hall had an outlet here in Anchorage. While I wouldn't buy a used car from the guy, I was grateful for the time the congressman gave me as well as the contacts in Fort Yukon and Chalkyitsik.

It was December 1984. The flight from Anchorage to Fairbanks was uneventful. Thanks to the Wien brothers, this has long since become routine. But in Fairbanks my first bush flight was about to begin and I excitedly hopped aboard an Arctic Circle Airways twin-engine Bandeirante for a flight to Fort Yukon. It was a Brazilian-built plane, though I don't know who built the engines. The pilot and co-pilot were bundled up in arctic parkas.

Wow, I thought, this was the real thing. As we pulled up to the active runway the co-pilot turned and reached across my lap to the door that had been ajar some inches from my left elbow. He gave it a tug and a click indicated closure. Gulp. I cinched my seat belt tighter.

In Fort Yukon we had to help Joe, the pilot, push the Cessna 185 out away from the hanger and get it turned around so we were in position to taxi out and take off. It was minus 20 degrees F. Tall and lanky, Joe Firmin was widely respected as the most experienced bush pilot in the vast Yukon Flats. He couldn't have been much over 30-years old, if that. He bragged how he'd never been outside of Alaska and then suddenly corrected himself – he'd been to the Yukon Territory of Canada once or twice.

I hopped into the co-pilot's seat next to Joe. Suddenly, the previous flight in the twin-engine Bandeirante seemed tame. Joe went through the requisite safety briefing and, lastly, pointed out the packet of emergency rations that was required to be on board. Then he turned around, laughed, and said, "If we go down and get hungry we'll probably start digging into some of those boxes."

The entire back of the plane, from the floor nearly to the ceiling and including the back row, was filled with groceries and various packages. I almost did a double-take when I glimpsed what looked like a disembodied human face among the packages. When I smiled, it smiled back. So, I thought, there's at least one more passenger on board besides me.

Joe got us to Chalkyitsik safely in the mid-day winter Arctic Circle twilight. Sadly, eight years later, while doing a fall moose survey with government biologists, Joe "bought the farm." That's pilot talk for "auguring in" and probably exactly how Joe would have described his final flight. I'm honored to have flown with the Yukon Flats legend.

We landed on a snow-covered gravel runway in the vast, flat boreal forest of Interior Alaska. Village residents came by snowmachine to meet Joe's plane. No cars here. One of them was 72-year old Reverend Chief David Salmon, who came to retrieve me. He had a sled behind his snowmachine. I grabbed my bag and jumped on for a slow, quiet ride to town.

Chalkyitsik was a sober village and a healthy one – physically, culturally and spiritually. And this was almost certainly due to the leadership of the Athabascan elder on the snowmachine who hauled me into town. David Salmon, born in Salmon village in 1912, was raised in Chalkyitsik. He was only 29 when he was chosen as Chief of Chalkyitsik.

I was given a place to sleep on a cot at the village health clinic (I had brought my own sleeping bag). The water for the village was hauled from a hole in the ice on the Black River. I spent several evenings at the home of David and Sarah Salmon sharing dinner and conversation. Sarah was very quiet, and usually busy sewing Indian mukluks. She shared with me, with the nodding consent of her husband, the secret thread for sewing Indian mukluks: dental floss. Probably waxed. My lips have been sealed until now.

It was my conversations with Reverend Chief David Salmon that I valued most during my visit. As the Dallas Cowboys blared on a flickering television from a corner of the room, David Salmon talked about the old days. He shared an apocalyptic prophecy of global destruction where the only place of refuge on earth for human survival would be the shores of Old John Lake far to the north. He also explained how just the right combination of green wood and dried wood in their barrel stove (made from half of a 42-gallon oil barrel) would keep their log cabin reasonably warm overnight at temperatures of minus 40 or lower. And from him I learned the Black River Gwich'in worldview of meat. According to David Salmon, there were two kinds of meat: moose meat and store meat. We ate moose at his home for dinner. On Sunday we attended services at the log cabin St. Timothy's church, presided over by (who else?) the ordained Episcopalian priest Rev. David Salmon.

Finally, I received the great invitation I'd dreamed of. The Reverend Chief and Elder David Salmon invited me to come along with him as he made the circuit to check his traps and snares. There were only a few usable hours of daylight at that latitude in winter. In interior Alaska (at least before global warming) winter temperatures were quoted without the "minus" sign. When I called David Salmon from the warm comfort of my Anchorage townhouse before my trip north, he told me the temperature had been "forty". When I hopped onto the sled behind his snowmachine that afternoon, it had warmed up to "twenty". Still cold.

To David Salmon a snowmachine was not a toy, it was a tool. A means of transportation. He drove slowly and carefully, following a trail through the stunted spruce and birch of the northern boreal forest. Not only steel traps, but also traditional Athabascan wood and wire snares, were set along the shore of a large lake and the streams emptying into it. No animals that day.

On our way back my feet started freezing up despite the heavy socks and felt-padded sorrels I was wearing We pulled over. David Salmon grabbed his axe and had a fire going in no time. And time seemed to stop as we sat around that fire in Alaska's vast snow-covered wilderness. There was no other place I wanted to be.

Back on the trail, David pulled over again after twenty or thirty minutes. He shut off the machine and, saying nothing, walked off on a side trail and up a very slight incline. After barely popping above the horizon, the sun had already set. The only sound was the squeak of our boots on the supercooled snow. I caught up with him.

I saw a frozen swamp. The septuagenarian Gwich'in elder saw a battlefield.

"A great battle was fought here," he told me, "before the white man came. Indians from the north swept down and slaughtered my people."

I stared out over a frozen swamp and tried to imagine snowshoe–clad Indians fighting and killing each other on the snow-covered ground in front of me.

"I've been trying to find out why this happened," he continued, "but nobody knows or remembers." He turned and walked back silently to the snowmachine. I followed.

We knew where. And we knew it happened before the white man penetrated this country. But the reasons for the "Battle of the Frozen Swamp", having lived on in the minds of old men, probably died with them.

EPILOGUE I

Some ten years later I was canoeing the Porcupine River in Canada's Yukon Territory. We started up north in Old Crow. My collapsible Ally canoe was comfortable, but when it came to speed it was no match for the two collapsible kayaks of my companions. I was perpetually behind and out of sight. But no matter, I enjoyed the solitude.

I had just shoved a candy bar in my mouth for a late afternoon energy burst before I rounded a bend and beheld a scene that nearly propelled me a century back into the "Twilight Zone". On a bluff to my right was a crude white canvas tent held down by rope and wooden stakes driven into the ground. A huge chunk of caribou meat was suspended from an 8-foot tripod over a small, smoky fire. Two Indians sat in front of the fire, looking off in the distance. And I wondered if Rod Serling, with his cigarette and bad teeth, might soon be stepping out from behind a nearby spruce.

There was no way I wasn't going to stop there. I beached my canoe and trudged up the slope. What I noticed, and I'll never forget, was that the two Indians were not reading paperbacks, or talking, or otherwise distracting themselves. They were simply sitting.

I had a quick flashback to when I was hoofing it with my backpack along Highway 100 through the small town of Moreville, Vermont. An elderly woman, sitting on her porch and, well, just sitting on her porch, said to me, "Good day." Vermont Yankees were known to be frugal in speech, but I wondered if there was some unseen connection here with the Alaskan Athabascans.

The two Indians welcomed me and shared their tea with me. We talked. David Salmon was their grandfather, they told me. Biological or spiritual, it didn't matter. I departed with a memory I'll never forget, pushed off in my canoe and caught up with my friends at that night's camp.

EPILOGUE II

David Salmon was elevated to the position of First Traditional Chief for the Athabascan people of the Interior in 2003. This followed the death of the previous chief, Chief Peter John of Old Minto, Alaska. The position was honorary and non-political, but held in very high esteem among the indigenous Athabascan people.

On October 11, 2007 Reverend Chief David Salmon died from cancer at his home in Chalkyitsik. He was buried next to his late wife, Sarah, in a hilltop cemetery near the spruce trees. Governor Sarah Palin ordered Alaskan flags to be flown at half-mast in his honor and said, "Alaska has lost a true treasure."

Sarah called that one right. And someday I want to canoe the entire length of the Black River in honor of this great man.

On the trapline with the Rev. Chief David Salmon. Chalkyitsik, Alaska December 1984

Rev. Chief David Salmon, his wife Sarah and their granddaughter in their cozy cabin. Chalkyitsik, Alaska December 1984

CHAPTER 38

FATHER JOHN AT MONK'S LAGOON (MARCH 1995)

It was the most sacred ground in North America to the Orthodox Christian Church. And probably the most difficult to reach, which may be a good thing. First one takes a commercial flight from Anchorage to Kodiak on an Alaska Airlines jet or a turboprop operated by ERA. A somewhat unpredictable journey in itself. Kodiak's runway is sandwiched between the rough waters of the Gulf of Alaska and a very tall mountain named Barometer Peak. It is very sensitive to weather and tailwinds. A U.S. Air Force F-15, capable of vertical flight, came to grief halfway up Barometer Peak. I'd flown into Kodiak several times to cover their hospital's radiology department when their radiologist was out of town.

From Kodiak one takes a puddle–jumper single-engine mail plane, which stops at several small villages (Kodiak is America's second largest island after the Big Island of Hawaii) before crossing turbulent waters to land on the gravel airstrip at Ouzinkie, Spruce Island.

Information previously gathered from a long-time Baptist preacher on the island led me to a local Aleut who would take me to Monk's Lagoon in his skiff for $50.00. I'd been forewarned that high swells and rough water prevented most boats from pulling into Monk's Lagoon nine days out of ten. There was no dock, just the shoreline. Fortunately, glassy water greeted us the entire way down the coast and we slid into Monk's Lagoon uneventfully. He dropped me off and departed.

Well, here I am, I said to myself as I hauled my bags up onto the beach. It was a chilly March day – still winter in Alaska, even in Kodiak. Twelve miles of temperate rain forest separated me from Ouzinkie. I was told there was a trail, though I had no map, no phone or GPS. And somewhere near the halfway point to Ouzinkie there was a monastery. But was there anyone here at Monk's Lagoon, any monks on-site? I was clearly counting on the divine protection of Saint Herman as I hauled my duffel bag, shivering, up toward the edge of the rain forest.

SAINT HERMAN

In 1794 a Russian missionary named Herman came to this island to convert Aleuts to Christianity and, eventually, to construct a small orphanage. It was a different time - George Washington was president in Philadelphia, Francis Paine was rotting in a French prison and Alaska belonged to Russia. St. Herman (finally canonized by the Orthodox Church in 1970) followed in the tradition of the Orthodox saints since Antony in 4th century Egypt. Dressing in deerskin, rarely bathing, using bricks for pillows and secretly wearing chains beneath his clothing, he prayed incessantly, mortifying the body to bring out and purify the spirit. Originally living in a self-dug cave, he later slept in a wooden hut. An ascetic monk, he drew a following. Shedding his body after some forty years on the island, the Aleuts buried Herman in his original cave. Later, a chapel was built over the site.

FATHER GERASIM

Things were relatively quiet for some 200 years. In 1935 a monastically–minded Orthodox priest named Father Gerasim fled from persecution by his fellow Christians on Afognac Island and came to Spruce Island. During World War II he was questioned by the FBI as a possible spy, but nothing came of it. He kept vigil over the gravesite of St. Herman for more than thirty years.

People who knew the solitary, ascetic priest told me he secretly wore chains and had a list of people he fervently prayed for every day. I had little doubt about the piety of this man. A decade later, up in Nome, I met an elderly woman at the museum who knew Father Gerasim. She confirmed my information.

Father Gerasim died in 1969 – one year before St. Herman was canonized, but not before meeting Gleb Podmoshensky.

ENTER GLEB PODMOSHENSKY, AKA ABBOT HERMAN

It was amazing how an apparently simple, pious monk now known as Abbot Herman could be revealed as so complex and controversial, and precipitate investigations on both sides of the Atlantic. Born in Latvia, he escaped Soviet persecution early on and immigrated to the United States. He began a correspondence with Father Gerasim and first visited Monk's Lagoon in 1961. They exchanged over a hundred pieces of mail.

Gleb Podmoshensky was ordained by the Russian Orthodox Church Outside Russia (ROCOR) in 1976. He was defrocked by ROCOR in 1989 for reasons unclear. In 1983, energetic and charismatic, he was invited to speak to the rapidly growing Holy Order of MANS – a somewhat fluid new-age church not without its own controversy. And over a few short years he effectively took over MANS and oversaw a mass conversion to Orthodoxy. He established the St. Herman of Alaska Brotherhood near Platina, California. A publishing house churned out works on Orthodoxy. The monastery was filled with monks and nuns, many of whom were young and fleeing from troubled lives and self-destructive lifestyles (this would provide fodder for those who would later cast aspersions at Abbot Herman). And fulfilling a promise to Father Gerasim, he quietly and respectfully re-established a small monastic presence at Monk's Lagoon.

The Blessed St. Herman did not let me down. As I approached a wooden chapel-like structure just inside the towering green forest, there appeared a young monk with a long red beard, well-worn flowing black gown and headpiece. He looked like he'd just popped out of a Dostoyevsky novel. Or perhaps I was walking into one. He smiled and graciously welcomed me in the name of Christ. Thus began my long friendship with Father John Marler.

At age 22, Father John was one of Abbot Herman's young recruits. Three years earlier, in San Francisco, he was a punk rocker who, during concerts, would swing dead animals round-and-round over his head before flinging them into the audience. Now he was a changed young man, and I was not going to judge him because he didn't have formal seminary training. He was keeping a solo vigil over Monk's Lagoon, following in the giant footsteps of Father Gerasim.

We drank hot tea and talked on the beach. A huge wooden cross overlooked the surging waters of the lagoon. Although it was March, it was still winter in Alaska, and a rather cold darkness soon settled over the land. Fr. John invited me to his shack for dinner.

The Orthodox (especially the Russian Orthodox) are very keen on liturgy and ritual. Fr. John was chanting from a large volume of the Holy Scriptures, as per schedule, when a mini-calamity occurred: the rice started boiling over. Suddenly in a quandary, he asked me to take over the chanting while he attended the rice. This I did, using my best Orthodox monotone. I found it refreshing.

We shared a dinner of beans and rice (monk food) and continued a thoroughly delightful conversation. Here was someone, I thought, clearly on the upward slope of a spiritual learning curve. Retaining a healthy modicum of skepticism, I remained open and engaged. I was on my own journey. When it started getting late, he found me a place to sleep in a small, unheated cabin nearby. Here they didn't burn wood for heat, only to cook.

At 1 am and again around 5 am the bell rang, and Fr. John chanted the requisite prayers loudly into the cold night air. The misty, moss-draped forest quickly absorbed the sounds. Before drifting back off to sleep, curled up in my sleeping bag, I wondered about the 200 years of prayer stored in the biomass surrounding this sacred cove.

The next morning, shafts of sunlight streaming through the huge, moss-draped spruce illuminated a mystical world. Icons, strategically and subtly placed, called out softly with their divine, other-worldly message. We stopped by St. Herman's well. A small stream of water spilled out from behind a pile of ferns and moss–cloaked rocks. Guarded by a small wooden cross and an icon, this same well sustained St. Herman 200 years ago and, blessed by him, flows to this day. It is said to have healing powers. I drank what I could and filled my water bottle.

We stopped by Father Gerasim's cabin hidden in the trees. Peering through fogged-up windows, we could see his furniture, desk, books and other simple personal items. Nothing had been disturbed since he died over twenty years earlier.

St. Herman's remains had been removed some time ago to the Orthodox Church in Kodiak. A simple, rough-hewn chapel was built over the site. Armed with a single seashell each, Fr. John and I squirmed through the three foot high crawl-space beneath the chapel to the approximate site where St. Herman's body had lain. I filled a couple of small film canisters with the soil, which is said to have great healing powers. I still have it, and it is available, free of charge, to any Orthodox believer who truly needs it.

A 6-mile hike through beautiful rainforest, punctuated by occasional glimpses of the sea, brought us to Sunny Cove where St. Michael's Skete, a small monastery, lies perched high above the water. It was staffed by the St. Herman of Alaska Brotherhood. A spartan place, it had no heat or electricity. Everyone was kind and quiet as they went about their work. I met two nuns, one a scholar of Greek and the other of Rumanian, who were translating old, holy writings. They shared a simple lunch with me. Then I had a plane to catch in Ouzinkie, and two of the brothers were kind enough to give me a ride to the airstrip in their skiff.

ENTER GLEB PODMOSHENSKY, A.K.A ABBOT HERMAN – IN PERSON

I was so impressed by my experience at Monk's Lagoon that I wanted to call Abbot Herman himself when I got back to Kodiak. It was surprisingly easy how quickly I got him on the phone. Divinity school researchers had difficulties scheduling interviews with Abbot Herman, but when I relayed my experience at Monk's Lagoon and told him I wanted to meet him, he hopped a plane and flew from northern California up to Kodiak! I was surprised and honored. I picked him up at the airport the following evening.

A black-robed monk with a large, bushy beard bounded across the terminal toward me, as if we knew each other. No Calvinist-debasement or austere sternness about him. I immediately noticed what I could then only characterize as a simple Christian joy that just flowed from him. The next day, over pie at a local Kodiak restaurant, I would bring up this observation. It seemed a no-brainer to Abbot Herman. "Why shouldn't we be happy and filled with joy? We have every reason to be," he responded. It seemed to make sense.

I'd figured I would just take Abbot Herman to his hotel after his long flight up from California. It was late and dark in Kodiak. Then he asked me for a small favor. The controversial Gleb Podmoshensky, investigated on both sides of the Atlantic, characterized as a "defrocked fraud" by Alaska's Orthodox Bishop Innocent and by Father Michael Oleksa as a "fanatical throw-back to pre-revolutionary Russia", was now asking me for a favor on the dark streets of Kodiak.

Would I kindly take him to the Orthodox Church, long since closed for the night, so he could peer through the window at the crypt housing the bones and relics of St. Herman? Of course, I would. I drove him there, parked my rental car and we scrambled through the brush to a dimly lit window. Abbot Herman saw what he needed to see that night. I then dropped him off at his hotel.

We returned the next day when the church was open. A service was just concluding. Oblivious to the local priest and parishioners, the black-robed Abbot Herman made a beeline straight for the crypt that held the bones and relics of St. Herman. He circled it reverently, knelt and prayed in his own language around all four sides. People looked at him with surprise and curiosity. The local priest did not look pleased.

Organized (institutional) Christianity, especially Orthodoxy, is a progression and a maze of often overlapping and competing jurisdictions. Finger-pointing accusations over who's not "canonical" and who strayed from the 2,000-year-old "apostolic line" fly every which way. Survival depends on authority (real or perceived) and submission. Renegade charismatics like Abbot Herman, no matter how pious, are a threat.

Abbot Herman chuckled as he told me how he was invited to join the Orthodox Church in America (demanded to submit would better characterize the offer). "Thanks, but no thanks," was his polite response, explaining that it was not necessary. The Russians, Serbs and Greeks got the same answer.

EPILOGUE 2011

The St. Herman of Alaska Brotherhood eventually came under the fold of the Serbian Orthodox Diocese of Western America. In response to my letter asking about Father Herman, I received a very courteous reply, dated May 21, 2011, from Hierodeacon Paisius at their monastery in Platina, California. Father Herman retired in 2000 and, while considerably slowed down by Parkinson's disease, remains cheerful and works on his Russian language journal "*Russky Palomnik*". The monastery continues its publishing activities.

Father John Marler left the Order many years ago and married.

Left: Father Herman, Kodiak, Alaska March 1995

Right: Father John at Monk's Lagoon March 1995

Taking the skiff from Monk's Lagoon back to Ouzinkie. March 1995

Monk's Lagoon on Spruce Island, Alaska March 1995

CHAPTER 39
THE ALEUTIANS I: HUMBLED BY A WILLIWAW (AUGUST 1985)

The three-quarter-inch-long squiggly blue line had looked deceptively innocuous on the USGS topographic map that lay open across my lap in my comfortable Anchorage townhouse. I'd been studying this map intently in preparation for my first trip "out on the chain." The Shaishnikoff River, emptying into Captain's Bay on Unalaska Island, appeared to originate from a small lake in the interior mountains about five miles inland. It seemed like a straightforward yet challenging hike, so I caught a flight to Dutch Harbor and settled in at the Sealaska bunkhouse.

It was nearly noon before I was finally satisfied that everything essential had been crammed into my backpack. This was to be my first overnight backpacking trip in the Aleutians - my first backpacking trip west of the Mississippi River, for that matter. And I would be going solo.

Packed and ready now, I headed down the long drafty hallway of the old Sealaska bunkhouse and out into the gray skies and fine drizzle of a typical Aleutian day. Unalaska is a hitchhiker's paradise. More often than not, just walking along the side of the only road is enough for someone to stop and offer a lift. Even cabs would stop and offer a free ride as far as they were going. Only when you really needed to get somewhere in a hurry was it necessary to stick out your thumb. Two rides got me past the airport, the Unisea Inn and across the bridge. I was on my own after bouncing along in the back of a pick-up for about five miles of dirt road toward the head of Captain's Bay. Thanking the pick-up driver, I began the mile or so hike to the end of the road. It wasn't long before I could see the rusted hulk of the USS Northwestern poking its bow out of the water at the head of the bay.

The Northwestern began service as an Alaska Steamship Company vessel in 1909. She had survived 16 groundings in the Inside Passage. Stationed at Dutch Harbor, the old ship had been driven ashore by a williwaw a few weeks before the Japanese attack. Two bombs scored direct hits on the deck of the beached ship, which was serving as a barracks for civilian construction workers. Then the Zeros strafed her. The resulting fires were brought under control by her dedicated deckhands, and she continued to serve the city for many months. Later the old ship was towed up to the head of Captain's Bay and scuttled.

I left the road at the head of Captain's Bay and hiked through the large swampy delta of the Shaishnikoff River. It was a sea of blowing wet, waist-high ferns and grasses. Reaching more solid ground at a series of small hills, I began to follow the river. There was no trail. When I would come up against a blind canyon I would have to backtrack, climb a hill, drop down into the adjacent valley and continue on, picking up the river further upstream.

Two bald eagles buzzed me for the first hour. A fine drizzle floated in the shifting breeze. Tall wet grasses and ferns swayed back and forth. The green tundra on either side of the valley reached finger-like up the sides of the mountains whose tops were perpetually hidden by the low, shifting gray clouds. It was at this time that I was struck by the beauty of the place. It was not the spectacular, awe-inspiring beauty of the Alaska Range, the kind that assaults and overwhelms the visual sense. Here was a more subtle, refined, beauty that struck right at the heart, imprinting itself. It was slowly pulling me in.

I continued hiking a steady, plodding and zigzagging course up a long incline, trying to keep the river in sight. Myriad small rivulets coursed hidden beneath the tall grass cover. I soon became adept at spotting these. Their banks, lined predominately by ferns, cut a dark green swath through the lighter green tundra grasses. A shallow depression in the center of this dark green stripe was confirmatory. Using these visual clues, I was soon able to jump across these narrow streams without even seeing them through the dense fern cover.

After about four hours of wet but exhilarating hiking, I finally reached the pass where my goal, the small inland lake, could be seen giving birth to the river I'd been following. It was a placid setting in the interior highlands. The small lake sat in a bowl surrounded by smaller but rocky peaks still streaked with snow. Not many miles beyond the low rocky outcropping on the far side of the lake lay the vast and wild expanse of the North Pacific Ocean.

I set up my tent on nice flat ground just above the beach and soon had a fairly decent meal of freeze-dried chili cooking on my camp stove. I remember thinking how safe I was there. There are no bears and no snakes on Unalaska Island. Shortly after this comforting thought I noticed the wind, which had been with me all day, starting to pick up. It didn't really bother me at first. I just laid back in my sleeping bag and started reading my Thomas Hardy novel. I sort of felt a kinship with him, in that his love of Egdon Heath, the flat grassland of his English home, was similar to my developing love for the treeless terrain of the Aleutians. The wind started getting stronger with occasional gusts that would ominously deform my tent before subsiding and letting it snap back into place. It was becoming more and more difficult to lose myself in the damp pages of my book. There was no sign of the wind subsiding and a quick look out the front of my tent showed three-foot seas and crashing breakers on my formerly placid little alpine lake. More concerned now, I laid down and tried to rest.

Around 10 pm a strong gust suddenly collapsed my tent. Flattened it like a pancake. Much more calmly than I ever would have thought possible under such circumstances, I reached about and fetched all my loose belongings as the wind molded the collapsed tent around me. Groping around, I found the opening and shoved my pack out. Then I wiggled out myself, much as one would get out of an oversized jumpsuit.

The wind was howling fiercely and blowing rain. I untwisted the last piece of the collapsed tent from around my ankle and kicked it free. To my surprise, it took off like a rocket, at a 45-degree angle, and flew across the river and down the valley. I watched in disbelief as it remained airborne, getting smaller and smaller, until it vanished into a distant swirling maze of dark gray storm clouds and faintly visible background tundra. It was a very sobering experience to stand alone in the howling wind and blowing rain. There was no shelter to be had anywhere on the wet and windswept treeless terrain.

I had several things going for me in the potentially dangerous situation I suddenly found myself in, and a few things going against me. In my favor was that I would have the wind at my back on the return hike,

I was fairly well-rested, well-fed, dry, and had the proper clothes. It was predominately a downhill hike. I was familiar with the route, and I had about two hours of usable daylight.

Going against me, I was alone, the weather and terrain were now very hostile and I had no shelter. Darkness would be upon me in two hours, and no one would report me missing for at least two days.

With these thoughts in mind I hightailed it for town. I made good time and found myself overlooking the swampy delta by midnight. By now it was dark. Overcast skies, wind and rain made visibility even worse and a flashlight was of little help. Trying to make my way across the maze of wet grass, standing pools of water and narrow, swiftly flowing branches of the main river, I was getting nowhere fast. I'd sink into mud up to my knees, struggle out, backtrack, ford a small branch of the river and make some headway, then be blocked by a small pool of standing water. At one point I fell into a hole up to my chest with my full pack on. By then I was getting frustrated and even more concerned.

Then I saw the road. I remember having a strong urge to strip off my pack and just dash straight for it. Common sense, however, told me to backtrack and head for higher ground around the perimeter of the swamp. This I did, following a series of small hills in an arc toward the road. I remember the final hill. I was on physical and emotional reserve. The wind was so loud and strong it felt as if I was being carried up the hill. I crested it and stumbled down the other side rolling in the wet grass. Coming to rest, I looked up to see the white wooden cross of the Russian Orthodox graveyard I knew lay alongside the road. Never was I so glad to see a graveyard. I took shelter briefly in the damp but roomy interior of an old World War II bunker located nearby and rested for a few minutes, trying to calm myself, and ate the rest of my candy bars. I still had five miles of hiking down the dirt road along the bay until I got to the main road, but now that seemed like nothing.

Around 2:30 am, in the "hitchhiker's paradise," I desperately flagged down a passing taxi. Arriving back in my small room at the bunkhouse, I resolved to do only day hiking for the rest of my stay on the island. It was a moot resolution, since my tent was probably halfway to Nome by that time.

Henry Swanson, who went on the last legal sea otter hunt in 1910, at his home in Unalaska, Alaska August 1986. We met on my return to Dutch the year following my "williwaw misadventure"

CHAPTER 40

THE ALEUTIANS II: CHERNOFSKY, VIA DUTCH (1986)

As they say, if you want to go to Chernofsky, first you gotta get to Dutch (Dutch Harbor, that is). Well, "they" never really said that. But I did. Just now. So I own the quote.

I've been to Dutch twice. First time I flew out with Reeve. Founded by the legendary and feisty bush pilot, Bob Reeve, Reeve Aleutian Airways had been flying "out on the chain" since 1932 and never had a fatal accident. Good odds. We were flying through milk in their old 727 jet before I could see the runway below us at Cold Bay. Cold Bay's 10,000-foot military-built runway was an emergency refuge for aviation over a large and stormy swath of the North Pacific.

Reeve bailed on us in Cold Bay and would fly no farther. My heart sank. We were shuttled over to a small twin-engine prop plane run by Peninsula Airways and flown by a bush pilot named Harold Wilson. He even resembled, just a bit, the former British Prime Minister.

We took off and backtracked for a quick stopover in Sand Point. Captain Wilson was in a hurry because the weather was closing in at Dutch. I didn't like the sound of it, but I found out later that the weather was always either closing in, or about to close in, at Dutch. If it hadn't already closed in.

Cruising at about 9,000 feet (from what I could read on the cockpit instrument panel), the cabin felt damp and slightly warm. We were unpressurized. Everyone's head was drooping, including the pilot's. Wait a minute, I thought, he's probably just studying an aviation map. As we circled in to land, menacing dark, gray clouds seemed to be everywhere and the wind swatted us about, banking the wings a good twenty or more degrees at times. Captain Wilson got us in.

About a year later I picked up the *Anchorage Daily News* and read a story about a PenAir pilot who had a seizure while flying to Dutch Harbor and how the passengers had to fly the plane with help from a nearby Navy P-3 Orion they contacted by radio (when the pilot slumped over he disengaged the autopilot, making it even more challenging for the non-pilot behind the wheel). They managed to roust the pilot in time and he landed safely. Yup, it was Harold Wilson. I was stunned! I'll never be able to shake the image of his head drooped over for several long minutes in the cockpit, and will always wonder if he was really looking at an aviation map. One explanation for his temporary loss of consciousness was a reaction to the artificial sweetener in the large amount of diet soft drinks he consumed.

My next trip to Dutch, the following year, was in a MarkAir jet. Non-stop from Anchorage, cabin comfort and a hot breakfast. As we descended into Dutch Harbor the captain came on over the intercom and alerted us to expect a "firm" landing. When a Boeing 737-200 jet lands on a 3,000-foot gravel runway with ocean on both ends, a "firm" landing is about the only landing possible.

I chatted with the pilot after our uneventful "firm" landing. He recounted how, after multiple practice landings prior to securing FAA approval, they had it down to where, from wheel contact to a dead stop, they could land in 500 feet. Extreme, but pretty darn impressive.

While in Dutch I had to check out the Elbow Room. It had been famously written up in Playboy Magazine as the wildest and most notorious bar in the USA. It was disappointingly sedate when I visited. Boring, actually. But I had run into a familiar face at the Dutch Harbor Airport who had seen the Elbow Room at its liveliest.

John Peavey had lived down the hall from me at Wadsworth Hall Dormitory, Michigan Technological University in Michigan's Upper Peninsula in the early to mid-1970s. So we were quite surprised to run into each other in Dutch Harbor more than ten years later. John was working for Exxon looking for oil. I was a radiologist in Anchorage and out in Dutch on vacation. John didn't buy it. "No one comes to Dutch Harbor on vacation," he said. "Well, meet the first exception," I replied. John described his experience at the Elbow Room.

Fishermen, after weeks at sea, finally came to port. Pockets flush with thousands in cash, they couldn't buy or drink $3.00 cans of Bud fast enough. So they bought cases at a time, popped them open, spilled them on the floor and did drunken belly-slides across the room. Wish I had been there. Hugh Hefner would have smiled at the decadence.

And, while it's not in the guidebooks, Dutch Harbor is home to a very famous (infamous?) Mexican restaurant - the Chili Pepper. Its claim to fame is that it was the shortest continuously operating Mexican restaurant in Alaska. From its grand opening until it was shut down by the local health department, it was in operation a full half-a-day. No running water, among other issues.

Mexicans are resilient, but the owner/proprietor of the Chili Pepper was downright entrepreneurial. After they shut down his restaurant, he founded a cab company. In Dutch at the time, whenever a cab was needed, the call went out over the radio to everyone: "Any cab, come to the airport" or "Any cab, come to the Unisea Inn". You guessed it - he named his single-car cab company "Any Cab" and claimed all the calls as his.

CHERNOFSKY

Chernofsky, a sheep farm on the far side of huge Unalaska Island, is one of the most isolated settlements in America. Two charter flights and one boat per year visit this remote community. It was a one-family town. I was lucky enough to get on one of those charter flights.

Tom Madsen, who had done a lot of flying in the Kodiak archipelago before coming to Dutch Harbor, operated Aleutian Air. About a half-dozen of us got into his amphibious Grumman Goose docked at the harbor. Self-assured, dressed in jeans and a T-shirt, Tom settled into the pilot's seat, carefully set down his coffee, and we took off.

We were flying west along the Pacific side of the island. Below, some of the roughest dark blue water I'd ever seen was pounding the steep, rugged shoreline cliffs. It was humbling in its raw, natural beauty. But up ahead a wall of crud forced us to turn back and fly along the more sedate Bering Sea side of the island. The coastal scenery was less frightening, more magical, in its beauty. It was a smooth landing in Chernofsky Harbor.

246

Chernofsky is a 200 square mile sheep ranch run by one family. Milt Holmes, a sheepman from Idaho, replied to an ad for a hand and came out in 1949. Later, he came to own it. Cora, a nurse from Idaho, replied to Milt's ad for a housekeeper and came out with her two young sons. Milt and Cora married a year later.

What splendid isolation, I remember thinking. They ordered food from Seattle every other year. Random fishing boats dropped off mail maybe four times a year. Income came from selling wool, mutton, and the occasional fox hide. And these small, twice-yearly tourist visits that I was now a part of helped provide some cash flow.

On the treeless terrain, and in so remote a location, fuel could easily have been the limiting factor. A massive mountain of coal left by the military after World War II provided fuel for heat and cooking and, some forty years later, showed no sign of running out in the near to mid future. A huge military warehouse on the grounds was filled with all kinds of mechanical equipment. Self-sufficiency was the rule in Chernofsky.

During our two days there we dined on freshly caught halibut, freshly slaughtered mutton topped with mint jelly, salad (flown in) and homemade bread baked in the kitchen's massive coal-fired cast iron stove. We talked, played pool, took tours of the ranch and learned a bit about sheep-shearing. Son Randy taught me how to ride a horse, and off I went – carefully. (There's a photo of little Randy hauling pails of coal on page 361 of the September 1983 issue of "National Geographic").

Tom Madsen came back for us as scheduled two days later, his plane filled with supplies. He half-beached the Grumman Goose's massive floats. After unloading, we all climbed aboard. Tom was given a massive side of sheep for his trouble. A little first-grader named Carl wandered up to the cockpit and started pushing buttons and yanking on levers. I yelled at the little bugger. We flew back to Dutch uneventfully.

Chapter 41

Attack of the Annelids

After a long day of paddling and portaging we beached our canoes and set up camp on the shore of Spruce Lake – the hub of the Swan Lake Wilderness Canoe system in Alaska's Kenai National Wildlife Refuge. My eight-year-old son, Brendan, was traveling with me and we were accompanied by our friends from church in another canoe. The faint, misty drizzle that dogged us all day had stopped as we finished our dinner, completed our chores and took our leisurely evening spin in the canoe – unencumbered by mountains of gear.

At this latitude in July the sun dipped below the horizon for about four hours, but not far enough to cover the land in darkness. When Brendan and I settled into our sleeping bags inside our blue dome tent around 10 pm it was still light.

I awoke suddenly about an hour later, eyes wide open, and realized our tent was under attack! No, the 3-inch claws of *Ursus horribilus,* the grizzly bear, were not ripping through the sides of our tent. Such an occurrence would hardly be newsworthy in Alaska. This was a far more bizarre predator. We were under attack by ... earthworms! The shadows of hundreds of slowly squirming earthworms could be seen through the translucent nylon skin of the tent, reaching to the very top. They had crawled into the nylon sleeves that anchor the tent poles. Coiled earthworm twosomes and threesomes, coated by cocoons of a saliva-like consistency, hung from exposed parts of the tent. Earthworms rained down on the back of my neck when I crawled out of the tent to pee. My bear spray and .357 magnum were useless. Brendan acknowledged the attack nonchalantly and rolled back over to sleep. I thought about some Alfred Hitchcock movies I'd seen. Earthworms are not noisy when they attack a tent en mass, so we were able to get a good night's sleep.

The next morning I spent some twenty minutes flicking earthworms off the tent with the tip of a plastic shovel before I could take it down and repack it (and I found several I'd missed at the following night's camp). The other tent, only about ten feet from ours, had only about a dozen worms on it. When I checked the water I had set to boil for coffee, there were two earthworms in it. No matter, camp coffee is camp coffee and it always tastes good, no matter what has been floating or swimming in it.

When I got back to Anchorage, I called the Extension Service and related the strange experience. It was a new one to them and we could only conclude that we had set up our tent in the middle of a massive earthworm mating ritual.

Years later I called Larry Kaniut, author of *Alaska Bear Tales*, and related this story. He'd heard all kinds of tales, such as the snowmachine that took off on its own, like the famous collie Lassie, to rescue its inept owner. But nothing about earthworm attacks. "Larry," I said, "this one might be something for your next book."

CHAPTER 42

CELEBRITIES, MORE CELEBRITIES, AND, FINALLY, A MEETING WITH THE HELMSMAN

I've had the opportunity to meet or shake hands with many interesting and famous personalities passing through Anchorage: President Bill Clinton, the President of the Dominican Republic, Ozzie Osbourne and Tiny Tim, for example. But no one quite like the Helmsman.

President Bill and First Lady Hillary Clinton stopped at Elmendorf Air Force Base in Anchorage to refuel – either going to or returning from Asia. It was late fall of 1994, just after his "shellacking" (an Obaman term) by Speaker Newt and the "Contract with America" boys. He was gracious enough to come out and greet the troops in a huge hangar on base. Being a member of the U.S. Public Health Service got me inside.

After his talk, and stories of Hillary working the "slime line" at an Alaska fish-packing plant, he proceeded to work the crowd. Hillary, smartly attired in a bright red dress, worked a smaller crowd at the opposite end of the hanger. I hesitated briefly before going after Bill and, with my long arm, snagged my first presidential handshake. Nice guy, sweaty palm.

There was much less hoopla when the President of the Dominican Republic swept through town. In fact, only the local Dominican community seemed to be aware. It was a friend who was married to a Dominican woman who invited me to come. The reception was held at a small dance floor/auditorium adjoining a Dominican restaurant in downtown Anchorage. President Hippolito Mejia walked up to the microphone. I'll admit I was expecting a tall, imposing, swashbuckling mestizo in a military uniform bedecked with medals. Mejia was a short, balding white guy in a gray suit and tie. Well, we shared one characteristic: we both had white skin.

He spoke in Spanish, which I did not completely understand. But then I was gratified to see him take questions from the audience. One woman simply wanted to have her son's photo taken with him and he graciously complied. Another questioner, apparently not satisfied by the President's answer, fired back another question. A spirited debate ensued. President Mejia - informed, confident and unruffled - held his own. I was impressed.

Finally, he had enough of the questions. The party began. Mejia turned to the band, which had been sitting respectfully silent, and snapped his fingers. Dominican music filled the room. And the President of the Dominican Republic literally jumped two feet onto the dance floor, grabbed a woman and started dancing. My kind of presidente. Afterward, in a surge of the small crowd, I found myself suddenly face-to-face with him. We shook hands and I welcomed him to Anchorage, Alaska. My second presidential handshake.

I was sipping my latte and reading the paper in the old Alaska Airlines Boardroom on the B concourse. Out of the corner of my eye I noticed a scraggly-haired man heading my way. His shuffling gait caught my attention. It was clearly abnormal. Acute impairment or chronic brain damage from drugs or whatever, I thought, reaching back to my days as a medical student in Detroit and as an intern in Buffalo. He quietly paused, as my crossed legs were blocking his way to the refreshment stand. I pay $200 a year for membership privileges here and they let in the street people, I thought, annoyed. I scrunched up my legs to let him pass and returned to my paper.

Not much later, again out of the corner of my eye, I noticed that at least two or three tall burly guys wearing black leather coats constantly hovered over the "scraggly shuffler." Something didn't fit. I got up, tapped one of them on the shoulder, and asked, "Who is that man?" "Ozzie Osbourne," he replied. "Ozzie Osbourne as in Black Sabbath?" "That's him," he said. "Will you introduce me to him?" I asked. "Sure," he said. This was one pleasant, tall, burly, black leather-jacketed Ozzie Osbourne bodyguard, I remember thinking. He even gave me an autographed photo which I gave to my son.

Ozzie was sitting by the doorway staring into space. We shook hands and I welcomed him to Alaska. No response. Ozzie was clearly zoned and seemed to be staring at something only he could see. No matter. He was the "Black Sabbath" and we just left it at that. Later I would see him undergo the most thorough pre– 9/11 pat-down before he hopped an Alaska Airlines flight to a gig in Fairbanks.

I was still in high school in 1969 when I watched, along with millions, the marriage of Tiny Tim and Miss Vickie on the Tonight Show Starring Johnny Carson. Johnny was always "Mr. Carson", and Tiny declined the postnuptial champagne in favor of milk and honey. And now here I was, decades later, at Chilkoot Charlie's Bar in Anchorage, Alaska some twenty feet away from Tiny Tim while he belted out "Tiptoe Through the Tulips" and "A Tisket a Tasket a Green and Yellow Basket" on his trademark little ukulele. I grabbed a 'Koots' napkin and got in line for an autograph.

The decibel level on stage had to have been well above OSHA's maximum and the bar should have been cited. Tiny Tim signed my napkin. He looked ill, uncomfortable and pained. His belly seemed swollen to me. As a physician, I knew illness would often express itself in a person's face. Instead of feeling excited about the autograph, I felt sadness. The ringing in my ears lasted almost 24 hours. Tiny Tim died not much later of a heart attack, in Minnesota, while singing "Tiptoe Through the Tulips."

George Takei is best known as Mr. Sulu, the Helmsman on the Starship Enterprise and its 5-year mission - abbreviated to 3 years (1966-1969) by the television studios. He dutifully executed the commands of Captain James Tiberius Kirk (William Shatner) and later, in the post TV movies, commanded his own starship.

George Takei had two strikes against him - he was Japanese and he was gay. To his credit, he overcame both. He was also a civic activist in Los Angeles, which is probably why (in addition to being Mr. Sulu) he was invited to Alaska by the Matanuska Electric Association in 1995 to jazz up their annual shareholders' meeting. I learned about the scheduled upcoming visit through my kids, who attended Sonrise Christian School in Anchorage at the time. It seems George, as a small boy, spent some time in one of America's shameful and notorious Japanese internment camps near the end of World War II. An elderly Japanese woman at their school also spent time at the same camp as George. She was to pick him up at the airport. It was a private visit.

Knowing the evening of his arrival, it only took a few phone calls to figure he had to be coming in on the United flight from LA. I hoped the Trekkies hadn't gotten word; they would have stormed the terminal. I remember how they mobbed Captain Jean Luc-Picard's "Warf" at an official Star Trek Convention in Anchorage. At the last minute, after dinner, I said to my kids: "Let's go to the airport and meet Mr. Sulu." I made sure my twelve-year-old son, Brendan, had a copy of "Star Trek" magazine so he could get an autograph.

We arrived at the gate I had predicted at the end of the old B Concourse. A few people milled about. The elderly Japanese woman was standing there. Bingo! We were right on and the Trekkies were in the dark. There was no mistaking Mr. Sulu when he walked out of the jetway in a beige trench coat. The first person he encountered was my young son.

His eyes widened, he smiled and extended his hand for a shake. He happily signed the magazine photo and chatted a bit with Brendan. Then he turned his attention to my daughter, Colleen. The little nine-year-old red-headed "Trekkie" stood by shyly to meet him. When he saw her he spontaneously composed a poem about her red hair. I stood back, spellbound. It was so fluid and sincere it was as if he had rehearsed it on the plane. I was really impressed. I wished I had a video camera.

Not wanting to take up any more of his time, I reached out to shake his hand and simply said: "Hi, I'm their Dad." And we let him be on his way.

A good man, the Helmsman. May his starship always take him where he needs to go.

Tiny Tim autographing a napkin for me at Chilkoot Charlie's,
Anchorage, Alaska February 1995

George Takei, a.k.a. the Helmsman, greeting my son Brendan at the
Anchorage International Airport. Spring 1995

CHAPTER 43

AUTHORS, MUSINGS ABOUT ASTRONAUTS, A DISABLED BUSH PILOT AND, FINALLY, A MEETING WITH LARRY KANIUT

Alaska Bear Tales was the rage of Alaska in the mid/late 1980s. The 1983 book became a national phenomenon and sold more than 100,000 copies. The author, Larry Kaniut, was a teacher at Dimond High School in Anchorage. When I arrived in Anchorage, Alaska in July 1984 with my wife and 18-month-old son, I was ready to begin the "Alaska Experience." So it wasn't long before I attempted to contact Larry Kaniut.

Imagine an East Coast resident trying to contact Leon Uris or Norman Mailer to arrange to have them autograph a copy of their book. Leon Uris displayed the haunting beauty and pride of Ireland in his books. I gave both my kids Irish names because of him. And Norman Mailer called the late astronaut Alan Shepard to the carpet for hitting a golf ball to unseen low-gravity oblivion on the surface of the moon. "An act so vulgar as to be obscene," said Norman, the alleged wife-beater. The club and ball cost the American taxpayers about $14,000 at the time. I'm not into exotic golf and I despise wife-beaters, but Mailer called that one right.

On the subject of astronauts, we discovered a legendary, disabled Alaska bush pilot named Jack Lee living down the street from our apartment on 42nd Avenue shortly after we moved in. Jack, I came to find out, embodied the hard-living, hard-drinking, wild bravado of the stereotypical Alaska bush pilot. Flying skills unquestioned, he used to ferry the Apollo astronauts to their hunting camps in the Alaska Bush.

"I'm lucky to be alive," Jack would say in the spastic voice of someone with significant brain damage. He was semi-immobilized and a physical therapy attendant was present. Stuffed exotic animals from Alaska and Africa filled his spacious living room.

I was told that Jack had made a difficult landing on Denali under extremely challenging conditions. In white-out situations, when there was no depth-perception, pilots were known to drop pre-collected spruce boughs and then circle around and re-attempt a landing.

Jack, skilled as he was, landed safely (this time with no astronauts onboard). But he was unable to perceive that he landed on a slight up-slope. The plane began to slide backwards, Jack was unable to restart the engine because it was already over-heated and the inexorable backslide continued. The plane flipped over into a small crevasse. Suspended upside down for countless hours, the damage had been done by the time rescuers got to him.

Jack, as I remember, always had a smile when I stopped by. He tried, with great difficulty, to share his stories with us. Once, he directed me to a photo of one of his clients hanging on his living room wall. It was a framed photo of astronaut John Young standing on the surface of the moon. There was a handwritten note on the black-and-white NASA photo that said: "Jack, the ballistics are great, but game is scarce." It was signed by John Young.

Kudos to astronaut Young, I remember thinking. At least he didn't smuggle his favorite hunting rifle aboard Apollo and take pot-shots at moon rocks. Though maybe that's because he already had been reprimanded by NASA for sneaking a corned–beef sandwich on an earlier Gemini spaceflight.

But, I digress...

Larry Kaniut himself picked up the phone when I called. (Yup, I just looked up his name in the phone book.) I stammered a bit. After all, I was talking to the *Alaska Bear Tales* guy.

The logistics of my driving to Larry's place somewhere in the wilds off De Armoun Road seemed difficult, so he said, "How about I just stop by your place?" Our townhouse, near Arctic and Dimond, was at the civilized edge of Anchorage at the time. Wow, I thought, a famous Alaskan author offers to drive to our townhouse and autograph his book. This ain't the Midwest and it certainly ain't the East Coast.

So one Sunday morning after church Larry Kaniut pulled into our driveway.

Unrushed Alaskans, then and now, have always had time for conversation. It was not an interview, I took no notes, and some thirty years have elapsed. But two things we spoke about I will always remember.

Teaching is an honorable, but often stressed and unappreciated, profession. He shared with us how, when one of his students showed up late again for class, he reprimanded him. He then learned of the dysfunctional and abusive environment at the student's home and back-pedaled, saying to the young man, "Your problems at home are far more important than anything I teach in this class." And he began to work with him.

No books had been signed yet, but Larry shared with us his "dream job". He would like to have an office with the door always open to troubled students. His only mission and full-time job would be to help young people with all their troubles and with full support from the State of Alaska and the Anchorage Board of Education. He would do whatever he could for each student who walked through his door. Wow, I thought, good for Larry. A real-life catcher-in-the rye.

Larry Kaniut did renege, though, on a promise he made us at our Anchorage townhouse that day in the mid-1980s. He said he was not writing any more non-fiction books about Alaska (bears or whatever). Well, that went out the window, but it is very easily forgiven. He autographed a couple books for us, we thanked him, and bid him farewell.

CHAPTER 44

FLOYD

I first met Floyd in the summer of 1984 – shortly after we moved to Anchorage from the Detroit area. On the C Street bike trail in south Anchorage I encountered a large, gentle Native Alaskan with a friendly face. "I'm from Barrow," he said, "top-of-the-world, top-of-the-world." Floyd would often repeat select phrases two or three times.

He was maybe in his mid-twenties when I first met him. From a large Inupiaq Eskimo family in Barrow, Floyd had been different since birth. Never talked well, didn't fit in. Hyperactive from six months old, he was always wandering off somewhere along the Arctic coast, and it soon became too much for his family. After a series of homes, special schools and hospitals, Floyd ended up in Spenard – a neighborhood in Anchorage.

Covered by social security and welfare, he settled into an adult residential care facility called The Lodge. Requiring only minimal supervision, Floyd was out and about most hours. He knew the Anchorage People Mover (bus system) like the back of his hand. But the Floyd who endeared himself to our community was the Floyd who planted himself on the southwest corner of Minnesota and Spenard Roads holding a cardboard sign that simply said, "SAY HI TO FLOYD."

A gas station/convenience store occupied the corner, but the asphalt stopped at a small, minimally tended garden with a few scraggly shrubs at the extreme edge. That was Floyd's turf and, flashing a toothy grin and waving and holding his sign, he poured out a simple good cheer. And Anchorage loved it. They honked and waved back.

Then someone threw the first coin. And the coins kept coming. Floyd may have been mentally impaired but he was not immune to the "capitalist bug." He made the connection and found a way to indulge (or overindulge) his twin addictions: coffee and soda. "Lotsa soda," Floyd would say. He was soon pulling in as much as $100.00 on weekends and the sign, inevitably, changed to: "PAY FLOYD."

A lot of the tossed coins landed in the street and Floyd couldn't resist darting out after them. His life was at risk and he could have caused an accident. Anchorage police had become concerned. So, he went and got himself a business license. His business? Panhandling. This, too, did not go over well. Knowing he could not actively solicit money, Floyd's sign changed again: "UP TO YOU. PAY FLOYD."

Floyd has had his low moments. He threw a fit in a downtown department store, raised a ruckus in a Spenard restaurant and punched a nose or two at the Lodge. But the Anchorage Police Department knew Floyd and, to their credit, knew the difference between someone who is mentally impaired and someone who is a criminal or a drunk.

I used to see Floyd occasionally at the Alaska Native Medical Center where I worked as a radiologist. At the Tundra Club cafeteria on the old campus at 3rd Avenue and Gambell I would treat him to coffee and pie. I last remember seeing him at the new campus on Tudor Road methodically checking the vending machines for coins inadvertently left behind. And he had a can of his beloved soda in his hand, repeatedly jerking his neck backward with the can pressed to his lips, sucking out every last drop – and the vapor as well. Top-of-the-world, top-of-the-world…

In the spring of 2004, Floyd died in Spenard of natural causes. Folks like Floyd grace Anchorage in a way that makes us a special place. And the small lot on the southwest corner of Minnesota and Spenard Roads remains disturbingly vacant. If I ever win the lottery, or maybe if I don't, I would like someday to commission a statue of the "pre-capitalist" Floyd on that very corner. It would bring needed good cheer to passing Anchorage motorists.

CHAPTER 45

AL

Alfred Clayburn Atkey was a fighter pilot for the Royal Flying Corps and one of Canada's most famous World War I pilots. He earned the British Military Cross for his gallantry and devotion to duty. He was also a journalist and a concert pianist. His young son Alfie (Al) reportedly adored him, but young Al's trajectory in life led him down a different path. Al became one of the most enigmatic and beloved members of Anchorage's homeless community.

Anchorage is Alaska's largest city, but in many ways it is a small town. It was only a matter of time before I ran into Al. No one will ever know how Al became the way he is, or how (why) he came to Anchorage. Stories abound and many of them are becoming cemented into the folklore and legend that has begun to stick to Al. Like how he rolled a tire down the Alaska Highway to sell, got a ride from a soldier and arrived in Fairbanks. Next stop, Anchorage.

Whenever I ran into Al I gave him my full attention and never regretted it. Once, in the Glen Alps parking lot for a wedding or a similar reception (Al was decked out in a bow tie), he launched into such a detailed and articulate account of corruption and conspiracy leading right up to the Governor's office (he named names, like the Carrs...or was it the Rasmusons...) that left me speechless.

Al was not a drinker. When I would run into him at a fast food joint like McDonald's I would always spot him a burger and coffee. I understand he loved music and would do odd jobs for tapes and CDs.

Al had a single remaining tooth in his mid-lower jaw that stood out, defiantly. It seemed to have a message. The others were gone, but this one was holding its ground, unyielding, like Al, against all the odds.

During the long, cold Anchorage winters Al would wear multiple layers of clothes so that he puffed out like a massive beach ball. At least he was warm (I remember seeing a similarly attired native in Kotzebue during several visits there for radiology clinics. I nicknamed him the "Kotzebue marshmallow". Unfortunately, I never learned his story).

It was outside the Denny's on Northern Lights and Bragaw one winter that Al and I had our last encounter and he explained his mission. It was Al's job, when he wasn't staying at the Brother Francis Shelter, to ride his bike up and down the Glenn Highway (braving temperatures down to minus 40°) and sell used paperbacks. "Somebody's got to do it," Al told me matter-of-factly, with a tinge of resignation to his fate, but not a shred of self-pity. Al never asked me for anything except, indirectly, for my time - which I was happy to give.

Ten to twenty white plastic Carrs bags hung from Al's bike – mostly on the handlebars, but also just about anywhere else you could hook a plastic bag. Pretty much everything he owned was either on that bike or somewhere in the six layers of clothes he was wearing. Al had his own filing system but apparently, at times, it was even too much for Al. He wanted to show me one of his books, reached into a Carrs bag, and pulled out a greasy aluminum plate. Oops. Several other interesting items came out of other bags before he found the dog-eared paperback.

Al explained how he had one or two backup bikes and other equipment stashed in the snowy forest along the Glenn Highway. He was about to embark on one of his trips north. I wished him well.

About an hour later I passed him pushing that massively overloaded bike through snowdrifts along Northern Lights Blvd. heading east (Mike Doogan would have been incensed upon seeing this. Unplowed sidewalks was the subject of one of the first of his 2,000 or so columns while working for the *Anchorage Daily News*). But I wasn't worried about Al at the time. Al is a survivor in his own way. And the folks up and down the Glenn Highway have been looking out for him.

Soviet-era playwright, Czech President and Gandhi Peace Prize winner (2003) Vaclav Havel once said that the best measure of a civilization is how it treats its poorest, most marginalized and disenfranchised members. He was probably referring to the Gypsies (Roma). Vaclav Havel would be proud of Anchorage. Folks like Al Atkey grace Anchorage in a way that makes us a special place.

Epilogue:

In May 2011 I visited the Alaska Room in the Loussac Library in Anchorage to pull up a little background on Al. The staff librarian knew right away who I was asking about. Apparently, Al spent a lot of time in the library reading and listening to music. She told me the last she heard was that Al was back with family in Canada.

CHAPTER 46

RABBIT

It was several summers ago that I first saw him pull up to the dumpsters in the alleyway between 26th and 27th just east of Minnesota in a beat-up old pick-up pulling a trailer behind. The most languid dog I'd ever seen crawled out of the passenger side, walked a few paces, then fell asleep on the warm pavement. Rabbit got out on the driver's side. Shirtless, dressed in soiled olive-green jeans, he always wore a woolen watch-cap, no matter how hot the weather. Most of his front teeth were missing.

I was absolutely amazed, watching from my third-floor apartment window, as Rabbit jumped into the dumpster in a motion so fluid it would have put Olympic gymnast Nadia Comaneci to shame. He began pulling out aluminum cans by the handful. Now, this was an all-purpose dumpster, which meant aluminum cans would be randomly scattered throughout, but it seemed as if they all came to Rabbit. Or he knew where to look. Then he paused to snack on a partial dried-up slice of pizza he found.

I grabbed a cold lemonade from the fridge and brought it down for him and introduced myself. He had the largest hands I'd ever seen. Long fingers with spatulate tips. I was looking at a pair of aluminum magnets. Either he developed these hands after years of dumpster-diving or he was born with them and gravitated into dumpster-diving. Either way, it was positively Darwinian.

Rabbit was also clearly a paranoid-schizophrenic. He was extremely articulate. I listened for almost thirty minutes to detailed accounts of the UFO base in the nearby Chugach Mountains, conspiracy theories, his time at the Alaska Psychiatric Institute and the multiple laser hits that left him implanted with chips which allowed him to monitor conversations on the police radio bands. One of those laser hits happened near the now-shuttered Northern Lights Hotel, he explained. During a following encounter he pointed out to me his two $5,000 Kevlar-diamond-dust dental implants, courtesy of the U.S. military. I didn't go in for a close look

After some years Rabbit dumped the old clunker and made the rounds on a bicycle pulling a long trailer. In all of our encounters Rabbit never asked me for money. He only asked me for something once. In the parking lot at Barnes and Noble he inquired whether I had any peroxide. Cuts and scratches from rummaging around in dumpsters could easily become infected. But I wasn't in the habit of carrying a bottle of peroxide around with me, so I couldn't help him out.

For several years, each spring, when the first junco filled the little Spenard parking lot with its song, I knew it wouldn't be long before I saw Rabbit in the dumpster. A cold bottle of lemonade with his name on it sat in the fridge.

The spring of 2011 arrived and summer slipped by quickly. The junco returned and sang for me, but there were no sightings of Rabbit in the dumpster. Granted, I was spending most of my time in Nome, but still, I was concerned. Dumpster-diving, fraught with the risk of serious infection, was not a healthy occupation. And neither was schizophrenia a healthy mental illness. Yes, I was very concerned.

Fall, winter and the spring of 2012 passed. Rabbit's cold lemonade in the fridge slipped past its expiration date and I had to give it the el tosso and replace it with a fresh one. Then, on a cool and drizzly afternoon in early July 2012, I looked out from my third-floor balcony and saw a vaguely familiar bicycle leaning against our dumpster. And inside I saw movement. Rabbit was back!

I grabbed his lemonade from the fridge and went out into the cool July day to bring it down to him. When I handed it to him, asking if he was thirsty, he politely declined. When I gently persisted, he accepted it, not with a "thank you" but with a "God bless you." Then he tossed it into the pack on his bike and went back to work in the dumpster. That was Rabbit. All business.

He had lost some hair on top since we last talked, though a huge and wildly disheveled shock of hair sprouted from the front of his scalp, just above the forehead. But it was the regal, gray and flowing beard – streaked with just the right amount of salt-and-pepper – that caught my attention. It would have been the envy of an up-and-coming young Hebrew patriarch 3,000 years ago.

I couldn't help but make a spontaneous connection between the willows in the tiny fenced–in lot behind the dumpster and Rabbit. I'd seen these willows razed to the ground twice since I acquired my apartment in Spenard almost ten years ago. And they kept coming back. Just like Rabbit.

Rabbit had given up on aluminum cans and was now going for copper and other metals that fetched a good price at the Anchorage Recycling Center. Wanting to make conversation, I volunteered how this dumpster had just been emptied a couple days ago, then immediately felt like an ignoramus for making such an inane observation. Of course, Rabbit knew the pick-up schedule of Anchorage's Solid Waste Services. But he showed no disdain for my ignorance of his profession as he explained how he timed his first visit to the dumpster a couple days after pick-up, when there would be only about two feet of garbage on the bottom. Easier to sort through thoroughly. A follow-up visit was scheduled for the second two feet of trash, and so on. So, when that dumpster was filled to overflowing just before pick-up, it had already been thoroughly gone through and picked clean by Rabbit – from bottom to top.

Folks like Rabbit grace Anchorage in a way that makes us a special place.

EPILOGUE

I ran into Rabbit some years later in the parking lot of the Brother Francis Shelter. He proudly showed me the new cell phone his sister had just bought for him. He gave me the numerical password and asked me to add up the numbers. It was a quick mental calculation. "Six," I said. "That's right", said Rabbit, "a hex. It's a hex!" His sister had apparently hexed his new cell phone and he lost me in the ensuing ten-minute explanation of how this happened.

As I walked back to my car Rabbit jogged up behind me and asked if I liked Jimmy Dean sausage. "Well sure," I said. Then he proceeded to give me detailed directions to a dumpster where I could find a stash of Jimmy Dean – not only which dumpster but where in the dumpster and at what level. Not sure how to respond, I joked, "We'll keep this our secret." A crestfallen look came over Rabbit's face as he said, "No, we have to share". Then he pointed over to a pile of tattered boxes on the steps to the shelter kitchen.

I cringed at the thought that our homeless need to be supplied with victuals by a dumpster diver middleman. Shame on the big box stores and all the food they waste. And kudos to the kind-hearted soul who goes by the name of Rabbit.

EPILOGUE II

On the day before Easter 2022, I stopped at Brother Francis Shelter to drop off some canned goods. And I inquired about Rabbit. Of course, they knew him, and told me he had been "housed". Yes, Rabbit has his own small apartment in Mountain View. Good for Rabbit and God Bless him.

CHAPTER 47

THE MONGOLIANS FOUR

It was the highest level official delegation from Mongolia to ever visit Alaska. For that matter, it was probably the first and only delegation from Mongolia to come to Alaska. Tserendembereliin Baasanjav was the deputy mayor of Ulaanbaatar, Mongolia's capital and largest city. Doobatyn Sengee was vice president of the Mongol Petroleum Company (MGT). Khurelbaatar Sandagiin was technical director of Mongolian Airlines (MIAT) and Dagvyn Batmunkh was president of Mongolimpex Corporation. Mongolia's movers and shakers.

It was the fall of 1991- only a couple of years since Mongolia emerged from the long, oppressive shadow of Soviet communist oppression and two years since the Dalai Lama was awarded the Nobel Peace Prize. Mongolia and Tibet share a bond, as they both adhere to the religion of Tibetan Buddhism. So it was no surprise that I got word of the delegation's upcoming visit from Denise Lassaw–Paljor, head of the Alaska-Tibet Committee.

Denise was a passionate advocate for Tibet, whose people and religion were being brutally persecuted by China. It was Denise who opened my eyes to this oppression when I naively wanted to visit "Shangri La" and contacted her for information. Her late husband Paljor was a Tibetan, as well as a scholar fluent in Thai, who took a construction job upon his arrival in Anchorage. He was tragically killed in an accident at the Port of Anchorage. Denise deeply missed him and it seemed his memory inspired her in her endeavors. She'd already met with the Dalai Lama.

It was also no surprise that she located the only known Mongolian in Alaska – an unemployed carpenter named Tschon Ombadykow in Fairbanks. He's on his way down, she told me, and since Denise lived in Anchor Point it looked like Tschon would be staying at our place in south Anchorage.

In 1978 His Holiness the Dalai Lama visited the small town of Howell in Monmouth County, southern New Jersey. Howell was home to one of the highest concentrations of Mongolians in America. These were Khalmyk Mongols, whose ancestors centuries ago had migrated west from what is now known as Outer Mongolia and eventually settled the northwestern shores of the Caspian Sea. This area, still predominately Buddhist, is now the Republic of Khalmykia – a part of the Russian Federation. (The only other Buddhist republic in Russia is Buryatia – bordering Lake Baikal and home to the Buryat Mongols).

Back then in Howell, I am told, a small boy named Eddie Ombadykow, age seven, broke free of parental restraint and ran up to meet the Dalai Lama and his entourage. Little Eddie spoke Mongolian and English but, to everyone's surprise, proceeded to converse with the Dalai Lama in a central Tibetan dialect. His Holiness immediately recognized him as the incarnation of the Dilowa Khutukhtu – a high-ranking Mongolian lama. With permission from the U.S. State Department he was taken to India at the tender age of seven for the training befitting such a high-level incarnation – all under the tutelage of the Dalai Lama. Young Eddie eventually became Abbot of the Mungood Monastery and traveled to Mongolia with the Dalai Lama. At present, he is revered as a Buddhist Saint and is the head lama of Khalmykia. Known as Telo Rinpoche, he lives in Colorado.

A car pulled into our driveway on a dark, cold fall night - a Ford Mustang without snow tires. A Mongolian with long, dark hair down to his shoulders got out. It was Tschon Ombadykow, Eddie's older brother.

Tschon had his own interesting resume. Born in Europe and brought up in Howell, NJ and a stint as a chef in a Chinese restaurant in Virginia Beach and as a manager for singer Bonnie Rait, among other interludes too numerous to mention. It became quickly apparent I was in the presence of a quietly self–confident jack-of-all-trades comfortable with the current socio-economic challenges of America and, at the same time, fully understanding and respectful of the ethnic and religious heritage of his Khalmyk origin. Every minute of conversation with Tschon was a pleasure. And Tschon brought along a very special gift for the head of the Mongolian delegation.

The Mongolian delegation's visit was sponsored by the State of Alaska Department of Commerce and Economic Development. Tschon, Denise and I had no role or invitation and no idea what their schedule might be. And, at least initially, the State had no idea we were planning a parallel welcome. Then, days before their arrival, there had been a minor shake-up in the Hickel Administration. Bill Noll, the Deputy Commerce Commissioner for International Trade and point man for the Mongolians' visit, was sent packing. A vacuum opened up and the State, surprisingly, dropped the ball. Prepared, we jumped in and took over.

Airports were friendlier places back in '91, so Tschon, Denise and I wandered over to the gate to await the Mongolians. It took a while to find the State's welcoming delegation, even though the terminal was not crowded. We finally founder her. That's right. They sent the office girl.

The term "office girl" does not do justice to Donna Logan, whose title was "Trade Specialist". She was one of those state workers who not only did her job well but finished other people's jobs, put out fires, changed course in mid-stream and improvised when she had to. Basically, she gave it her all to get the job done and did so cheerfully. I was shocked to learn that Commerce Commissioner Glenn Olds, who had just returned from an out-of-state trip, was "too tired" to come to meet the Mongolian delegation. And that Donna's small car could not possibly have accommodated four men and their luggage. Fortunately, I had driven my Plymouth Voyager, which was quite spacious, so our guests did not have to cab it. Donna was very happy to see us.

When one meets with the Dalai Lama or other high-level Tibetan lamas or officials there is usually a mutual exchange of katas, which are white ceremonial silk scarves. They are placed over the person's neck or onto the palms of their outstretched hands. The Mongolian version of Tibetan Buddhism has a similar tradition, only the scarves are blue and called khadags.

Tschon's younger brother – incarnate lama and monastery Abbot in India – blessed a khadag and sent it to his family in Howell, New Jersey, who forwarded it to Tschon in Fairbanks, who brought it to Anchorage in his Ford Mustang (sans snow tires). He presented it to the delegation upon their arrival. Although nominally communist, they still had an understanding and respect for their religion and culture. They were surprised, touched and honored to receive it and learn Tschon's story. We split them between my car and Donna's and got them to their downtown hotel.

We filled in the gaps (they were several and lengthy) between scheduled meetings with government officials and business leaders. Another thing the State overlooked was the need for a translator. The members of the delegation were Khalkh Mongols and Tschon was a Khalmyk. Fortunately, we linguistically lucked out. Khalkh and Khalmyk were similar enough and Tschon was shanghaied into the role. He chuckled one night as he told me how strange and ironic it was to have been a promoter of the Recall Ball (the movement to recall Governor Wally Hickel) in Fairbanks and then, two weeks later, translating before the same governor in Anchorage.

Tschon wanted to put his culinary skills as a former chef to use and prepare a home-cooked banquet for the delegation. He made up a long list of ingredients and I took him to Carrs and then turned him loose in our kitchen. He came through with a tasty feast – an adhoc combination of Chinese and Mongolian cuisine. The entire delegation was over for the evening for their first visit to an American home. We ate, toasted, talked and shared small gifts. It was relaxed and memorable. Friendships sprouted that night.

On Saturday morning Mr. Dagvyn Batmunkh had a plane to catch before the others, leaving for Seoul, South Korea. I showed up at the quaint Anchorage Hotel, just up from the Hilton, to pick him up. He was in the process of checking out when they handed him his room bill. He balked, surprised.

"Wait a minute," I said, "he is a member of an official delegation from Mongolia invited by the State of Alaska. This should have been taken care of."

"Who are you?" the desk clerk asked me. I had no good answer.

Mr. Batmunkh, if I recall correctly, had prior diplomatic experience. He certainly had the manners and sensitivity not to want to skip out on an unpaid hotel bill and leave the country. So, I asked to borrow their phone and rang up Alaska Governor Wally Hickel in Juneau. Ever try to call a governor on a Saturday? Futile, to say the least. So I tried Bill Noll, the official forced out in the shake-up, and reached him at home. He didn't speak for the State anymore, at least not officially, but maybe he could help.

Bill Noll listened patiently to the problem and then laughed – the kind of laugh that says an awful lot. He said he'd take care of things and within minutes he did. A good man, I remember thinking. The hotel bill was canceled and Mr. Batmunkh was wished a pleasant journey to South Korea.

No sooner had we gotten to the door when a young man appeared and introduced himself. And he was from – you guessed it – the State of Alaska Department of Commerce and Economic Development. Could he accompany us to the airport, he asked me. What a bizarre question, I remember thinking. But after the last few days it needed no further analysis. "Sure," I said, "hop in." We got Mr. Batmunkh to his plane and the others left Alaska uneventfully.

EPILOGUE

I finally got to Mongolia some two years later. Mr. Baasanjav was now the mayor of Ulaanbaatar and Mr. Khurelbaatar was president of MIAT Mongolian Airlines. They took me to dinner at what was probably the ritziest restaurant in Mongolia at the time. It was nestled halfway up a forested hillside overlooking the sprawling city of Ulaanbaatar. Some 400 years earlier a Mongolian khan had the foresight to declare this area a forest preserve, and it remains such today. I remember apologizing for my casual attire at such a nice place – I hadn't known we'd be coming here directly for dinner and they were both attired in their workday suit and tie. They brushed off my concern by saying we weren't here to negotiate the purchase of a Boeing jet for MIAT, just old friends getting together. I thought back to our time in Anchorage and realized they were right.

When it was time to leave Mongolia Mr. Khurelbaatar drove me to Buyant Ukhaa Airport. Now, years later and working in Nome, I've become a little spoiled with the MVP Gold Status I achieved with Alaska Airlines - free upgrades to First Class, free drinks, being catered to by the flight attendants. But MVP Gold pales in comparison to the VIP status I got when I departed Mongolia that day.

I was due to fly Air China, a mainland China carrier, to Beijing. We drove to a private parking spot and walked into Mr. Khurelbaatar's spacious office. The walls were of dark wood paneling and decorated by the requisite portrait of Chinghiss Khan and various Mongolian pastoral scenes. In a word, decorum befitting the office of the president of the national airline. A decanter of whiskey and two glasses sat on the table.

Mr. Khurelbaatar picked up the phone and spoke in Mongolian. Minutes later a young woman arrived with two black coffees and set them down before us. As instructed, I gave her my luggage, plane ticket and passport. Mr. Khurelbaatar poured whiskey from the decanter. We drank and we talked.

Mongolian is a difficult language – unrelated to neighboring Russian or Chinese. I was able to master about a half-dozen words. But I could speak conversational Russian, so Mr. Khurelbaatar and I conversed in a Clockwork–Orangish amalgam of Russian and English that was unique to the two of us. It worked.

The young woman returned with my boarding pass, luggage receipt and passport – already stamped. I could get used to this. Conversation continued between sips of black coffee and whiskey until I looked at my watch and realized the flight was due to leave in five minutes - not board, but leave.

No problem, my calm friend assured me. They are waiting for you. He escorted me out of his office and we walked onto the tarmac to the base of a stairway that led up into the cabin of the Air China jet. We shook hands and I boarded. No sooner had I sat down and buckled my seatbelt than the engines revved as we taxied out to the active runway and took off for Beijing.

EPILOGUE II: FROM VIP TO NOBODY

I arrived in Beijing as a nobody. "Emperor" Deng Xiao-Ping had only recently opened Pandora's capitalist and economic box and I was about to be sucked into it. I simply needed a hotel room for the night before I flew off to Japan.

I stopped at a Traveler's Assistance desk inside the airport lobby where they spoke some English and inquired about getting a hotel room nearby for the night. A young man spoke rapidly to his colleague and then literally hopped across the desk and told me to follow him. Across the lobby, out the door, onto the street and into the back seat of a private car driven by someone he seemed to know. Something just didn't seem quite right. We drove for almost an hour to the outskirts of Beijing.

I was getting a little concerned, as they were not forthcoming about our destination and spoke poor English. Finally, we pulled up in front of a nice 3-star hotel. Crossing the lobby, we bypassed the reception desk and went straight to a room on one of the upper floors. He asked me if I liked it. I liked it. I liked it very very much. I loved that room. I … time to follow my friend again. To another floor and down a long dark hallway to a room. He knocked, then let himself in. A guy wearing only boxer shorts and a white T-shirt was sitting at a makeshift desk eating noodles from a Styrofoam container. I was told to pay him for the room. It was a good price and they didn't even hit me up for gas money. I got my key and was good to go. I looked over my shoulder a few times and no one was following me. After securing my room I took off to find some Tsingtaos. I needed a couple beers. It had been a long and interesting day and I was already missing Mongolia.

Future Ulaanbaatar mayor (center) and fellow delegation officials opening gifts at our home in Anchorage, Alaska Fall 1991

Vodka break with some nomads we met on the Mongolian steppe.
MIAT Mongolian Airlines President Khurelbaatar on the far left.
September 1993

Dinner with S. Khurelbaatar, the President of Mongolian Airlines
(center) and T. Baasanjav, the mayor of Ulaanbaatar, Mongolia's capital
and largest city (right). Ulaanbaatar, Mongolia September 1993

CHAPTER 48

NANAO SAKAKI

The hippie movement was building to a crescendo during my high school years (1966-70), reaching to within 25 miles of our secluded "Leave It To Beaver/Ozzie and Harriet" suburban New Jersey town (100% white, except for Mrs. Duncan, the typing teacher. She taught at the high school but must have lived elsewhere). Greenwich Village may have been only 25 miles away, but those were long miles. I only remember one hippie in our high school: Larry Hopp. Larry had long hair and he'd been to the Village. That's all it took.

The epochal Woodstock in 1969 was way beyond where I was at the time, but I did make it to Watkins Glen in 1973. With 600,000 others I saw the Grateful Dead (yes, Jerry Garcia), the Band and the Allman Brothers (well, at least Greg – Dwayne was killed in a motorcycle accident two years earlier).

Only years later, after discovering Jack Kerouac, did I realize the hippies owed a great debt to the beatniks who paved their way: Jack Kerouac and his friends Allen Ginsberg, William Burroughs, Neal Cassady and Gary Snyder – and their works are cultural classics.

Kerouac lived his life to the fullest and then pushed the boundary farther. He paid the price, though, mostly with alcohol. Sitting in his mother's Florida apartment in his later years with a can of tuna fish and his daily allotted shot of whiskey his esophageal varices exploded in a bloody mess. And Jack left us. I think it was mountain climber Willie Unsoeld who said, "Death is not too high a price to pay for a life well-lived". Unsoeld, who died in an avalanche on Mt. Ranier, called that one right.

And it was years later still that I found out the beatniks had a Japanese compatriot - Nanao Sakaki. Nanao seemed to be more a Japanese Walt Whitman than a beatnik, but definitions are fluid. Certainly, he is the most famous Japanese poet outside Japan (I have yet to meet a Japanese who has even heard of him).

Nanao wandered the globe, spending a lot of time in the American West. He accepted hospitality when he found it. And he wrote poems. Most were written in Japanese and later translated back into English.

Nanao's signature poem, and the title of his book, is *Break the Mirror*. Nanao is an ageless child, filled with the wonder and awe of life, in a man's aging body. It was a body he could not see, or be reminded of, until he looked in a mirror:

> "In the morning
> After taking cold shower
> ⁃ What a mistake ⁃
> I look at the mirror."

Nanao's advice closes the poem:

> "To stay young,
> To save the world,
> Break the mirror."

Gary Snyder concludes his forward to *Break the Mirror* as he describes Nanao: …

> "he has bony knees, dark tanned face, odd toes, a fine chanting voice, a huge capacity for spirits, a taste for top-quality green tea, and four beautiful children. His work or play in the world is to pull out nails, free seized nuts, break loose the rusted, open up the shutters. You can put these poems in your shoes and walk a thousand miles".

It was Denise from the Alaska-Tibet Committee (the same Denise who told me the Mongolians were coming) who called to alert me that

Nanao was in Anchorage staying with some friends. Denise read some of his poems to me over the phone. I drove over one evening to meet him.

I've written a few haikus, but Nanao deserves a "double", so I dedicate my first "double haiku" to Nanao:

Drinking white wine
with Nanao Sakaki in Anchorage,
I took no notes of our conversation.
Didn't need to.
Nanao handed me
the Swiss Army knife
that Allen Ginsberg gave him.
I held it for a minute, then gave it back to Nanao.
It was enough.

In a July 2004 e-mail Gary Snyder promised to take my greetings to Nanao when he went to Japan later that year. Nanao lives in a small hut on the flank of Mt. Fuji.

Bill Cox and Japanese beat poet Nanao Sakaki in Anchorage, Alaska
August 2000

CHAPTER 49

NARA

I wasn't there when she slipped on the ice half a world away. I couldn't hear her cry out when the large bone in her forearm (the radius) snapped in two like a dried twig. But news of the accident somehow reached Nurse Esther Petrie, Providence Hospital's "Angel of Mercy", who's been sending help and tons of medical supplies all over the world for years going on decades. And Esther tipped off the U.S. National Park Service (NPS) that I might be potentially helpful. Thank you, Esther! I was soon happy to have another focused mission on my hands.

It seemed that the Park Service, with support from USAID, was involved in a joint venture with Hovsgol National Park in Mongolia. Hovsgol Lake, Mongolia's largest freshwater lake, was pristine and pure and surrounded by a recently created national park.

The NPS was working with their Mongolian counterparts on the administrative, management and financial aspects of sustaining a national park. Non-sexy issues. Then there was also access, poaching, violence, arson – sexy issues where they needed some outside help. NPS was fortunate that an incorruptible dynamo named Tumersukh was superintendent of the park.

When the Japanese wanted to set up a polluting tannery on the shore of Lake Hovsgol Tumersukh gave the project the axe, even though it had already been approved in Ulaanbaatar, Mongolia's capital. The tannery didn't happen, but there was another issue that did happen and needed to be attended to: Tumersukh's wife, Nara, slipped on the ice in the Mongolian winter and fractured her radius. Nara had been working with NPS in setting up the Park's Visitor Center in Hatgal – the small, haphazard log cabin village that was the gateway to the vast Hovsgol National Park.

Tumersukh took his wife to the hospital in the larger town of Moron – about three hours away by jeep. They splinted the fracture, but never set it, and it did not heal properly.

Tumersukh, Nara and their family could not survive on their meager Mongolian Park Service salaries alone. But by milking their small herd of cows twice a day during the summer months and chopping piles of firewood, they got by in the harsh and beautiful land. Winter must have been tough. But with Nara's fracture not healing it was becoming increasingly difficult for her to perform the daily chores her family depended upon for their survival.

Ulaanbaatar, Mongolia's capital and largest city, did not seem prepared at the time to deal with a malunion/nonunion mid-shaft radial fracture. One local consultant even recommended exercise. It clearly needed surgery, so it was either Singapore or America, and America, all things considered, was the better choice.

I walked into the National Park Service office on Tudor Road and the New Seward Highway - the building coated with the "fuzzy brown rust" look. And I sat down with NPS official Clay Alderson and his colleague, Kevin Apgar. Ennui, my ever-stalking and pervasive enemy, was bearing down upon me again. But I was now encountering opportunity after having completed my last assignment of getting a church bell, ensnared in Moscow's red tape, to a Polish Catholic village in the vast forest of southcentral Siberia.

The NPS officials I was now sitting down with were active in the collaborative project with Mongolia and wanted to bring Nara to Anchorage to have her arm fixed. They knew it would require surgery. Could I help? Of course I could. I thought for a minute and made a proposal: "I'll find an orthopedic surgeon willing to operate for free and convince Providence Alaska Medical Center to waive all operating room and inpatient fees. And I'll also find a place for Nara to stay in Anchorage while convalescing." "You guys," I said to the NPS folks, "gotta arrange and cover her transportation from Mongolia to Anchorage – and transit through Seoul, Korea." They agreed and we had a plan.

And I suddenly had a lot on my plate. I called my former colleague, Dr. Steve Tower, from the old Alaska Native Medical Center on 3rd and

Gambell. An orthopedic surgeon, Dr. Tower was now in private practice in Anchorage. He readily agreed to operate gratis, provided Providence gave it their blessing. And he took the time to send a personal appeal to the Providence CEO.

I then contacted the pleasant and helpful Kathe Boucha–Roberts, Director of International Medicine and Telehealth at Providence Alaska Medical Center. In our e-mail exchanges and telephone calls she gave me hope that Providence would write off Nara's inpatient expenses.

Ultimately, in a letter to NPS official Clay Alderson dated February 27, 2001, Gene O'Hara, the CEO of Providence Alaska Medical Center, confirmed that Providence would cover Nara's operating room expenses and 1-3 days of inpatient services. Bingo. Two out of three on my end of the deal.

There was an International Hostel I knew of just down the block from Anchorage's West High School where a lot of foreign students resided. A scenic location with a large balcony overlooking Westchester Lagoon. It was supervised by a board of directors. With Providence's "angel of mercy" nurse Esther and the NPS behind me, I petitioned board member Andrew Crow to allow Nara to stay there while she recuperated. We were informed that there needed to be an "educational" justification for her to stay at the hostel. The NPS put forth the argument that Nara, in setting up the Visitor's Center in Hatgal, Mongolia was involved in educating people about Hovsgol National Park. She could give a short talk in Anchorage. Also, since the surgery was limited to her forearm she would not be a burden to other residents. The board approved and Nara had a place to stay for $150.00 per month while she recovered.

The NPS kept their end of the bargain and Nara arrived in Anchorage. I accompanied her to Providence Hospital and sat with her until she was wheeled into the operating room. Dr. Tower performed an osteotomy at the fracture site, realigned the fracture fragments and transfixed them securely and permanently in place with a metallic plate anchored by multiple threaded screws. Another Nara from Mongolia just happened to be staying at the Hostel, which made for great company and emotional support. Nara recovered well and, sooner than anticipated, received Dr. Tower's blessing to return to Mongolia.

EPILOGUE: A FOLLOW-UP VISIT TO MONGOLIA TO CHECK ON NARA

In August 2004 my wife Amy and I made the long journey to Hatgal, Mongolia to visit with Nara and Tumersukh. Hatgal was a log-cabin village right out of the old TV Series: "Gunsmoke". The surrounding scenery was simply stunning. Low green hills partly covered with forests of dark, green larch. Jeeps and horses came to the small airport to pick up incoming passengers. The only toilet was a weathered, wooden double-latrine maybe some thirty meters from the terminal. We spent nine days at the two-story log-cabin home of Nara and Tumersukh and their four children.

Family chores began at dawn and resumed at dusk. Milking the cows twice a day was critical. The "white diet" of milk-derived products sustained rural Mongolians during the summer months. We were served fresh Mongolian yogurt each morning and it was delicious. My rice-eating Taiwanese wife liked it so much she scarfed down five bowls one morning – and later paid the price: several urgent and extended trips to one of the two wooden latrines at the corners of Nara's property. A day later Amy was good to go. And we made sure to stop at the only store in town once a day and leave a bag of groceries on Nara's kitchen table.

Nara and Tumersukh's kids spent virtually all their waking hours outdoors. When not doing chores they were riding old bicycles about and shooting hoops through an old rusted basketball net set up on the property. Being two meters tall, I couldn't help but challenge them.

The number one requirement for life-as-we-know–it is water. Oxygen is nice too, if you're not an anaerobe. There was plenty of oxygen in the pure, fresh air that filled and surrounded Hatgal. And at least a half-kilometer away was a virtually endless supply of some of the purest water on the planet: the mouth of the Egiin River.

The Egiin River, emptying Hovsgol Lake, was quite large. Empty barrels on wooden carts pulled by horses regularly made their way to the river to be filled. We drove there in Tumersukh's jeep.

Landlocked Mongolians and island-bound Taiwanese seemed to have one thing in common (other than Asian facial features): an inability to swim and a fear of the water. Using liter-sized plastic scoops at the river's edge, it was taking folks forever to fill their barrels. Having worn my bathing suit I grabbed our barrel, raised it over my head, and walked out into the cold water until it was chest-deep. I filled the barrel with the even purer water just off the mid-channel flow. When I got back toward shore our driver was willing to get wet up to mid-calf and help drag the heavy filled barrel onto dry ground.

Two other Mongolian families out to haul water were standing by in amazement. So I grabbed their barrels and filled them the same way. Water hauled ashore, I filled one of their liter-sized scoops and chased after their little kids – threatening to douse them. They laughed and ran off. I was careful not to catch them. Their parents stood there, beaming.

Later that evening Amy and I joined Nara and her family for the evening milking. It was a chore that could not be skipped. After a quick lesson I was sitting on a small wooden stool milking my first cow. Turns out it's all in the thumbs. Squirt…squirt…squirt… I had filled the pail about an inch, but after ten minutes my thumbs became numb. And then the sides of my forearms started throbbing. I was finished.

I could simply not imagine milking a cow with an ununited fracture of my radius – the loose ends of the bone in my forearm scraping together with every squirt. A heartfelt thanks to all of you who helped get this situation remedied for Nara.

Bill Cox blending in with the locals in Nara's backyard, Hatgal, Mongolia. August 2004

Bill Cox exchanging snuff boxes with Mongolian nomad, Hovsgol
National Park, Mongolia. August 2004

Tumersukh and Nara sharing Mongolian tea, Hovsgol National Park,
Mongolia. August 2004

Nara milking her cow. Hatgal, Mongolia August 2004

CHAPTER 50

ANCELMO VALENCIA TORI, CARLOS CASTANEDA AND TOM BROWN, JR.

Ask a student of literature who was the most reclusive author in America in the 20th century and you'll almost certainly hear: J.D. Salinger. Wrong answer, but I wouldn't take away any points from them. It's just become standard fare. The correct answer: Carlos Castaneda. Castaneda was not only reclusive, but controversial.

There is no doubt that J.D. Salinger was born and that he wrote the widely acclaimed novel: *The Catcher in the Rye.* How intertwined he was with the fictional character Holden Caulfield will be the subject of papers and theses till the 1-K asteroid makes its inevitable hit. There are uncontested and published photos of J. D. Salinger, though not many, and he died a mortal death.

Castaneda is a different animal. Born in Brazil or born in Peru? His early background is mostly obscure, though he unquestionably received a B.A. in anthropology in 1962. In 1968 his best-selling book, *The Teachings of Don Juan: A Yaqui Way of Knowledge*, exploded onto the national scene. A year before Woodstock, a book about a Yaqui Indian sorcerer who travels through higher planes of reality with the aid of psychedelic drugs was ripe for a disillusioned young generation of Americans looking for alternatives to the Establishment. Perfect timing? Coincidence?

His first three books were written in the first person as the journal logs of an apprentice (Castaneda) to the Yaqui Indian sorcerer Don Juan Matus. His third book, *Journey to Ixtlan*, was presented as his doctoral dissertation and earned him a Ph.D in 1973. Academic legitimacy bestowed, he was praised by anthropologists and remained wildly popular with the public. In all, his 12 books sold some 8 million copies in 17 languages. But no one (besides Castaneda) had seen, or been able to verify, the existence of Don Juan.

Cracks began to appear after some six years of academic acclaim. Native American critics stepped up to the plate, albeit timidly. The lack of any Yaqui vocabulary or Yaqui terms for his experiences was pointed out. But nothing so devastating as the work of Richard DeMille, who published *Castaneda's Journey: The Power And The Allegory* in 1976.

DeMille discovered published sources for just about everything Castaneda wrote. And he painstakingly laid out the dated journal entries that comprised his books and cross-referenced them with Castaneda's stack requests from the University of California libraries. He showed Castaneda to be in two places at once. Astral projection as taught by Don Juan? Doubt it. When he was supposed to be sitting in a hut in the Mexican Sonoran desert sharing a peyote ceremony with Don Juan he was… well…sitting in the library reading someone else's description of their experience with the peyote ceremony.

An interview with "Time Magazine" described Carlos Castaneda as "an enigma wrapped in a mystery." He disappeared from public view afterward. He is reported to have died in April 1998 and that after cremation his ashes were sent to Mexico. An obituary didn't appear until two months later in the "Los Angeles Times." And immediately the doubts began about whether he really lived at all. The only photo anyone could come up with was one of Carlos with his hand over his face. And so it goes. . .

ANCELMO VALENCIA TORI

In the late 1980s the International Indian Treaty Council (IITC) sponsored a conference of indigenous peoples from the Western Hemisphere in Palmer, Alaska.

The Seminoles from Florida drove up. The Sioux were in attendance. The Miskito Indians from Nicaragua were there. A Mayan priest from Guatemala who I later drove to the airport. An unforgettable California Indian woman named Mary Baker Pilgrim who explained to me, on the long ride afterward back to the airport, that in her people's worldview there was no difference between animate and inanimate. Everything had a spirit. Even the rocks, she explained, will absorb the sun's warmth and radiate it back later when needed. And Ancelmo Valencia Tori, the Chief, Medicine Man and Spiritual Leader of the Yaqui Indian Nation, was there.

Ancelmo was a small man with a bronzed and wizened face. Maybe in his early 80s. And he had this otherworldly look about him. Before he spoke he stated that he was a Medicine Man and politely asked that his picture not be taken. And left it at that.

Ancelmo's Yaqui-Irish goddaughter, one of the conference's top organizers, is a friend of mine. Some two or three years after the conference I was Arizona-bound for a medical meeting. I asked her if she could arrange a meeting for me with her godfather down there on the Yaqui reservation. And she did.

I arrived at the Yaqui capital in the remote desert wildlands of southern Arizona. It would be more properly termed an "administrative center." Indian nations didn't have capitals in the western sense. And Tombstone was a metropolis compared to this sand-blasted array of single–storied, strung-together functional buildings. Yes, bingo and gambling were available and secured.

Floyd Westerman, a Sioux actor and singer who also attended the Palmer gathering, liked to joke about how the Indians stole bingo from the Catholics. He is probably best known for playing the role of the old Sioux chief next to Kevin Costner in "Dances with Wolves." I met him at a pot-luck dinner at an Anchorage home. Good for them, I remember thinking, before Floyd launched into a song in fluent Sioux. But they needed to steal more than bingo – and not just from the Catholics - to get back even a minuscule portion of what was wrongfully taken from them. But I wasn't in the Arizona desert for bingo or to advocate for reparations. I was there for the final word on Castaneda.

Ancelmo reminisced briefly about the old days and still remembered fighting the Apaches. He described how fierce they were. Wow, I thought at the time, this guy is the real thing. And then I brought up Carlos Castaneda and sat in rapt attention. The U.S. Supreme Court be damned, the 85-year old Chief, Medicine Man and Spiritual Leader of the Yaqui Indian Nation (USA and Mexico) sitting before me was about to deliver the final verdict on Carlos Castaneda.

"I never met Carlos Castaneda," Ancelmo told me, "but some of his students dropped by once. I did read his first book." Pure fiction, he said of the book, "it was pure fiction." Castaneda's Don Juan was a Yaqui Indian sorcerer, but Ancelmo informed me, "We don't have sorcerers in our Yaqui culture or religion. If we did, I would know about them. I'm the Chief, Medicine Man and Spiritual Leader." 'Nuff said, I remember thinking.

Ancelmo did volunteer that he was indebted to "fictional" author Carlos Castaneda because his sensational books popularized the Yaqui Indians at the time they were definitively consolidating their binational land claims. So it was helpful.

Thanks, Carlos, whoever you were, or are. Time to move on.

AND TOM BROWN, JR.

A story exploded in a 1978 "Reader's Digest" article about a seven-year-old boy named Tom Brown, Jr. who, twenty years earlier, with his friend Rick, began a ten-year "apprenticeship" with an 83-year old Lipan Apache Indian scout named "Stalking Wolf" in the vast Pine Barrens of southern New Jersey. They were both from the town of Toms River, perched on the edge of the Barrens.

Tom had just started his own Survival School and May 1989 found me sitting on a wooden bench in a barn in rural Asbury, N.J. The haystack in the loft behind me was my sleeping quarters for the week. It was Tom's Tracker School Standard Course. Right out of "Reader's Digest" Tom, age 38, walked into the room. Articulate, charismatic and convincing, he "wowed" everyone in that barn. The one sentence I always remembered, right out of Tom's mouth, was "No, I have not read Carlos Castaneda."

I've read about a half-dozen of Tom's books and taken five of his week-long courses. I knelt in the dirt next to Tom as he pointed out the track made by the front left paw of a mouse in the forest debris (had to take his word on that one). Swam down a river with him. Talked with him. Did a sweat lodge with him. His skills and experience seemed genuine, yet inscrutable. But I could never shake the fact that there has never been any independent verification of Stalking Wolf or Tom's boyhood friend, Rick. It burrowed under my skin like a chigger…and festered. Still, I took more of his courses

This was the city of Toms River in southern New Jersey from 1958 – 1968, for crying out loud. Cameras were everywhere: Kodak Instamatics, Polaroids… I know, I was one year younger than Tom and living in northern New Jersey during that time. And we had a great-aunt we used to visit in Toms River. Tom's parents and Rick's parents would have piles of old black-and-whites developed at the local pharmacy. Stalking Wolf reportedly healed people, using native techniques, throughout the Pine Barrens. No one seems to recall. What was Rick's last name? No one knows. Tom's younger brother Jim, later a Ph.D microbiologist for the Department of Health of the State of New Jersey, remains mum and coy.

Am I dealing with another Castaneda in Tom Brown, Jr.? No, no way. Tom is very real. Is "Stalking Wolf" a Don Juan Matus? My ongoing challenge. So far, everything seems to support Tom. I need to, and intend to, remain securely rooted in a healthy, rational skepticism, but I secretly hope, in my heart, that Tom and Stalking Wolf will be fully vindicated.

Tom Brown, Jr. at his Tracker School in Asbury, NJ May 1989

CHAPTER 51
CHENA HOT SPRINGS AT MINUS 72°F

Uncle Dave and Brucie flew to Anchorage from the Midwest for two weeks of winter adventure here in the Last Frontier. I was determined not to disappoint them and I had a little help. It was early February 1993 and the biggest cold snap in maybe a decade (I'd been waiting for it since my arrival in Alaska in 1984) was about to descend upon Interior Alaska, courtesy of a Siberian high-pressure system.

I first met Dave in the weight room at Wadsworth Hall, Michigan Technological University in Michigan's Upper Peninsula in the early 1970s. At the time it was the second-largest all-male dormitory in the world behind one in Moscow, USSR. Dave was a couple years behind me. Hailing from the north side of Iron Mountain, Michigan, he was obviously Italian. We were pumping iron and the "Italian Stallion" continuously out-bench-pressed me, maybe by twenty to forty pounds or more. We didn't shoot 'roids, but we enjoyed our beers. He later snared himself a lovely wife named Lianne and had some kids. And as I was also having kids, I adopted them as Uncle Dave and Aunt Lianne.

Bruce was a friend of Uncle Dave's who I met at the in-laws' in Rochester, Michigan back in the 70s. Bruce and his wife Mary (who later tragically died from ovarian cancer) were planning to build their own house. Bruce had that innocent little boy "Dudley Moore" look about him, so I adopted him on-the-spot as a "nephew", christened him Brucie, took him under my wing, but never said anything to anybody. He did really well for himself over the years and I was proud. If he reads my book (and he better because he's getting an autographed copy) he will finally learn of this magnanimous gesture on my part.

Soon after their arrival in Anchorage we had a hearty, non-heart healthy breakfast at Denny's on Benson and A Street before hopping into my 1987 Isuzu Trooper for the long and challenging ride north. The temperature was rapidly dropping. First stop was Bill Davidson's Susitna Dog Tours at mile 91 & 1/4 on the Parks Highway.

I'd gone on an overnight dog-mushing trip with Bill several years earlier. After a few hours of training he gave me my own dog team. I remember we camped tentless alongside the frozen Susitna River. I enjoyed every minute of our trip, even when I had to stop and disentangle the dog team from ropes and harnesses while Bill was out of sight ahead of me. Bill and I talked over the small fire in the vast snow-covered and frozen wilderness landscape.

Bill did hazmat clean-up work for the EPA during the summer months, which required hours in protective suits and masks. He was OK with that, but preferred to be outdoors with his dog teams in the winter. "No mosquitos then," he said. He called that one right.

I frost-nipped my toes on that trip with Bill and blame it on not drinking enough water. "Frost-nip" is not an agreed-upon or defined medical term, but it was generally accepted as just shy of frostbite. After a month of numb toes I decided to see the guy at the top, Dr. William J. Mills, Sr. – an internationally acclaimed orthopedic surgeon and frostbite specialist. He had an office in Anchorage and I'd been driving his little granddaughter Jennifer, who is now a nurse, to school for years. Dr. Mills had the warmest hands. To make a long story a bit shorter, he cured me. When I last saw him at a medical meeting several years ago he was almost ninety and following up on the sequelae of frostbite injuries among Korean War veterans from almost sixty years ago.

Musher Bill Davidson introduced Uncle Dave and Brucie to his dogs and harnessed up two teams. He allowed me to lead one because of my past "experience". Poor Uncle Dave drew the short straw and got me. I had a little fun with him. We all went out on a short loop – the dogs knew where to go. Uncle Dave was hunkered down in a sled behind the dogs and I was standing in the back of a second sled attached to the back of his. Inexplicably, his sled suddenly flipped ninety degrees to the right and he disappeared under a heavy spray of kicked-up snow for several dozen yards as the dogs kept going full-speed. Then it suddenly righted. Fortunately, I didn't have to stop, secure the dog team and go perform

CPR on Uncle Dave for massive snow aspiration. It would have been difficult, as I was laughing too hard. Afterwards, we all warmed up and talked in Bill and Rhodi's cozy cabin. Brucie remembers her applesauce cake. We couldn't linger long in the friendly warmth of that Alaska cabin – we had a long drive ahead of us to Fairbanks.

It was at least minus 20°F, getting dark and the wind was picking up. We were driving through some very remote countryside. Hours later, exhausted from concentrating on the road, we pulled into Skinny Dick's Halfway Inn - an Alaska roadhouse located halfway between Nenana and Fairbanks. We still had a bit of a drive to Fairbanks. I really wanted a beer at that crazy place but, being the driver, had to settle for some stale black coffee. Amazingly, we hit the jackpot: Skinny Dick himself was behind the counter!

Anchorage's legendary Mr. Whitekeys once called Skinny Dick a legend. Since Mr. Whitekeys, a phenomenal piano player who invented the Spam daiquiri, was an icon in his own right, that made Skinny Dick a "double legend." According to one story, Skinny Dick was stopped by Alaska State troopers somewhere between Anchorage and Fairbanks on suspicion of drunken driving. As part of the field sobriety tests, the troopers ordered Skinny Dick to jump up and down on one foot. "Hell," replied Skinny, "I can't even do that when I'm sober."

The walls in Skinny's Halfway Inn were covered with framed autographed photos. Mostly from women. They were all addressed to "Skinny Dick" and the content was mostly double entendre.

Skinny Dick had just gotten out of the "pokey", he informed us. Can't remember for sure, but it must have been a parole violation or another run-in with the law. He seemed nonchalant about it – apparently Skinny doesn't let stuff like that bother him. We still had a ways to go in the increasingly extreme cold, so we bid Skinny Dick a fond farewell and took off for Fairbanks.

Exhausted, we checked in at the Fairbanks Hotel downtown. It was quite the dive, but that's what you get for $15.00 a night. A drunken and toothless local hanging out in the lobby christened me "Too Tall". I was OK with that and shook his hand. Of course, my two friends seized upon my new nickname. I was given the key to a small room on the 4th floor. Uncle Dave and Brucie got a room with a king-sized bed on the second floor, but the front desk could not come up with a set of keys. They were assured, though, that the room was unlocked. It did not inspire confidence.

My friends were less than pleased with their accommodation for the night. I ribbed them for their fastidiousness and explained that this was not 4-star. "Just because there are big clumps of black hair in the sink and dried bloodstains on the bed's headboard," I explained, "doesn't mean there is anything to complain about. This is, after all, downtown Fairbanks and we mustn't behave like stuffy Midwesterners." Brucie recalled how they barricaded the door with a chair and whatever else they could pile up against it. And how they slept on top of the bedspread, each with one eye open, lest someone return for the stash of coke, or whatever, hidden under the bed or behind a loose wallboard. And Uncle Dave later opined how much he had looked forward to a hot shower in the morning – after a long day of driving, an afternoon of dog-mushing and a fitful night in a Fairbanks flophouse. The tap provided only cold water.

I had a different challenge up on the 4th floor that night. When we pulled up to the hotel it was minus 45°F and I had thought it curious that all the windows on the 4th floor were open. Well, almost all of them. But I forgot about it in my concern to get my Isuzu Trooper plugged in, knowing otherwise we'd be going nowhere the next morning. Later, when I entered my room, I realized it was the one with the window closed. The hot-water heating on the 4th floor seemed to be going full-blast, hence all the open windows. But mine was absolutely frozen shut. It must have been almost 110°F in my room and there was nothing I could do. The negative degree weather outside beckoned to me. I stripped to my underwear, laid on top of the covers, sipped every hour from my Nalgene water bottle and hoped I would not succumb to dehydration or heat exhaustion before morning.

Another hearty non-heart healthy breakfast to get us moving in Alaska's frozen interior (especially after a night at the Fairbanks Hotel). We had planned to drive the Steese Highway to Circle Hot Springs but were told the road was closed. This was probably due to conditions on one of the two high passes where heavy-duty snow removal equipment, tackling ten-foot drifts in high winds, was known to have been blown over the side. So we chose to pursue the more sedate Chena Hot Springs. After all, my friends had families and kids (and, as my daughter did not hesitate to remind me while editing this story, so did I). My Isuzu Trooper operated like a charm, so we just changed directions and headed east. We arrived late, checked into our room and then hit the hot tubs. They were most relaxing. Outside, the temperature was dropping through the minus 50s.

The next morning the outdoor thermometer read minus 65°F. First order of business was the "water toss" – something I'd waited eight years to try, but it had never gotten cold enough until now (it really only works reliably at temperatures below minus 40°F). Uncle Dave was standing there with a cup of warm water and I had my camera ready. He tossed it into the air, it made kind of a muffled "whoosh" and instantly froze into a visible white cloud of very fine ice crystals. And there it hovered, about six to ten feet above the ground, dissipating very slowly. Not a drop fell back to the ground.

The air at minus 65°F is so dry and dense that sounds carry a long distance. They say you can hear the sound of an axe against a tree a mile away (that axe isn't going to penetrate very deeply into that frozen tree). This likely explains the muffled "whoosh" I heard when that cup of warm water was suddenly converted to ice crystals. The sun was just starting to shine from below the horizon – it wouldn't come up more than a couple degrees above the horizon for a couple hours – but enough to "warm" the frozen landscape to a daytime high of minus 40°F. It was sufficient for us to set off into the nearby forest to build a snow cave.

We spent hours outdoors building a snow cave, with short forays up a nearby hill and into the frozen boreal forest, just for fun. The super-cooled air was dry and comfortable (there's something to be said for humidity being the discomforting factor). Fortunately, after hours of toil, the snow cave collapsed on Brucie and we were released from our collective vow to spend the night in it. We had been too vigorous in hollowing out the interior and there was not enough moisture inside. A pot of water should have been vigorously boiling for at least an hour, steam wafting upward, freezing and cementing our roof, but I hadn't brought my camp stove. Uncle Dave and I mobilized and were able to rescue Brucie from the collapsed mounds of snow. No serious injuries, maybe a little PTSD, but nothing that a few beers couldn't cure. We hauled him off to that warm and comfortable room at the Chena Hot Springs Resort – an establishment many stars above the Fairbanks Hotel.

We woke up the next morning and, after bottoming out overnight at minus 72°F, it was still horrendously cold. We needed to drive to

Fairbanks and then on to Anchorage. My 1987 Isuzu Trooper, fortunately, was still plugged in. It actually started, but the foam-based upholstery was frozen solid like hardwood. And no matter how hard I pushed I could not move the stick-shift that I had left in neutral. I had to let it warm up for a good fifteen minutes or so. The bottoms of the four tires, naturally flattened by the weight of the car, had frozen into place. When we started out they went "kerplunk kerplunk" until they heated up and became round again. Finally, we were on our way.

Driving along the wilderness highway from Chena Hot Springs to Fairbanks at a temperature of minus 60°F is a bit dicey no matter how well prepared you are. And we were prepared – sleeping bags and blankets, food and water, matches and fire starters. There were plenty of spruce trees to torch with siphoned gasoline from the car if we really got stuck (a tip from George, a miner in Circle). But I couldn't imagine changing a tire at that temperature.

I had cardboard covering three-quarters of the radiator. The 1987 Isuzu Trooper has a very weak heater and I had the defroster going full-blast to try to keep the windshield clear, but it kept icing over with the breath of three men. We stopped at the first place we saw and purchased a straight-edge razor to use as a scraper. With no warm air going to the floorboards we had to stuff chemical warming packs into our boots to keep our feet from freezing. Brucie, in the passenger seat, had to reach across and scrape off the thin layer of ice that continuously formed on the windshield in front of me so I could see the road. No sooner had he scraped a small porthole for me to see through than he had to start over again. The interior of the car never warmed up.

Once, we slowed down as we passed by a moose grazing along the side of the road. We marveled at its ability to survive in these temperatures, but they had been doing so for millennia. No Bunny Boots on their four hooves. Amazing creatures.

The Trooper's heater may be weak, but its durability and reliability is strong. (I'm still driving it, as I edit this, in July 2016 – and still in August 2021 as I review this story pre-publication). We made it safely past Fairbanks and detoured to Gakona. The Gakona Lodge was on our itinerary because room #5 was one of the most famous haunted places in Alaska.

The Gakona Lodge goes back to 1904 when it was Doyle's Roadhouse. Notwithstanding the site's original location valued by the Ahtna Indians of the Copper River Basin, it later became the main stop for the Orr Stage Company at the junction of the Valdez-Eagle and Valdez-Fairbanks trails. Doyle sold out in 1912 and the property passed through several owners, including a mining company. The last of them was Arne Sundt.

World War II came and went. Then in 1976 Jerry and Barbara Strang purchased the lodge from Henra Sundt. And then on that cold February day in 1993 Uncle Dave, Brucie and I pulled into the lodge looking for a warm room. We requested room #5 because it was written up in "The Ghostly Register."

Since coming to Alaska in 1984 I'd stayed alone in room #5 twice: once in the light of the northern summer and once in the dark of winter. No action. Years later my brother, nephew and daughter stayed in the same room with me on our way to McCarthy. Again nothing, although downstairs in the bar the jukebox suddenly turned itself on. Pretty lame, but we decided to attribute this to the ghost and proceeded back up to room #5 for a good night's rest. My 8-year old daughter had a scary dream, but otherwise it was pretty flat.

In the quiet bar folks were shooting darts when we arrived. Must've been a tournament. Otherwise, things were pretty dead and we had time to talk with owners Jerry and Barbara Strang. Jerry was the police chief of Watkins Glen, New York during the famous rock concert featuring the Grateful Dead, the Band and the Allman Brothers in 1973. I was there, but he didn't remember me. Probably because I mostly stayed out of trouble and was only one of 600,000 rock fans who converged on the place. It was the first, last and only time I ever scored some weed, but the occasion called for it (Gallo wine just didn't cut it). I remember the blurry-eyed dealer sitting on the hood of a car among the crowd, opening a large hinged wooden box and showing me a veritable cornucopia of drugs (all I wanted was the $6.00 bag of Colombian) while going on and on about the war in Armenia – about which I knew next to nothing and wasn't interested. In a strange twist of fate I was able to redeem my former ignorance, decades later, by bringing Professor Michael Papazian, chair of the Department of Religion and Philosophy at Berry College in Georgia, to Anchorage to speak on the Armenian Genocide. His lecture to the Alaska World Affairs Council on Oct. 17th, 2008 was: "After Nine Decades: the Enduring Legacy of the Armenian Genocide." I learned a lot from him. And for the record, I took my last toke in the spring of 1977.

I didn't mention any of this to former police chief Jerry Strang and assumed the statute of limitations had long since expired. And the only action that night in the lodge was some clown running up and down the hallway draped in a white sheet. Since it was only the three of us at the lodge, I can narrow down the list of suspects to two people.

It was a safe and uneventful drive back to Anchorage. Uncle Dave and Brucie recall some interesting last-minute urban wildlife (or rather, nightlife) viewing at the Great Alaska Bush Company #2 - a major strip joint on International Airport Road - before heading back to the relatively tame Midwest. On the way to the airport we concluded it had been a fun, interesting and fulfilling trip, and I had no doubt their "carry-on baggage" included memories of a wild and crazy two weeks in Alaska's frozen winter north – memories that would be recalled and maybe (slightly) embellished over the years, decades.

Uncle Dave and Brucie huddle in our unfinished snow cave.
Temperature minus 45 degrees F and dropping. Chena Hot Springs,
Alaska February 1993

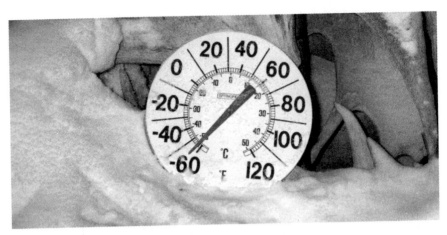

A cold morning at Chena Hot Springs Resort, northeast of Fairbanks, Alaska February 1993

At a temperature below minus 60 degrees F our wet bathing suits froze solid on the short walk from the hot tub to our motel room. Chena Hot Springs, Alaska February 1993

At a temperature of minus 65 degrees a cup of hot water tossed into
the air instantly freezes into a cloud of ice crystals
Chena Hot Springs, Alaska February 1993

CHAPTER 52

TO MCCARTHY, WHERE I MEET WITH
TONY ZAK (AUGUST 1987)

In the mid-1980s McCarthy, Alaska was still a hold-out of the Wild West. Kind of like a northern Tombstone. In August 1987 I set out for the historic and legendary town of McCarthy in my 1975 Volkswagen Rabbit.

A mostly civilized drive on the Glenn Highway takes one to the interior town of Glennallen, 189 miles northeast of Anchorage. Hang a right on the Richardson Highway and it's a short trip to the Edgerton Highway for the straight shot to Chitina. Mt. Wrangell (14,163 feet) and Mt. Blackburn (16,390 feet) welcome you, in the distance, to the vast Wrangell-St. Elias mountain range. At Chitina the fun begins.

Chitina started out as a mining supply town on the Copper River in 1908 for the Kennecott copper mines outside McCarthy. As the terminus for the Copper River and Northwestern Railway, it boomed until it went bust in 1938 when the mines closed. The most famous red salmon in the world come from the Copper River and once a year Chitina is a salmon–dipnetting mecca for Alaska residents only.

The 62-mile "road" to McCarthy begins after crossing a bridge over the Copper River. Built over an old railroad bed, it is barely one-and-one-half lanes wide with lots of potholes, frost heaves, washboarding, loose rocks and sharp turns. Not mentioned in the many printed warnings is the fact that it is littered with old railroad spikes that work their way to the surface with the intent of puncturing one or more automobile tires.

After about twenty miles of challenging driving through stunning scenery I came to the notorious Kuskulana Bridge. I pulled over. Not having done my homework, I gaped in acrophobic horror at what I had to drive across if I was to get to McCarthy. This old railroad bridge, built almost entirely from felled timbers in 1910, was approximately 525 feet long and soared an eye-popping 238 feet above the gorge of the Kuskulana River, which emptied into the Chitina River.

The bridge, apparently, had been converted to automobile traffic. That meant that the iron rails had been removed, lifted up maybe six to eight inches and re-bolted as rather flimsy guardrails at the extreme edges of the wooden railroad ties. Enough, theoretically, to gently redirect a veering automobile to the center span. (I was later told by Gary at the McCarthy Bar that it worked for Tony Zak's careening car on multiple missions to secure more spirits in Fairbanks. "Check out the scratch marks on your way back," Gary told me. I never followed through – no way was I going out on foot on that precarious span with a magnifying glass).

Side-by-side 2x4 planks the width of car tires had been placed on each side of the railroad ties to serve as a driving surface. I went for it. The flimsy iron guardrails were not visible to me on either side. I was basically driving over wooden railroad ties with a couple hundred feet of wide-open drop-off on either side. And then I saw it: an eight-foot length of the 2x4s on the right was rotted out up ahead! Fortunately, the underlying ties were solid. I could see the Kuskulana River hundreds of feet below and I braced for the inevitable.

My Rabbit tipped to the right about five degrees as I drove over the rotted wood and struggled to keep her pointed straight. Soon, another bump and we were again level on solid wood. And I arrived safely at the far end of the bridge without wetting or soiling my pants.

Forty more miles of breathtaking scenery brought me to the shore of the Kennicott River, with all four tires still miraculously inflated. The last mile to McCarthy would prove interesting, as the bridge across the Kennicott - a raging glacial torrent - had washed out in 1978 and was never rebuilt. A solitary, thick steel cable spanned the river. From it was suspended a self-propelled tram to the opposite bank.

Unlicensed and uninspected, the tram was quietly maintained by the locals while the State looked the other way. I parked my car, grabbed my pack, hopped into a flimsy metal chair and across I went. Churning masses of silty gray water pushed up waves several feet high, though I had plenty of clearance. On a whitewater scale that maxes out at six, this one looked like at least a nine. Safely across, I walked the last mile into McCarthy.

I stayed at the McCarthy Lodge. Gary, the manager-bartender-jack-of-all-trades, told me that Mrs. Johnson might pay me a visit sometime during the night. Intrigued, I slept with one ear open and listened. Alas, the ethereal one was a no-show. Decades dead, the spirit of old Ma Johnson apparently still haunted the old hotel. So, at the bar the next day I asked Gary if there were any living people I should meet. I always went for the local color and I knew there had to be some interesting characters in a town like this. "That would be Tony Zak," Gary said without hesitation. Tony was a drinking man, a character and definitely the local color here in McCarthy. And Gary plied me with a seemingly endless number of anecdotes about him, including driving drunk across the Kuskulana Bridge. I went off in search of Tony that afternoon.

Tony Zak was a Pennsylvania coal miner until he came down with black lung disease. A merchant marine during World War II, he drifted up to Alaska in the late 1940s where he worked with the International Brotherhood of Electrical Workers. In 1952, the year I was born, he purchased his small piece of paradise in McCarthy. A summer resident, his cabin was an old Kennecott mine bunkhouse.

There was no mistaking Tony Zak soaking up some August sunshine in a chair on his small lawn. He looked a bit like Bhagwan Shree Rajneesh. I introduced myself and he invited me inside. Alaskan informality and hospitality.

I expected the cabin of a guy like Tony Zak would be, well, just this side of a pigsty. But it was spotless. The dishes were all washed, rinsed and stacked to dry. The kitchen counter-top, and even the floor, were so clean one could have eaten off of them. Tony reached into a small, propane-powered refrigerator and offered me a cold beer. We talked unrushed, Alaskan style. When I felt it was time to leave I thanked him for his hospitality. And I promised him that on my next trip to McCarthy I would bring him a bottle of his beloved Slivovitz (despite being born in Pennsylvania, Tony Zak was an old Pole to the core).

EPILOGUE

Tony Zak died in 1999. The Kuskulana Bridge has been boringly and sedatingly upgraded. A pansy-ass pedestrian footbridge replaces the now dismantled steel cable trolley across the Kennicott River.

Cell phones have gotten a foothold and I won't be surprised if a Starbucks is next.

But old Mrs. Johnson is probably still making her ghostly rounds at the McCarthy Hotel. And the vast Wrangell – St. Elias National Park (13.2 million acres – a total of almost 20 million acres if you include the adjacent Kluane National Park in the Yukon Territory of Canada) beckons from the very edges of McCarthy.

Tony Zak at his cabin in McCarthy, Alaska August 1987

Wooden railroad bridge across the Kuskulana River converted for automobile traffic. Not for the acrophobic. August 1987

CHAPTER 53

ON THE YUKON RIVER WE MEET DICK COOK, ALASKA'S QUINTESSENTIAL SOURDOUGH

To anyone who has spent any length of time in Alaska the term "sourdough" has two different meanings. The first, also understood by many from the lower 48, and most San Franciscans, is the yeasty starter that was often cultivated and passed on through generations. Kept at ambient or cooler refrigerator temperatures it hosts live organisms which impart a tangy flavor to our Alaskan pancakes, biscuits and bread. Sourdough cultures were shared.

I had a culture once, from my friend June in Nome, that supposedly went back not only to the Klondike folks in 1899 but to the Oregon Trail twenty years earlier. Unfortunately, it tanked on me, as did the one from my friend John, a US Navy SEAL-turned-naturalist/birder. My bad - I probably didn't feed and nourish them enough.

Then there is the human sourdough, who this story is about. I've been in Alaska long enough – over thirty years – to have a good idea of who a sourdough is and, out of principle, refused to Google it. (Well, I'll admit I tried but kept coming up with bread and pancake recipes).

A common misconception (maybe now part of Alaska folklore) is that a sourdough is one who peed in the Yukon River. Lame. Been there, done that many times, but I'm no sourdough. A sourdough is one who witnessed seven successive freeze-ups and break-ups on the Yukon River is a definition that is getting closer. For example, Fabian Carey, Lake Minchumina trapper, was unquestionably a sourdough. His son Michael (the former editorial page editor of the *Anchorage Daily News*), who introduced me to Robert Ingersoll, still occasionally writes about his dad.

Alaska natives do not, and cannot, qualify as sourdoughs. They are one with the land, having been here forever – or at least since their forebears crossed over on the Bering Sea Land Bridge over 10,000 years ago. Sourdoughs come in from the outside, like the Klondike Pass in the late 1890s, and demonstrate tenacity and staying power in the Alaska Bush. A century ago there were few options for return, but in recent decades many idealistic "sourdough wannabes" skedaddled back to whence they came after their first winter in the harsh Alaska wilderness – if they survived.

Dick Cook lasted 37 years in the Alaska Bush, with just the occasional visit outside to family or to a courtroom in Fairbanks to fight his "enemies" - mostly the National Park Service and the Bureau of Land Management. The totally clueless sourdough wannabe Chris McCandless froze and starved to death in an abandoned bus in far more accessible Alaska wilderness after only 16 weeks. And Sean Penn played him in the movie! (I think Sean Connery, if he's not too old, would make a great Dick Cook)

Richard Okey Cook was an old marine who, even in his younger days, had difficulty fitting in. He got into trouble more than once for picking fistfights with his superiors in the military. Not so strange, then, that many decades later he'd be picking legal fights with his superiors in the state and federal governments.

Enlisting in the Marine Corps at age 17, Dick saw hard time in Korea. His family says he returned as a changed and uncomfortable man. Working a job in real estate provided little satisfaction (well, duh), so he split from Ohio and headed for the Great Land (Alaska and its vast wilderness). He arrived in Eagle, just downstream from Canada on the Yukon River, in the spring of 1964. I was in elementary school in New Jersey at the time and the Beatles had just appeared on the Ed Sullivan Show.

It's been pretty much established that Dick Cook was not a consummate woodsman, nor a skilled mechanic when it came to maintaining the few internal combustion items he needed for his decades in the Alaskan Bush - a chainsaw and an old outboard engine he was given for his 19 foot Grumman Canoe. But he had spirit, stubbornness, resilience and/or that Robert Pirsigian term "gumption". Whatever, Dick kept plowing along.

Author John McPhee, who later would write about New Jersey's Pine Barrens, came across Dick in the 1970s. His seminal book, *Coming into the Country*, was the Bible-small-b and required reading for anyone heading to the Great Land. I devoured McPhee before I came to Alaska.

Dick fished for himself and his dogs. He trapped over an area of 250-300 square miles. He hunted, raised chickens and tended a small vegetable garden. When the federal land managers made his life difficult he never backed away from confrontation. In the late 1970s he was threatening to shoot down BLM (Bureau of Land Management) planes. Later, after apparently mellowing a bit, he would just sue them, which required a trip to the courthouse in Fairbanks. Dick was no hermit and loved the occasional company; it gave him the opportunity to vent and rant and be his uniquely opinionated self. But he preferred to spend the vast majority of his time alone in the bush.

In June 1999 a lightning strike started a blaze on Hardluck Creek, part of the Nation River drainage. Progressing to a full-blown forest fire, it crossed the pass over to Pass Creek, which emptied into the Tatonduk River. It was there Dick had a cabin where he had been stockpiling supplies for summer renovations. The advancing fire caught Dick by surprise and he barely escaped with his life. His precious journals, which he had no time to retrieve, burned to cinders. Dick hightailed it to his fish camp at Drew's cabin on the Yukon's main channel.

Unbeknownst to Dick during his emergency escape, the federal land managers he loved to hate also had Drew's cabin in their crosshairs. They were prepared to save it. They swooped in with helicopter support and set to work carving a wide fire-suppression ring around the cabin by clearing brush and setting any necessary backfires. Industrial-strength hoses encircled the cabin, connected to industrial-strength pumps ready to suck water from the Yukon. The cabin was saved and I doubt Dick ever got an itemized bill.

I was on the Yukon River only a couple weeks later, in July 1999, with my 13-year old daughter Colleen and two other canoes with friends from the Midwest. We were canoeing from Eagle to Circle. After pushing off in Eagle we had to quickly scurry off the river while a sudden thunderstorm passed over. Back on the water, we paddled into the twilight seeing fire damage everywhere. It was tough to find a campsite.

A day or two later we set up camp on the right bank of the Yukon at the mouth of the clear Nation River. The sun had come out. Massive trees - scoured, abraded and abandoned by the mighty river - served as natural drying racks for our damp clothes. Even in death they served us.

Warmed by the sun, these became shirtless hours on the Yukon (well, excepting the only female member of our entourage). After finishing our dinner and chores, strangers suddenly appeared at our campsite. It was the firefighters who had previously saved Drew's cabin and were doing suppression work at the Nation River cabin, just a short walk from our multi-tent campsite. My ever-sociable daughter, delighted to meet them, invited them for tea. They would return, they promised, as soon as they finished their duties.

And return they did, as per-promise, just around midnight. A July Yukon River twilight-midnight. I was dog-tired from a long day of paddling, but when the firefighters show up at your campsite on the Yukon River for midnight tea and conversation, they get, well, midnight tea and conversation. Colleen had the water boiling and I summoned a second wind. I still fondly remember the setting and camaraderie.

Little did we realize at the time that we would be hopscotching and re-rendezvousing with our firefighter friends as we made our way downriver over the next couple of days. When they left the Nation River several hours after we did the following morning, the prop wash from their chopper sent a pair of water boots flying into the Yukon. A firefighter jumped out and grabbed them. Turns out Uncle Dave (a college buddy I christened as an uncle) left his water boots behind at our campsite.

And when we next met up on a wide bank of the river downstream around midday, Uncle Dave earned himself some major bragging rights about how his water boots were helicoptered downriver by a rugged team of firefighters and personally returned to him. I was a little worried, but Uncle Dave is pretty laid-back and cool, so his head just barely swelled into the next larger hat size. But my head practically burst when firefighter Mitch casually mentioned that Dick Cook was at Drew's cabin just a short paddle downstream on the left. "Dick Cook?" I exclaimed, "as in THE Dick Cook?!" "That's him," he answered.

I was the only one on our team who knew the significance of this tip. We were now on a beeline to meet an Alaska legend. The huge riverside pumps and thick white hoses leading uphill marked the location of the cabin. And then I recalled a tip from one of many books about Alaska I'd read over the years. The famously crusty and fiercely independent denizens living along the Yukon River are more than happy to meet with strangers passing through, but with two provisos: leave your weapon and your camera in your watercraft before approaching their abode. This I did, and asked the others to wait behind while I first went up alone.

I followed the white firehose, about as thick around as a giant boa, up a short, steep slope to the top of a bluff. And there was Dick, sitting in a crude lawn chair under an equally crude Visqueen lean-to. I introduced myself and he was most cordial. I explained I had some friends waiting down below who would like to meet him, and we would not keep him long. He indicated that they were welcome. Dick never stood up, but sitting on that tattered throne under that tattered canopy, with 35 years of sweat equity behind him, he didn't need to. This was his fiefdom. The view of the Yukon and the wilderness extending beyond the opposite shore was expansive and pristine.

I ran down the bluff and brought up the rest of our crew. Brucie and John, fishermen from Dick's old stomping grounds in the Midwest, bonded with him quickly. Fishermen will do that. A remarkable summer vegetable garden in front of the cabin was visible from where we all stood under Dick's lean-to. And we were surprised when he pulled away a small piece of plywood and revealed a subterranean cache in the semi-permafrost above the Yukon River. Loads of salmon in there were probably for his dogs the coming winter.

Dick was certainly a man with his opinions. It's been said that "He (Dick) was prone to overstatement, and that's an understatement." He sure was a fearless old cuss. Only two things would send Dick running for his life. Forest fires, obviously, were one. The second one surprised me. It was not the interior grizzly bear. It was the urban hunters who came up the river every fall during hunting season.

Dick said how they would shoot someone's horse thinking it was a moose. Shoot at his dogs thinking they were wolves. No doubt there was the possibility, I thought, of them shooting at Dick, mistaking him for a giant wolverine. They scared the bejeezus out of him to the point where he would hightail it off to a remote, off-river cabin until fall hunting season was over.

We kept our visit reasonably short before bidding Dick farewell, as per unspoken protocol. And departed sans photos, also per unspoken protocol. But we had met the legend - sourdough extraordinaire and high swami to the river people. We pushed our canoes into the Yukon's current and were back on the river.

We caught up with our firefighter friends one last time at the historic two-story wooden Slaven Roadhouse. Actually, they were headquartered about a mile inland up Coal Creek in some old, well-built but long-abandoned government buildings being slowly encroached upon by the boreal forest. But they had quite the mini-NORAD command center set up, what with primitive laptops, satellite phones, etc.

We spent the night above the river in a clean, well-maintained cabin with a propane stove. Gratis, courtesy of the folks Dick loved to hate – the National Park Service. Chef Brucie went to work on a multi-course feast. The on-site caretaker joined us with a salad of locally grown greens and fresh-baked bread. And we invited Kenji, a solo Japanese rafter who was the only other guest on-site.

After dinner I felt it was the appropriate and opportune time to allow Uncle Dave to open his belated birthday present. I had insisted he carry it unopened in his canoe until we were approximately halfway through our stretch of the Yukon. I was the trip leader and therefore the boss. He did as he was told.

We hung out on the cabin's porch, which was dappled in the warm, evening sunlight that filtered through the surrounding birch and spruce. Uncle Dave reverently opened his gift. It was a nearly 3-inch thick copy of the Tokyo Yellow Pages which I had (shamefully) ripped off from a phone booth in Narita a couple years earlier. Kenji, a look of befuddled bewilderment on his face, sat there quietly. Another night on the Yukon River.

EPILOGUE:

In June 2001, after a long search, they finally found Dick's body floating near the mouth of the Tatonduk River. With hip boots on but, characteristically, no life jacket. Apparently, he set off downstream from his cabin at Pass Creek in what was still high water from recent rains. Flipped, but made it ashore. Tried again, but didn't make it the second time.

Dick was cremated. Half of his ashes were scattered in the region of his fish camp at Drew's cabin, where we had met him two years earlier. And Dick's friends afterward motored his two daughters, who had come up from the Lower-48, up the Tatonduk so they could spread his ashes at Dick's Pass Creek cabin site.

But on the Tatonduk the prop snagged on an underwater sweeper, killing the engine. The boat turned sideways to the current and flipped. After a near-Dick experience they all got to shore (they were wearing life jackets) and survived.

Much was lost, however, including the second parcel of Dick's ashes destined for his maybe now charred Pass Creek cabin.

I have no doubt Dick was out there somewhere laughing when half of him drowned a second time in the Tatonduk River.

Midnight tea with the firefighters (kneeling, front) on the Yukon River. July 1999

A small black bear takes down a moose calf on the road to Eagle, Alaska July 1999

Canoeing the mighty Yukon with my daughter Colleen in the bow.
July 1999

CHAPTER 54

FATHER DONALD J. MCGUIRE, S.J. - MOTHER TERESA'S CONFESSOR

The Jesuits (Society of Jesus), founded by St. Ignatius Loyola in 1540 when the Jesuit Constitution was adopted, are widely regarded and respected as the intellectual arm of Roman Catholicism. And the Reverend Donald J. McGuire, S.J. was one of the premier Jesuits of his time. His stellar resume details his work as a teacher at the Jesuits' Loyola Academy in Chicago and later in San Francisco. He organized and led dynamic Ignatian and other retreats. He was chaplain of the National Federation of Catholic Physicians in the early to mid-1990s.

Mother Teresa herself, leader and founder of the Missionaries of Charity, selected Father McGuire to be their advisor and her personal confessor. I had spent a half-day volunteering at Mother Teresa's Home for the Dying Destitutes in Calcutta in 1987. So, when my Catholic friends in Anchorage invited me to an evening mass by this famous Jesuit I jumped at the chance.

Father McGuire was well into a rousing sermon on St. John the Baptist. I was impressed by his obvious intellect, dynamism and oratorical skills. He didn't just talk from behind the pulpit. He preached with his legs, darting back and forth and lunging forward toward the folks in the first pew. He preached with his arms, pumping them and gesticulating.

He was drawing me in. Then he used the term "the scourge of homosexuality." I can still hear it clearly. Not the scourge of HIV/AIDS. Not the scourge of poverty and starvation in the third world. And certainly not the scourge of hateful rhetoric and spiritual violence that leads to harassment, bullying, physical violence, murder and suicide among the gay community.

I remember as a kid (and yes, a grown-up in front of kids) blowing up a balloon and releasing it before tying it off. It goes off crazily, shooting in haphazard loops around the room before collapsing, flattened and out of air, on the carpet. The Reverend Donald J. McGuire did the very same before my eyes. All the respect, like the air in the balloon, was gone. But I had no idea at the time that he was also a practicing pedophile.

His comment apparently went unnoticed by my Catholic friends which, in retrospect, is disturbing but, sadly, not surprising. After the sermon they excitedly ushered me in to meet this great man. I remember his hand was very soft, but ours was a very weak handshake. My trusted hand, channeling my moral disapproval, had gone limp. I avoided eye contact.

And that's how I left it. Over the years, after reading Christopher Hitchens, I've re-evaluated Mother Teresa. Some folks finally summoned the courage to challenge this formerly untouchable icon. She was probably the Roman Catholic Church's biggest cash cow. She took contributions from the likes of Lincoln Savings and Loan mega-swindler Charles Keating and the wife of Haiti's brutal dictator, Jean Claude "Baby Doc" Duvalier. She raked in millions, almost all of which remains unaccounted for (when you're on an inevitable track to sainthood you become embraced by the Vatican and don't have to account for anything). In a comprehensive 399 page book entitled *The Untold Story* Aroup Chatterjeee follows up on Hitchens, exposing in detail Teresa's Calcutta charade, including her skill at manipulating the media that fawned over her.

And then it hit me. The dying destitute they brought in for me to examine in Mother Teresa's Home for the Dying Destitutes in Calcutta back in 1987. All those millions and her damn nuns couldn't even produce a thermometer so I could check him for fever or heat exhaustion. Yes, they seemed more concerned about saving souls and glorifying poverty and suffering in the name of Jesus. Germany's "Die Stern" once decried: "Mother Teresa, where are your millions?" Fortunately, I didn't see her non-medically trained and tightly controlled nuns rinsing hypodermic needles for reuse, as reported by Lancet and the British Medical Journal — two publications I trust as a physician.

And then dear Mother Teresa, who decried artificial contraception as "unnatural", allowed herself, when in a sudden personal medical crisis, to be flown away from her beloved destitutes suffering in the name of

Jesus and directly to the best hospital in Italy where she was implanted with an "unnatural" cardiac pacemaker. As Christopher Hitchens said to me in an e-mail dated May 12, 2006, "she (Mother Teresa) was a racket and a fraud, plain and simple, and a very heartless one at that". Hitchens comes on strong, but I was tending to agree.

PEDESTALS

Mother Teresa has fallen off her pedestal and landed flat on her face. And her homophobic, pedophile confessor, the Jesuit Father Donald J. McGuire, never had a chance to climb up onto his. Two empty pedestals, what to do?

My buddy, "rambling" Dr. Jack Preger, climbs up on one. He's doing what Mother Teresa should have been doing – providing real health care to the poor in Calcutta. And my friend Father Joe Maier, a real Roman Catholic priest who provides nourishment, health care, non-judgmental education and compassion to the poorest of Thailand's poor – the children and their families in Bangkok's Klong Touey slum - climbs up on the other one.

EPILOGUE

Father Donald J. McGuire is currently serving 25 years in federal prison for child sexual abuse. It's too bad the scores of Jesuits who condoned, ignored or looked the other way aren't there behind bars to keep him company.

Here's wishing the former Jesuit, who will likely spend the rest of his life in prison, to experience some of the hell he inflicted on his multiple victims - a hell that will perpetuate into future generations. The same hell spread by the despicable pedophile Jesuit Jim Poole, who founded the radio station KNOM in Nome, is already spreading - dysfunctional families, substance abuse and probably worse to come. Poole, probably doddering and slobbering in some Jesuit-protected home for the Vatican's ecclesiastical waste in Oregon, escaped the statute of limitations.

These may be harsh words on my part, devoid of forgiveness, but when innocent and precious children are sexually assaulted, I become infused with a passion for lex talionis.

EPILOGUE 2020

Father Donald J. McGuire died in federal prison in January 2017. Good riddance. Dr. Jack Preger, after serving the poor of Calcutta some forty years, retired recently and moved back to England. I rang him up after he retired and we had a nice talk. Mother Teresa died some time ago but many may have missed it since Princess Di, who was killed within days of Teresa's passing, got far more attention. Fitting. And Father Joe is still going strong in the Bangkok slum.

CHAPTER 55

THE KURDS COME TO NOME

It all started on a flight to Sitka, Alaska where I was heading to work as a locum tenens (temporary) radiologist at Sitka Community Hospital. My seatmate in first class (I was MVP Gold and Alaska Airlines bumped me up) was George Cannelos, at the time director of the Anchorage Heritage Land Bank. (A word of advice to those flying to southeast Alaska destinations, especially Juneau: choose your seatmate carefully. You're likely to spend a half-hour or more circling in weather before landing – and you may not land at your destination at all. I made a good choice).

George was intelligent, well-read and had a wide worldview. We had hours of potential conversation in reserve (far more time than the 737-400 had fuel). I was telling him of my work with the Roma (often called Gypsies) and how they were the largest transnational ethnic group in the world when he politely interjected with a question: "What about the Kurds?" Hmm, I had no answer but vowed to educate myself when I got back to Anchorage.

My inquiries led me to the American-Kurdish Information Network (AKIN) and its patient and passionate executive director, Kani Xulam. I learned a lot from Kani and George was right - there are some 30-40 million stateless Kurds, as compared to 14-16 million Roma, in the world. About half of those Kurds live in Turkey, where they have been persecuted and politically and culturally oppressed. The remainder live in Iraq, Iran, Syria, some in Armenia and Russia and the rest mostly scattered in European and North American diaspora. Kani is a Turkish Kurd.

I invited Kani to Anchorage and Nome, Alaska in the winter of 2003 to talk about the Kurds. He enlightened a lot of people. But for someone who has fasted on behalf of his people, Nome's minus 10°F temperatures tested his somewhat frail constitution. He did well.

Kani once set up a mock Turkish prison cell in Lafayette Park, across from the White House in Washington, D.C., identical to those where Kurdish political prisoners were confined in Turkey. Turkey's Foreign Minister leaned on U.S Vice President Dick Cheney to have it dismantled but Cheney responded that as long as Kani had a permit from the U.S. National Park Service, which required 24-hour occupancy, it was legal. Kudos to Dick Cheney and the American rule of law.

After Kani's departure I set my sights on a follow-up visit to Alaska by Qubad Talabani, the official representative of the Kurdistan Regional Government (Iraq) to the United States. The Kurdistan Region is a Switzerland-sized and highly autonomous region in northern Iraq. In the interim Qubad's father, Jalal Talabani, became the President of Iraq. I felt my chances of nabbing Qubad diminished, but I was not about to give up.

In November 2008 Qubad Talabani, son of Iraq's President, arrived in Nome, Alaska, understandably jet-lagged after a long flight from Washington, D.C. He came alone, at my invitation. My wife and I greeted him at the small airport holding up a cardboard sign saying: B'kher-hati, Mr. Qubad Talabani. B'kher-hati is "welcome" in the Latinized Kurdish script used in Turkey. He'd recognize it.

My beat-up Toyota and the snow on the ground reminded him of winter in his Kurdistan homeland. We took him straight to his hotel so he could get some rest. He offered to pay for his room, but I pulled out my credit card – he was my guest.

Qubad's staff in D.C. had politely requested I give him as much downtime as possible to relax and engage in his passion for photography. I could understand the need for someone in his position to de-stress. A noon talk at Nome Rotary and an evening talk to the public at Nome Elementary School was all I scheduled. The rest of the time we were out-and-about in my beat-up Toyota driving as far as we dared down the semi-plowed roads in the outskirts of Nome. Once, we stopped and slogged across snow-covered tundra on the shore of the nearly frozen Bering Sea so Qubad could photograph some driftwood fish-drying shacks.

Later, we climbed up the outside of an old gold dredge and, maneuvering across the rotted and collapsing timber floor on the upper deck and holding on to rusted steel cables for support, we made our way to the control room (Qubad photographing all the way). When I later introduced Qubad to the Alaska World Affairs Council in Anchorage I briefly related our adventures in Nome, then paused, expressing my concern that if his father, the President of Iraq, found out I might get in trouble. The audience laughed, and so did Qubad, who assured me that I was okay.

Once we drove out just past the semi-shuttered Rock Creek Mine on the Glacier Creek Road. I stopped when wind-blown snow drifts made the road seem too dicey. It was a clear, calm day and we stepped out of my car. This point was about as far away as I could get Qubad from the intensity of his job and responsibility in Washington, D.C. He seemed to sense it and quickly took off up and down the snow-covered road to photograph. The remaining yellow-brown leaves on the stunted tundra willows were lightly dusted with snow. Small animal tracks could be seen everywhere if one looked closely. Quiet wilderness surrounded us for 360 degrees. It was as serene as you could get.

When we settled back into my Toyota I was more concerned about being able to back up through the deep snow till we got to the mine so I could turn around. But I paused to ask Qubad a question that had been on my mind: "Qubad, do you have a cell phone?" "Yeah," he answered, "and my voice-mail is full. And I think my dad has been trying to reach me the last two days."

"Good for you, Qubad," I responded, maybe a bit too loudly but it was an issue I was passionate about. "You have the right," I said, "to carve out for yourself a chunk of free, uninterrupted downtime - a week, a day, four hours, your choice." He had just done that.

No slacker, and dedicated to his job, he was already checking messages as we pulled into Nome. Dinner that night was at the home of Jana Varatti and her husband, the Honorable Judge Ben Esch.

When Kani Xulam came out in 2003 we also had dinner at Ben and Jana's. The theme at dinner then was "Kurdish". Kani's friend Chiya – a Kurd and master chef from Turkey resident in Washington, D.C. - supplied recipes. I had dropped Kani off at Jana's and slipped away for a short nap. With Chiya's recipes and Jana's cooking skills they set to work.

But Jana had an ulterior motive. She plied poor Kani with red wine to get him to confirm rumors of my "romance and upcoming marriage" with a Taiwanese woman. Poor Kani stood no chance and he "spilled the beans". When I found out I laughed and forgave Kani instantly. He was no match against Jana.

When Qubad arrived for dinner five years later the theme at Ben and Jana's was "Native". Among the many delicacies were two species of whale – beluga and bowhead (both legally harvested by subsistence Eskimo hunters). Qubad relished them.

I met Qubad late the next morning at his hotel. I was sure he hadn't eaten breakfast. We took off on foot for some short appointments (we had a mid-day plane to catch for Anchorage). I had his breakfast in a 12-ounce used plastic bottle: a smoothie of homemade soymilk, fresh-ground flax seed, wild tundra blueberries and non-fat organic yogurt. Can't get much healthier. He was a few paces ahead of me, crossing Nome's Front Street, when I yelled out: "Qubad, your breakfast." And I tossed it to him. Like a pro, he caught it effortlessly, drank it down and thoughtfully looked for a trash can to dispose of the empty container. And I remember thinking, this guy is no spoiled, stuffed-shirt Saudi prince.

But no visit to Nome from the lower-48 goes off without a glitch, even a small one. Usually, it's the weather. For my brother, a southcentral volcano grounded him in Nome an extra few days after Iditarod 2010. Qubad's case was different. The son of the President of Iraq was summoned to Alaska Superior Court. Not wanting the media to find out and make it an international incident, and having a pretty good idea what it was about, I accompanied Qubad and offered my services pro bono.

Seems Jana had a pair of polar bear mittens that she was very proud of but had forgotten to show them to Qubad at dinner the night before. A late riser, she gave them to Ben to bring to court in the morning so he could show them to Qubad. Yes, the summons had come from Jana, but it was not to be trifled with–although the long-term consequences of ignoring it would be much less than ignoring a summons from her husband, the short-term was an entirely different matter. Qubad and I showed up at Alaska Superior Court in Nome and were ushered into the chambers of the Honorable Judge Ben Esch.

The smile on Ben's face suggested this was not the first "polar bear mitten" incident. He thoughtfully donned his black judicial robe, Qubad slipped on the mitts, I took a photo and we had a nice conversation. The Judge's chambers were lined with law books and Ben pointed out the slightly singed 1934 edition – it had survived the devastating fire of that year - the worst in Nome's 100-plus year history.

Appointed by my old canoeing buddy, Governor Tony Knowles, Ben was the Superior Court Judge for northwestern Alaska, one of four state judicial districts. And he embodied the patience, honesty and integrity that makes our third branch of government – the Judiciary – a vigorously independent model to the world.

I remember thinking that we have Doctors without Borders (they won the Nobel Peace Prize in 1999) and Reporters without Borders, but what about "Judges without Borders"? Retired U.S. judges could go overseas and help other countries strengthen their judiciaries. They needn't worry about boning up on the intricacies of local law, as we're talking "institution building". Fairness, political independence and the rule of law. Nor need they worry about challenging living conditions - Singapore needs as much help as Chad or Niger.

And the indefatigable and amazing Jana, whose activities range from escorting high-profile political candidates through Nome to cooking for Nome's homeless, has an incredible ability to make her varied guests feel welcome and equal in her home.

Qubad and I got to Anchorage on time. And after his talk to the Alaska World Affairs Council (AWAC) we headed to the snow-covered Chugach Mountains above the Glen Alps parking lot near the edge of town. As we trudged through knee-deep snow on the steep, mountain hemlock-studded slopes Qubad photographed, pulling increasingly long lenses from his padded bag. I was becoming increasingly worried about the damp, obscuring fog that was descending upon us. Sure, it was all downhill to Anchorage, but it was a long downhill.

Qubad's schedule called for dinner that evening with Jim*. In my beat-up 1987 Isuzu Trooper II (more beat-up than my 1990 Toyota pickup in Nome) we were headed for downtown Anchorage, but were soon jammed into stop-and-go rush-hour traffic on northbound Lake Otis Blvd. Qubad's cell phone rang. It was Jim.

Jim had heard about Qubad's upcoming trip and called the Alaska World Affairs Council asking if they could meet for dinner. He apparently worked for the U.S. Department of State. Neither I nor the Council's executive director ever met Jim, but she assured me that she vetted him through the governor's office and "one other source" and he came up kosher.

I pulled into the limo slot at the front entrance to the Anchorage Hilton (if anyone hassled me I could always make a case that Qubad was a VIP). He had just finished his talk with Jim. "You know," Qubad said, as he turned to me, "I don't think he works for the State Department. He knows _____**in _____***. "Oh," I replied, "so you think he works for _____****?" Qubad nodded. I found out later that guys like Jim will masquerade as State Department officials – it's part of their cover. And "Jim", not the name he originally gave us, probably wasn't his real name but, well, since the name he originally gave us probably wasn't his real name either there's a small chance that the name I gave him, "Jim", was his real name. But it's really not important and I'm way out of my milieu...

I had little doubt Qubad was in safe hands and wished him an enjoyable evening with Jim, but then added, "Call me in the morning and let me know all is well." He did.

Qubad has much to offer the Middle East, especially Kurdistan and Iraq. During the AWAC question-and-answer session he promised not to run for president. He did not specify which country he would not run for president of – Iraq or Kurdistan. Clever.

Qubad's only real concern in Nome (and it was a minor one) was the extensive spider-web of cracks on my Toyota windshield. Over the years, on bitter-cold mornings, I got a kick out of hearing (and maybe seeing) them spread when I put my defroster on full-blast heat. As a former auto mechanic, Qubad matter-of-factly explained the physics and dynamics of auto windshields and how the entire thing could implode on us without warning.

* not the name he gave us
**redacted by the author at the author's request
***ibid
****ibid again

In August, 2010 I finally got my windshield replaced and afterward I faxed Qubad in D.C. with the good news. I got the following response from Brenda Kinser, Qubad's Executive Assistant, in an e-mail on Sept 7, 2010: "Hi, Dr. Cox, nice talking to you last week. I passed your msg to Qubad and here's his response: 'I thought your previous windshield had a certain charm about it'."

Sometime after Qubad's visit I started finding a flyer (usually in a ziplock plastic bag) tucked under the windshield of my 1987 Isuzu Trooper II every time I got back to Anchorage, sometimes under four inches of snow. These flyers advertised free removal of junked vehicles and they really hurt my feelings. Granted, my Anchorage Trooper makes my Nome Toyota look like I'd just driven it out of the dealership's showroom. But me and the old rust-bucket go back a long ways. After all, I rescued her – an unsold Japanese orphan – off the lot at Alaska Eero Volkswagen on Gambell Street for just under twelve grand. And she continues to serve me well.

I poured out my hurt feelings in a letter to Qubad, reminding him that she served him well too when I escorted him about Anchorage. Qubad responded in a personal letter dated Feb. 28, 2012. He began with the disclaimer: "I write to you not as the Representative of the Kurdistan Regional Government to the United States but as a former car mechanic." And he continued: "I would like to state for the record that whoever left the note offering 'free removal of junk vehicles' knows nothing about cars. Your 1987 Trooper is a fine automobile. Don't let anyone dissuade you otherwise."

Qubad's letter lifted my spirits and I am still the proud owner of an Anchorage rust-bucket.

My wife and I greet Qubad Talabani at the airport in Nome, Alaska
November 2008

CHAPTER 56

THE FBI

I could see the FBI building on 6th Avenue in downtown Anchorage when I parked my car just across the street from my dermatologist. That looming building always reminded me to feed the parking meter – usually with an extra quarter just to be on the safe side in case I got delayed (not that the FBI ever issued any parking tickets).

When in Anchorage from Nome I would stop by my trusted dermatologist to have actinic keratoses and "pre-actinic actinics" (basically, pre-cancerous sun-spots and very faint pre-cancerous sun spots) on my face or arms sprayed with liquid nitrogen. At a temperature of minus 320°F the liquid nitrogen was heavily shielded in an insulated metal canister. It's the same stuff that dribbles from the sky on Saturn's moon Titan, only here in Anchorage it costs a pretty penny. Thank goodness for health insurance.

What does the FBI have to do with liquid nitrogen? Absolutely nothing, but their building kept reminding me (in addition to feeding the meter) that I should share with them a conversation I had with a neighbor in Nome. She had previously worked for Bill Allen's VECO.

Passing in the hallway of our Nome apartment building one afternoon, Josie (not her real name) ended up relating to me an incident involving Allen and a prominent Alaska politician (pssst…that would be U.S. Senator Ted Stevens, but you didn't hear it from me). As she talked, and as I asked questions, she became more indignant and angry. I could understand why. Seems Uncle Ted's grandson worked for Allen and committed an infraction serious enough that an immediate dismissal was mandated. So Uncle Ted got on the phone with his buddy Bill and Bill made everything go away. I knew there was an ongoing investigation against Stevens for corruption and what she shared with me in that cluttered hallway was clearly incriminating. "You should share this with the authorities," I suggested. But she was far too cynical and disgusted. I filed it away, but it kept coming back to me.

Back in Anchorage again for a few more blasts of liquid nitrogen, I saw that building again: the thin, slit-like vertical windows and video cameras mounted every ten feet or so around the perimeter. It kept reminding me of the Ministry of Love in Orwell's 1984. Only these were the good guys. The conversation with Josie came back, so I walked across 6th Avenue to the front door of the FBI building, and paused. Then I sucked it up and walked through the door.

I gave a uniformed guard my ID and he proceeded to write my name and identifying information on a paper ledger. As he was doing this I found myself staring down at a list of names of everyone who had been there before me. It was upside down to me, and I didn't have on my reading glasses, but if I had been inclined I could have made out a few names. I really didn't care who had been there before me, but I didn't want the next guy to see my name on top of the list. Seems to me it should have been shielded, but I was hesitant to criticize the FBI's security procedures.

Then I emptied my pockets, went through the metal detector and was escorted to a small sitting room on the second floor. A huge pane of thick plexiglass separated me from what looked like the "active" section of the floor. A thin slit at the bottom above a shallow, curved metal tray allowed for papers to be passed back and forth. Reminded me of the 7-Elevens back in inner-city Detroit. Back then, in the 1970s, I could understand the fear in the Black and Hispanic shopkeepers and cashiers behind their plexiglass. But here, both sides of the thick plexiglass were within the security of the interior of the FBI building. Another question that would go unanswered.

My waiting area was spartan. There was an old Alaska tourism VCR sitting on a low shelf and a dog–eared copy of "Field and Stream." That was about it. Nothing like the waiting room at my dermatologist's two blocks away where I could peruse "Business Weekly" or pick up a copy of "People" and catch up with the latest on Brad and Angelina and Jennifer Aniston. So I waited. Then I wondered how long it would take me to get back out on the street if I panicked. I reminded myself this was not the Iranian Embassy (which I walked into once in Bangkok). These were the good guys and I did nothing wrong. So I waited some more. Their big computers were probably running a check on me.

After maybe almost thirty minutes an agent appeared behind the plexiglass clutching a long paper print-out. Since I hadn't told him anything yet it had to all be about me. I gulped. It was surely all there. Everything. They probably knew about that pesky kid across the street in the old New Jersey neighborhood who my brother and I used to beat up at least every other week - that is, until a pre-adolescent, hormone-fueled growth spurt kicked in and leveled the playing field, forcing us to back–off.

And the Feebs almost certainly knew about that ticket I got in Florida for running a red light - a red light that you could not see until you were driving directly underneath it immediately after making a left turn on green. At 4 am. Cop car sitting right there. An obvious set-up.

(After returning to Anchorage from Florida, for the following several weeks, my mailbox was stuffed with glossy brochures from every ambulance - chaser (a.k.a. attorney) in northern Florida offering to get me out of the ticket. Their fees were all greater than the value of the ticket. Everyone in Anchorage was probably going to find out so, frustrated, I wrote to Miami Herald columnist Dave Barry suggesting he write a column and let the entire country know about my ticket. I promised to follow up with BBC and Al-Jazeera for international exposure. I got a postcard back from Dave at the Herald that simply said: "Dear Dr. Cox. It's dangerous criminals like you that give Florida a bad name". Dave's a funny guy! I treasure that card and it is hanging next to my autographed photo of the Three Stooges and a Chilkoot Charlie's napkin autographed by Tiny Tim)…

But, getting back to the FBI, the first thing I noticed, after the long print-out in his hands, was that the FBI agent was wearing a white shirt. I thought the white shirt requirement went out the window after J. Edgar Hoover bit the dust. Maybe it's optional now. I didn't bring this up either. My reason for being there was to relate some incriminating information I had learned, but I also had a side goal. I wanted to make an FBI agent laugh, or at least smile. I made North Korean diplomats laugh – on more than one occasion. People should laugh more. I liked challenges and I didn't do crossword puzzles. So when the agent introduced himself I saw my chance. "I'd shake your hand, but I don't think

I can get my arm through that small opening," I said. He didn't even crack a smile.

The interview lasted almost half an hour. The agent seemed very interested in what I had to report, asked a lot of questions and took a lot of notes. And while we were talking I realized that, despite the thick plexiglass barrier separating us, we were really on the same side. These guys need help from the average citizen to do their job. Sure, we always hear about the rogue cop or rogue FBI agent. It's because they got arrested and it hit the papers. But the vast bulk of our law enforcement people are quietly and honestly going about their work – much of it non-dramatic grunt work like here in this interview. If I need a cop he's a phone call away and will put his life on the line to help me. While I slept in the day after 9/11 thousands of FBI agents were mobilizing to protect this country. I felt proud to be an American. God Bless our law enforcement people.

The interview over, I had one last chance to meet my side challenge. I told the agent that I hoped the information I provided would prove helpful to the investigation. "Unfortunately, you'll never know," he responded. I looked him in the eye, pointed a finger at him and said, "Ah, but I'll be reading the *Anchorage Daily News*." He cracked at least half a smile and I thought I even heard a muffled chuckle. Success? Maybe...

Some months later neighbor Josie was sitting at our dinner table when the conversation turned to Alaska politics. She suddenly blurted out: "Guess who I got a call from? The FBI!" I quickly broke eye contact and adopted my best poker face: she had no idea I was the one who ratted her out to the Feebs. (It was the same poker face I successfully employed many years ago passing through American customs on my way back from Canada with an untaxed liter of Crown Royal and a real Cuban cigar under the seat and saying I had nothing to declare. There's nothing like kicking back and sipping a snifter of Crown Royal while smoking a real Cohiba!) With a little nudging I was able to steer the conversation away from politics.

EPILOGUE

Some years later I got a better chance at "success" with the FBI. A television news alert about a terrorist attack in the Middle East jogged my memory. A ho-hum incident a few years ago in a large East Coast

328

city suddenly presented itself to me in a new light. I needed to share my concerns with the FBI.

I had been able to walk from point A (the street) to Point B carrying a black backpack. All I had to do was sign my name with Security. Security? No ID check, no scan or X-ray, no pat-down, no questions or call to my "intended" destination. It should not have been so easy.

This time I was met by two armed FBI special agents and escorted into the "inner sanctum". It required them to swipe their badges and punch in code numbers on a panel adjacent to the door handle. I wondered if there might be more interesting reading material in the "inner sanctum". But this was no time for reading.

We walked into a large conference room with an impossibly long table, just the three of us, and they told me I could sit where I liked. I had a quick flashback to that Eddie Murphy movie where he plays a prince and has a meeting with his father (played by James Earl Jones) and the two of them sit at opposite ends of a similar table and have to talk through walkie-talkie-like microphones. I was tempted, then gave myself an internal pinch that said: "Get serious".

I explained to the two special agents what I could have had in my backpack if I was one of the bad guys and what I could have done at Point B. It would have taken just a few minutes and there would have been national and international repercussions. I drew them a map. I noted the video cameras, which would have resulted in my eventual capture. But the damage would have already been done and I'd have been hailed a martyr for the cause by some dark group. Hopefully, security at Point B has since been tightened up.

After our interview the two special agents escorted me out as far as security and reminded me to turn in my guest ID badge. When you enter the FBI building past security you wear a guest ID badge. If you flip it over there will be a 3 digit number on the back. I always check my number – just curious, I guess. Now I saw my chance. Before I turned it in I flipped it over and said to the two special agents: "Ya know, the last time I was here I was 007, now I'm only 002. What gives?" They laughed and said that was a good sign, that I was moving up. Bingo. My bucket list just got one item shorter.

Chapter 57

Tony Knowles

Tony had a smile that probably eclipsed Jimmy Carter's. Nothing like a mouthful of well-set white teeth when you're running for political office. Tony Knowles was twice elected as mayor of Anchorage.

After Tony's two 3-year terms he went back to the Downtown Deli, which he owned. There was little doubt that he would run for governor of Alaska in the near future.

Each May, as a member of the Alaska Sierra Club's Outings Committee, I would contribute to a public slide show illustrating the coming summer's scheduled outings. They were free and open to the public (transportation and expenses were shared). Tony stopped by and signed up for my 3-day Kenai National Wildlife Refuge-Moose River canoe trip.

We all drove down to Sterling, where the Moose River empties into the Kenai River, then ferried our canoes 25 miles into the Refuge to the West Entrance of the canoe system. Tony brought his seven-year-old daughter Sarah as his "bow girl". My "bow girl" was my seven-year-old daughter Colleen. Three other canoe teams joined us and we took off. We had nine lakes to cross (all connected by portage trails) over two days before we would put in on the upper Moose River for an eight-hour paddle down to Sterling.

It rained incessantly the first two days. There were no voters perched among the dripping spruce and birch trees, but Tony never stopped smiling. He helped two older women haul some gear across a difficult portage. He sat in the mud fiddling with his camp stove like everyone else. Wow, I thought, this guy is the real thing.

Paddling across Swan Lake – the largest in the system – we were all spread out. We were ever on the alert for sudden winds on a large lake and though none came up, dark wet clouds still filled the sky. Colleen and I, in our canoe, converged with Tony and Sarah in theirs. We paddled alongside each other and had a leisurely talk – mostly about family. Tony said something that, to this day, still stands out clearly: "You know, from the day our kids are born we should begin preparing them to be independent, leave home and be on their own successfully, someday." It was an expression of selfless love. Tony is a family man par excellence.

We camped on Swan Lake the second night and got an early start the following morning. Several of us took off first down the narrow, winding Moose River. With minimal rapids it was considered flat water, although there were sweepers and debris, and in several areas overhanging trees created a tunnel-like effect. We would beat our paddles on the gunwales to make enough noise to spook any downstream moose or bear.

Several hours later a vicious hailstorm struck, forcing us off the river. We took refuge under the spruce at a campsite I was familiar with. We were all accounted for, except for Tony and his daughter. I had my binoculars trained on the spot where they should appear at a bend in the Moose River I knew well.

The weather let up amazingly fast. And then a canoe came into view. It was Tony and his daughter, wet with rain, a boat filled with hail, and still smiling.

Tony served two terms as governor of Alaska from 1994 to 2002.

CHAPTER 58

FRANK MURKOWSKI

My first in-person introduction to Governor Frank Murkowski was a little awkward. But first, some background...

Frank Murkowski had been one of Alaska's U.S. senators in Washington, D.C. for 22 years and became Alaska's Governor in 2002. We mostly disagreed on environmental issues and many social issues, but I came to find out he was a strong supporter of human rights, freedom and democracy, especially in Taiwan. No small thing, that. He had principles and was capable of great political courage.

Lee Teng-hui was the President of Taiwan from 1988-2000. One of Asia's shrewdest and most enigmatic politicians, Lee almost single-handedly turned the tables on his own authoritarian party (the Chinese Nationalist Party, or Kuomintang) and ushered in Taiwan's modern democracy. He was a colossus and a hero of democracy and freedom.

President Lee made his first visit to the United States in 1995, while he was president of Taiwan. It was billed as a visit to his alma mater, Cornell University. The Clinton administration had opposed granting him a visa. This was the same Bill Clinton who, during his presidential campaign, excoriated President George H. W. Bush for "coddling tyrants from Beijing to Baghdad." Clinton was now kowtowing to Beijing, but with the House on record 396-0 and the Senate 97-1 in favor of granting the visa and Clinton having granted visas to the likes of Irish Republican Army "terrorist" Gerry Adams and the PLO's Yasser Arafat, it was hard to deny a democratically elected president. Clinton relented. Lee flew to Syracuse, N.Y.

President Lee's plane stopped to refuel in Anchorage. Governor Tony Knowles had the moral courage to personally greet him. "I tried to keep it under the radar," former governor Knowles told me recently, "but they found out about it."

Deborah Bonito confirmed to me in a phone call after the visit that the Knowles administration had been hit with the usual flak from Beijing. Later during Lee's visit, Chinese missiles were fired toward Taiwan. In Syracuse, Clinton's subservient State Department tried to keep Lee's plane on the far side of the runway – away from the throng of reporters and supporters waiting to greet him. The mayor of Syracuse was furious and overruled them. Three U.S. senators came up from Washington D.C. to greet President Lee in Syracuse: Jesse Helms, Alphonse D'Amato and Frank Murkowski.

Communist China (a.k.a. The People's Republic of China or mainland China) has long pursued a policy of divide-and-conquer against Taiwan, attempting to isolate the island nation into oblivion. Corporate America, where integrity, morality and ethics have long been in chronically short supply, has gone along with this, stiff-arming Taiwan as they salivate over the potential profits to be made in mainland China's booming economy.

As Alaska's governor, Frank Murkowski publicly hosted the current Taiwan President Chen Shui-bian, the opposition candidate whose rise to the highest office in Taiwan was made possible by President Lee's policies. President Chen was a major thorn in Beijing's side due to his pro-independence sentiment. And Governor Murkowski also dared to host His Holiness the Dalai Lama, a "notorious splittist" from Beijing's perspective. It was now October 2005 and Governor Murkowski was hosting a public reception for former President Lee, who was on a speaking tour in the United States. I was on my way downtown to attend, but first had to stop and make a special purchase.

The ballroom at the Hilton was filling up fast. Governor Murkowski and President Lee sat together at the head table up on a small stage. There was plenty of security about, both Taiwanese and American. My wife and I had just met with President Lee in Taiwan four months earlier. During our long conversation, when I remarked on the variety of delicious fruits available in Taiwan, President Lee volunteered that his favorite was the small green grapes. I walked into the Hilton ballroom with a bunch of fresh green grapes I had just purchased at Carrs.

I recognized President Lee's chief of security - a tall, thin Taiwanese man with the little coiled wire hanging from his ear. I went up to him and asked if I could bring a gift to President Lee. He remembered me and waved me through. Security parted and I walked straight toward President Lee clutching a brown plastic bag. Out of the corner of my right eye I thought I saw the governor's face go a bit ashen and his jaw drop a bit. Understandable. He didn't know who I was or what I had in that bag.

"Hello, President Lee," I said, "welcome to Alaska." "Ah, Dr. Cox," he responded. I was honored and impressed that he remembered my name without hesitation. "I brought you your favorite fruit," I explained as I handed him the bag. And then I quickly realized I needed to acknowledge Governor Murkowski, who I had not yet met in person, or I'd be both rude and violating protocol. I introduced myself, we shook hands and chatted a bit. It looked like the color was returning to his face as I excused myself and scooted back to my table in the audience.

I've kept in touch with Frank over the years. He is widely respected in Taiwan. Yet, as former staff member Isaac Edwards reminded me several years ago in a phone call from D.C., Frank Murkowski – both as senator and governor – always maintained good relations with Beijing. This is as it should be. Taiwan is Taiwan and China is China.

I was attending a medical conference in Palm Springs, California in November 2009. Frank and Nancy Murkowski keep a winter home in nearby Palm Desert and invited my wife and me to join them for lunch at a nearby restaurant. We talked for some two hours under the warm California sun and could have easily talked another two. Everything from cross-stitching (that was Amy and Nancy) to Frank's meeting with Saddam Hussein and lots of Alaska in between.

My wife (center) with Frank and Nancy Murkowski in Taipei, Taiwan,
when Frank was there to monitor the presidential election.
January 2012

CHAPTER 59

WALLY AND ERMALEE HICKEL

On June 25, 2011 I attended a dinner reception for the Japanese Ambassador to the USA, Ichiro Fujisaki, at the Sheraton Hotel in Anchorage. I had no assigned seat, so I sat down next to a tiny gray-haired lady I didn't recognize at one of the tables. I had no idea she was the widow of a former Nixon cabinet member and also Alaska's second First Lady.

I'd barely downed a mouthful of salad before she turned to me and introduced herself. "Hi, I'm Ermalee Hickel," she said, extending her hard. "ERMALEE," I responded a bit too loudly, my surprise having gotten the better of me. "Ermalee," I repeated, a bit more quietly and subdued. We shook hands. I felt bad that I didn't recognize her.

I had a lot to share with Ermalee and it had been years since we last talked, but out of courtesy we were silent while Ambassador Fujisaki spoke. But later I reminded Ermalee of the critical role she played back in the early 1990s in freeing a church bell from bureaucratic red tape in Moscow and getting it to the small log cabin church in Vershina, a tiny Polish Catholic community in the vast birch forests of southcentral Siberia. We talked about her son, Dr. Jack Hickel, who provided medical care to the poor in Swaziland and was recently involved in similar projects in South Sudan. And we talked about Dr. Ted Mala, who almost single-handedly melted the ice curtain between Soviet Russia and Alaska and was instrumental in getting that church bell to its destination after hearing from Ermalee.

Ermalee shared with me how she was born in Alaska – her father had been sent here in 1918 as a military officer because of concern by the U.S. government at the time that Japan had designs on the Territory of

Alaska. I looked over at the Japanese ambassador, who honored Ermalee in his introduction, and marveled at how times had changed.

We could have continued talking, but the room was emptying out and her handlers were trying to suggest it was time to leave. "I really miss Wally," I blurted out to Ermalee. "Well, so do I," she responded in a very sweet and matter-of-fact tone. Then the 80-something former First Lady thanked me for our conversation, saying how nice it was to be able to talk with someone about the old days. She meant well, but suddenly I felt older than I wanted to.

Her husband Wally, as legend would have it, arrived in Alaska from Kansas with eleven cents in his pocket. A former boxer, he was a "doer" and so did well for himself in the construction industry in the young new state of Alaska. He was also an original thinker who defied categorization.

As a republican, he was elected Alaska's second governor in 1966. In 1968 he was offered, and accepted, the position of Secretary of Interior in the cabinet of America's new president, Richard M. Nixon. Environmentalists were alarmed, though he showed a delightful independent streak. But he didn't last long. He famously chastised the paranoid Nixon in a letter for not listening to, and heeding, the increasingly loud voices of America's concerned and vociferous youth, especially their alarm at the situation in Vietnam. And Wally received a one-way ticket back to Anchorage.

One of the first speakers I brought to Anchorage to address the Alaska World Affairs Council was Chinese dissident and astrophysics professor Fang Li-zhi. An up-and-coming academic in Beijing, Fang Li-zhi arranged the first trip to China for his friend and colleague, the famous cosmologist Stephen Hawking. And then along came 1989.

Professor Fang played such a high-profile role in the Tiananmen Square protests that he had to flee for his life ahead of the massacre that followed. He took asylum in the U.S. Embassy in Beijing. After a year of high-level negotiations (during which he penned four scientific papers), he was permitted to come to the United States. An Air Force plane flew him to Washington, DC with a brief stopover in Anchorage.

Driving around Anchorage with Professor Fang, I offered him a little background and then said to him, "You know, you and our former governor, Wally Hickel, have something in common." He looked at me, puzzled. "You both told the leader of your country to listen to the young people, and then you both ended up on a plane to Anchorage." He laughed.

Governor Hickel was ramping up speaking his mind publicly and a deluge of "Wallyisms" spilled forth over the ensuing decades. Fortunately, long-time Hickel aide and good friend Malcolm Roberts collated them into a book entitled: *The Wit and Wisdom of Wally Hickel.* A great read for those who wish to understand the mind of Alaska's elder statesman.

I never agreed with Wally Hickel's "bulldozer" approach to Alaska's development and his "big project" agenda. A transoceanic "water pipeline" to California?! And the scar of the notorious "Hickel Highway" lingers in Alaska's fragile tundra, but it will recover over time.

Anyone as outspoken, intense, caring and impatient as Governor Hickel was bound to put his foot in his mouth on occasion. And I was witness to one real doozie. The Interior Committee of the U.S. House of Representatives was holding a public hearing in Anchorage. Representative Gerry Studds of Massachusetts, as I recall, went out of his way to praise our notoriously ill-mannered Congressman Don Young. I didn't buy it, but I respected him for the gesture. And when it came his turn to speak, Governor Hickel declared that "it would be a crime against Christianity if we didn't drill for oil in ANWR." I'm sure *Anchorage Daily News* columnist Mike Doogan had fun with that one.

I was talking with Wally once in his spacious, second-floor office in the Hotel Captain Cook when the subject turned to his son Jack. Jack, whom I'd known for many years, was a missionary physician in Swaziland and Wally had just recently returned from a visit. Patients would start lining up at daybreak to get a chance to be seen in Jack's clinic. Wally told me he had made the observation to his son, "Jack, you're on the wrong end of the line." I blinked a few times, puzzled, before I understood. It was an insightful observation, laden with implication. Wally was questioning the political structures and social institutions that not only allowed so many people to get so sick, but forced them to wait long hours in line to see a single volunteer foreign doctor.

On another occasion he squinted pensively and stared out his office window a few seconds before turning back to me and saying, in a slightly raised voice, "I'm sick and tired of all those people out there criticizing big government, saying big government is bad. It's not a question of big government or small government, it's a question of better government.

And that might mean bigger, or it might mean smaller." Bravo, I thought, well said.

In the last free-wheeling conversation I remember in Wally's office a visiting Kurdish activist accompanied me. Wally was describing a cabinet meeting with President Nixon where Henry Kissinger was also in attendance. Wally always maintained his friendship with Nixon despite having been fired by him. But it was clear from our conversation that, to put it mildly, he did not hold Kissinger in high regard. (Another point of agreement - I've always detested Kissinger). Wally could do a great Kissinger imitation, mocking the former Secretary of State's thick German accent.

Kissinger was also widely detested in Kurdistan for betraying the Kurds in 1975 with his realpolitik Algiers Accord. And I was in Kurdistan, northern Iraq, when I learned that Wally passed away (Malcolm Robert's wife, Cindy, kindly informed me by e-mail). The above conversation with Wally flooded back. I fired off my own eulogy via e-mail from our hotel in Irbil to the *Anchorage Daily News* and it was published, half a world away, the next day.

I would say that, more than all other Alaska governors, Wally Hickel belonged to the world. And as I said in my letter, the world is a better place for the 90 years he spent here.

In January 2001 I brought famous Chinese dissident Wei Jingsheng to former governor Wally Hickel's office. Wally welcomed him. Mr. Wei's translator David Ma (to the left) turned out to be a Chinese spy. Ooops

CHAPTER 60

SARAH PALIN, STARRING IN "THIRD FLOOR ANTICS"

In March 2009 I was escorting Lobsang Nyandak, the Dalai Lama's envoy to North and South America, through the Alaska State Capitol in Juneau. He had just addressed a special joint House-Senate committee co-chaired by Senator Lesil McGuire and Representative Jay Ramras, and was well received. Representative Ramras proudly held up a photo of himself with the Dalai Lama, who he met when His Holiness visited Anchorage. After securing permission from the Legislature's parliamentarian, I had hung a copy of the Tibetan flag from the small table where Lobsang sat while he talked with the committee. I wanted to honor Tibet and (secretly) tick-off China at the same time.

We had some time to kill before my friend and colleague, Senator Dr. Donny Olson, was going to introduce Lobsang in the Senate Chambers. So we wandered up to the third floor to see if our request for an audience with Governor Sarah Palin had been approved. It had not, and the young receptionist guarding the long hallway that led to the governor's office was not very friendly. The request was supposed to default to the lieutenant governor, so we walked to the opposite end of the third floor to Lt. Governor Sean Parnell's office. They politely told us nothing had come through.

I was on my way back to pester the governor's unfriendly receptionist again when I ran into Major General Craig Campbell, Adjutant General of the Alaska National Guard. He stood out in his full military uniform. We had met and talked briefly in the past and I introduced him to the Dalai Lama's envoy. He was gracious with his time and I also made it a point to thank him for the Guard's cooperative efforts with Mongolia.

(Sixteen months later in Anchorage, as Lt. Governor Craig Campbell, he would be equally gracious with his time when I introduced him to former Taiwan Vice President Annette Lu).

No sooner had we finished our brief chat with General Campbell than a buzz swept the entire third floor. It was almost palpable. Faces lit up in excitement and anticipation and people began to scramble. Our famous governor, Sarah Palin, would shortly be giving a press conference. (This was after her highly publicized, unsuccessful 2008 bid for vice president and she was already somewhat of an international celebrity). Lobsang and I were maybe just twenty feet from the press room. I was probably violating protocol, but I couldn't resist. "Follow me, Lobsang," I said to the highest-ranking Tibetan official in the Western Hemisphere, "I'll see if I can get us in."

There were two doors from the main hallway into the press room, one on either end. Each was guarded by a formidable-looking woman. I wondered if they were packing heat. I went to the one I thought was Meghan Stapleton. Don't know if I got it right, but I politely asked if we could attend the press conference and we were allowed in. Lobsang and I took a seat along the wall on the opposite side of the table from where the governor would be speaking. The place was packed, microphones and cameras everywhere.

A third door, a private side door, also led into the press room. It came directly from the governor's office. The door opened, a hush fell over the room, and in walked Sarah. Perfectly coiffed and camera-ready, she walked into that room like she was walking onto the set of Letterman. Eyes on the cameras, always, connecting with a wider audience. I figured as much and wondered how long she would last in Juneau.

I'll admit, never having seen Sarah from so close, that I sort of expect-ed a pretty-faced version of Janet Reno. But Sarah was very petite and yes, very attractive. The media must have been angling their cameras to make her look more imposing than she really was. Something she can thank the media for?

As per script, I assumed, she allowed her minions to talk first about oil and gas issues while she smiled at the many cameras. She had no idea the Dalai Lama's top envoy to North America, who could have easily been mistaken for an Alaska Native, was sitting directly across the table from her. Lobsang, ever the humble and respectful diplomat, tried to keep a low profile and blend in. (I felt a little guilty, but in that carnival atmosphere it was easy to blend in). I was getting bored fast, but fortunately Lobsang and I had a commitment down in the Senate Chambers. It was easy enough to slip out of that stuffy, overcrowded press conference.

I was disappointed in Sarah. She could have arranged to slip out of her office with a few hairs out of place, acknowledge and welcome the Dalai Lama's North American envoy who flew out from New York City, apologize for how busy she was, pose for a photo, then slip back into her office. It would have been enough, more than enough. Not from Sarah. But all was not lost.

Lobsang and I boarded the Alaska Airlines flight from Juneau back to Anchorage and our seats were in the back of the plane. Just as I cinched my seatbelt I noticed Alaska Lt. Governor Sean Parnell get onboard and take a seat in one of the exit rows over the wing. (To his credit he wasn't flying first class).

When we reached cruising altitude and the seatbelt sign clicked off, I got up, walked forward and tapped Alaska's lieutenant governor on the shoulder. He was sitting in a middle seat working on his laptop. I think he remembered me - we had previously talked about North Korea. I re-introduced myself. "The Dalai Lama's envoy to North America is in the back of the plane with me," I explained, "Can you greet him when we get off in Anchorage?" He agreed.

When you're sitting in the back of the plane it takes a while to exit. Luggage comes from below the seat in front of you. Luggage comes from the overhead bins. When we finally broke free and exited, Lt. Governor Sean Parnell was standing there at the gate, patiently awaiting us. I introduced Lobsang and stepped back. They talked a bit, shook hands and he welcomed Lobsang to Alaska.

EPILOGUE:

Sixteen months later former Taiwan Vice President Annette Lu (2000-2008) stopped in Alaska for a three-day private visit at my invitation. (It felt really cool to get a special pass and accompany the Taiwanese diplomatic contingent - up from Seattle - backwards through every level of security at Anchorage International Airport, and right up to the very door of the China Airlines 747, to welcome V.P. Lu and her four-member security detail as they exited the big jet).

Well before her visit, Vice President Lu expressed a desire to meet Sarah Palin. It only made sense – a former female Taiwan Vice President and a former female American vice-presidential candidate. Uh-oh, I thought, here we go again. But I was determined to give it the old college try.

Meghan Stapleton and her indispensable blackberry were still both working for Sarah. She responded promptly and helpfully. Thank you, Meghan.

I soon received an e-mail from Sally Heath, Sarah Palin's mom. The Palin family would be at their Bristol Bay fish camp during V.P. Lu's scheduled visit, she told me. And they would be unreachable. Good for Sally and the Palin family, I thought; they had their priorities right. Family fish camp came first. I responded and wished Sally and the gang an abundant catch.

Major General Craig Campbell had become Alaska's new lieutenant governor under Governor Sean Parnell, who succeeded Sarah after she resigned. And he graciously spent almost an hour with V.P. Lu and the Taiwanese diplomatic contingent in his Anchorage office, discussing bilateral trade and Taiwanese tourism to Alaska.

As Taiwan's vice president for eight years, Annette Lu was Taiwan's face to the world. Fluent in English (she was a former exchange student in Illinois), she traveled widely and met many international leaders, though mostly from countries that still had diplomatic relations with Taiwan. She even bumped into Fidel Castro once in South America - someone she was not authorized to meet. She told me how Fidel was polite, cordial and inquisitive. And how he finished their off-the-record conversation with a comment that made both of them laugh. Yet, despite all her international travels, she had never seen a glacier. I remedied that by arranging for her to see two in one day: Portage Glacier and Exit Glacier. She was one very happy camper.

At her speech to the Alaska World Affairs Council's assembled evening audience, Vice President Annette Lu warmly acknowledged Sarah Palin's contribution to the further empowerment of the world's women by having reached into the highest levels of America's political establishment. Credit where credit is due.

CHAPTER 61
W.A.R. (WAYNE ANTHONY ROSS)

He is probably the most flamboyant criminal defense attorney living in Alaska, although some might have ascribed that honor to Edgar Paul Boyko. But Mr. Boyko, after decades of energy and theatrics on behalf of his clients in Alaska's courtrooms, has passed on. But there's no doubt Wayne Ross was the shortest-serving Alaska State Attorney General in our history – two weeks and a couple of days – until he was "non-confirmed" by a vote of the Alaska State Legislature. Governor Sarah Palin should have known better than to nominate him. And Wayne should have known better than to accept. Wayne was too big for the job.

Wayne is known for his outspoken and unabashedly conservative political views and views on the social issues. And maybe even more so for his passion for guns and the Second Amendment. A member of the National Rifle Association since 1964, he was elected to its executive board in 1980 and became first vice president of the 3 million-member organization in 1990. On a trajectory to become president, he found himself, a few years later, on the wrong end of an internal power play.

Closer to home, Wayne – an Alaskan since 1967 - has provided free legal services to local anti-abortion activists for decades. And he is always available for a colorful quote on one of his three favorite topics – guns, gays and abortion. A quote usually guaranteed to make liberal blood boil.

Wayne is certainly a showman which, in the criminal lawyer business, can be a benefit in the courtroom. With his cowboy boots, bolo tie and tweed jacket he seems to be cultivating the image of Teddy Roosevelt. The vanity plate WAR emblazons the hummer he proudly drives around town.

344

Three adjectives and a noun seem to be the most common descriptors bandied about describing Wayne by those who know him, or have encountered him. Arrogant, opinionated and belligerent. And integrity. And they would all agree, I am sure, that the noun trumps the adjectives. Also to Wayne's credit is that he loves books – indeed, he owns maybe ten times as many books as he owns guns. That being said, though, his personal library in his Hillside home is said to have about 6,000 volumes.

Many articles have come out about W.A.R in the Anchorage newspapers over the years, including one in December 1995 by Sheila Toomey of the *Anchorage Daily News*. (Sheila is the longtime author of the gossipy *Alaska Ear* in the Sunday paper). At the time, Wayne was contemplating a run for governor. Sheila's story prompted me to write a letter to the editor, which was published a few days later.

In my letter I acknowledged Sheila's article and noted how W.A.R and I were at complete opposite ends of the political spectrum and the social issues spectrum. There was no way that I would ever vote for him if he ran for governor. But, I added, he is exactly the kind of person I would welcome as a neighbor, and no, that has nothing to do with the awesome firepower at his disposal. It's that he is an honest, ethical, hard-working, solid citizen – a man of integrity. And I'd be the first on his doorstep with a welcoming plate of chocolate–chip cookies (not that he's moving down from the Hillside to Spenard anytime soon). I concluded by saying that we need to separate people from their opinions (political or otherwise) and that if W.A.R. and I ever met we'd have a great conversation and probably finish up as friends.

The evening of the day my letter was published (*Anchorage Daily News* is a very early-bird newspaper), the phone rang. The caller did not initially identify himself. It was just a very gruff voice asking: "Wadda ya mean you're not gonna vote for me when I run for governor?"

Uh-oh, I thought.

What felt like several long minutes of frosty silence (it was actually only a few seconds) was suddenly broken by laughter. Yup, it was Wayne. He wanted to invite me to lunch.

I showed up at his law office on Fireweed Lane a few days later. Most of the photos on his wall were of Teddy Roosevelt chumming up with famous Alaskan state and federal politicians. And maybe a U.S. President or two, all of them conservative republicans. Not a democrat in sight. (Well, maybe it was just Wayne channeling Teddy in those photos).

Wayne grabbed a handgun from his desk drawer, made sure it was loaded, then stuffed it into his pocket. We took his car to the Sea Galley restaurant. When we arrived, knowing the Sea Galley sold liquor, Wayne took out his loaded handgun and locked it into his glove compartment. I took note of this, and respected it. He was following the law.

We had a great lunch and talked for an hour. And we found three things we had in common: 1) We were both unafraid to stand up to Alaska's all-powerful U.S. Senator Ted Stevens, although Wayne's problems with Uncle Ted were different than my disagreements with him, 2) both of our wives at the time were librarians, and 3) we both had a high regard and respect for Anchorage surgeon Dr. Steve Kilkenny. Not bad for a busy hour of conversation.

But what struck me most from our conversation, and it came to me, I believe, through careful listening, was an insight I am convinced exposed the very core of who Wayne was and where he was coming from. Sure, he had a passion for guns, and a great respect for them, but it went much deeper. No, I saw a man with a great respect and concern for the freedom of the individual against an arbitrary, unpredictable, or tyrannical government. And the need for eternal vigilance to protect that freedom. That's where the guns came in. It was like I was speaking to one of our traumatized founding fathers arguing for a citizen's militia to protect against any future attacks from the British. Clearly, Wayne had followed the seventy-year Soviet debacle.

Wayne volunteered to me that, if government agents ever came to his home to confiscate his guns he would, as a law-abiding citizen, turn them over, but he would probably empty them first. It took me a minute, with a little coaxing from Wayne, to get his half-joke. It was vintage Wayne.

When the black helicopters start circling overhead and the G-men start breaking down my door, Wayne Anthony Ross is my man. I got his number on speed-dial.

Oh, and next time lunch is on me!

Chapter 62

Hans, a Swiss fairy tale, or where the Wanderlust began

Summer 1972

As the train screeched to a halt at the small station in Interlaken, Switzerland I prepared to put into action a plan that had served me well during several months of backpacking through Europe. I would just follow the people with the blue jeans and backpacks and they would inevitably lead me to the local youth hostel or some equally inexpensive accommodations. This I did, following them across the small lobby, out the door and down a narrow and surprisingly rural road. Captivated by the countryside I slowed my pace, lagging farther and farther behind. To my right were a series of small cottages, each surrounded by neatly manicured gardens. A few farmers were out tilling their fields. Off to my left were woods leading up to some foothills and off in the distance, hidden by clouds, the mighty Swiss Alps.

I finally arrived at the youth hostel only to find it filled. I remember standing there with a few others in the gravel parking lot, feeling angry and depressed. I didn't want to leave such a beautiful place, yet I couldn't afford more than a few dollars for a night's lodging. What had often happened in such situations in the past was that fate intervened and things worked out for the best, sometimes even better, than I would have expected. Well, fate intervened again, within minutes, in the form of a white Volkswagen Beetle which came screaming into the parking lot and skidded to a stop in a massive cloud of dust. A man got out. It was Savann.

Savann was a Swiss-Italian who owned a chalet in the next valley, in the small village of Lauterbrunnen. He was apparently having some difficulties making his mortgage payments during the slow summer months, so he had taken it upon himself to pick up the overflow from the youth hostel in Interlaken and drive them over to his chalet where he would let them stay for the same price they would have paid at the hostel. By now there were quite a few of us milling about in the parking lot. We all piled into Savann's little VW (many more of us than I would have thought possible) and off we went.

By the way he drove it was soon obvious that Savann had quite a bit of Latin blood coursing through his veins. I remember a high-speed, breathtaking ride along narrow, winding mountain roads in rapidly approaching darkness. I don't remember seeing much, although even in bright sunlight I doubt I could have seen through the tangled mass of bodies packed into the back seat. What I do remember seeing, though, is my life passing in review before my eyes and concluding that it had been a good summer so far and I'd really gotten to see quite a bit of Europe.

We arrived safely and pried ourselves out of the car. It was very dark and I could see very little, but I sensed that we were in a special, almost magical place. I just sort of felt it. I could hear loud gurgling nearby. (Lauterbrunnen means "loud brook" in German). Confirmation would have to wait until morning, so we retired to the chalet for the night.

I was up early the next morning and outdoors just as the mist was beginning to burn off. We were in a long, narrow valley. Off to one side was what looked like a sheer granite face, over which a waterfall dropped hundreds of feet onto the rocks below. The opposite side of the valley was more gently sloped, covered with the brightest green grass and dotted with picturesque chalets. It all seemed unreal - as if the hills were carpeted with giant rolls of bright green pool-table felt and the chalets carefully and deliberately set down on this by a giant hand from above. I felt like I was standing at the foot of a huge department store Christmas display.

The people staying at the chalet were a typical cross-section of American hippydom at the time, with a few Europeans mixed in. Communal-style cooperation ensued almost automatically; everyone had a role and got along. I remember a girl named Sunshine who talked about her uncle who farted a lot and liked to pull his pants down on elevators. (I remember thinking that Sunshine's uncle had a problem). I'd made friends with a guy from Toronto I nicknamed Red because of his hair and we set off to explore the town, ducking into various cheese and chocolate shops, cafes and clocksmiths. Over the course of the morning we'd begun to hear stories about a local "cheeseman". We inquired further and soon learned about an old man named Hans who lived alone in a cabin way up in the mountains where he made cheese.

Well, this story, in this particular setting, was the closest thing to a real-life fairy tale I'd ever encountered, so by noon we had decided we were going to find Hans. We made the rounds once again, asking how to get to his place. Everyone warned us not to go up into the mountains by ourselves, certainly not dressed the way we were. Someone finally admitted that there was a trailhead less than a mile down the road, and we started off.

We located the trailhead without difficulty and plunged into the forest. We had nothing more than the clothes on our backs (mostly cotton at that). We had no rain gear, no extra clothing, no matches, no flashlight, no compass, no map and no food. Nor had we told anyone from the chalet where we were headed. The going was fairly easy through the woods, then the trail started to switchback up a much steeper rocky face. Wire guard rails strung between steel posts anchored in the rock provided safety and support on the more treacherous parts. Then we passed through a second wooded area and finally broke out onto an alpine meadow.

Many years ago, as a child, I remember reading a book about climbing a mountain. The journey in that book started in the forested valley floor and progressed steadily up the mountain, broke out above timberline and continued on up toward the snow-capped summit. Somewhere along the way it crossed an alpine meadow. I don't remember if there was an illustration in the book, or if I created one in my mind, but the image of that alpine meadow always remained with me. Now here I was in the mountains of Switzerland, standing before that alpine meadow of my childhood.

Before heading on we happened to glance off to the right where a sudden high altitude gust of wind cleared away the clouds, and there stood the snow-capped peak of the Jungfrau, clear and sparkling like a diamond against the dark blue sky. It was a majestic, but fleeting, moment, for the giant massif soon enshrouded herself in clouds again. We headed for the two cabins we spotted at the far end of the meadow.

We peered in the window of one of the cabins, then knocked on the door and were invited inside. And there was Hans standing before us. He was an older man with gray hair and a gray mustache, dressed in dark green lederhosen. He spoke only Swiss-German. An American couple was staying with him, helping with the chores in return for lodging. We sat and drank coffee and talked. Then we were invited to go make some cheese.

We followed Hans and his assistants to the small barn behind the cabin where he kept his two cows. He milked the cows quickly with his calloused hands, filling an old pail about two-thirds full of fresh milk. The American woman then offered me the pail. I hesitated, then drank. It was deliciously warm and somewhat sweet. She then poured the milk into a metal container inside Hans's rucksack and we hiked up the trail to the cabin where the cheese was made.

The milk was poured into a large iron cauldron which hung over a small fire. The fire was stoked and the milk was heated, we were told, to the temperature it had been when it came out of the cow. The small cabin was filled with all the implements of cheesemaking, many of them wooden and handmade. Hans had spent his summers up in these mountains making cheese since he was a boy of fourteen. His father and grandfather had done the same before him. He was in his early seventies now, an old bachelor. Sadly, because of his age and health, this was to be his last summer there.

When the milk was just the right temperature Hans reached up and grabbed a jar containing an orange-colored fluid off a high shelf. He filled a wooden ladle with the fluid and poured it into the warmed milk. Reaching in up to his elbow, he swirled the milk around and around, then set the empty ladle floating on the swirling mixture. As the empty wooden ladle spun around in the center, we were told to watch closely, that the ladle would come to a sudden stop, then reverse direction just under a quarter turn. It did just this, as the whole mixture suddenly gelled. Hans then plunged his hands into the curdled glob, burying his arms up to the elbows. Minutes later he pulled out a soft, but cohesive, blob of what looked like white bread dough. This was put into a wooden cheese press which had multiple holes in it, like a sieve. Pressure was applied and water was forced out several times. It was then taken to the curing shed a dozen yards away.

The whey that was left was saved for the pigs. Red and I reached into our pockets for a few Swiss marks and each bought a wedge of fresh cheese from Hans, eating some and saving the rest. It may be the best cheese I have ever tasted.

Munching on cheese and talking outside the cabin, we suddenly noticed that it was getting dark rather quickly. This caused us some concern, ill-equipped as we were. We bade Hans and the two Americans a hasty farewell and headed for the forest on the far side of the meadow. We hadn't gotten far before it got very dark. The sky was heavily overcast, so there was no light from the moon or the stars. We could barely see our feet on the ground in front of us and in the rough terrain we were forced to slow our pace to a near crawl.

It started to rain hard, soaking our thin, cotton clothing. Then came the thunder and lightning. Bright flashes of lightning were followed by deafening thunderclaps that rolled and echoed up and down the huge valley. The storm turned out to be a blessing, since the lightning provided us with the illumination we needed to find our way back. A flash of lightning and its brief afterglow would illuminate the trail for about twenty to thirty yards. We'd imprint the appearance on our minds, dash ahead as far as we felt comfortable, then grab onto a rock, a small tree, or an upright anchored steel post and wait for the next flash of lightning to lead us farther. We literally used the lightning to guide us through the steeper, exposed and more confusing parts of the trail. (Not the safest way to hike down a steep mountain, by the way). We finally stumbled onto the road - cold, wet and tired - but warm inside with the glow of adventure.